Ancillary Police Powers
in Canada

Law and Society Series
W. Wesley Pue, Founding Editor

We pay tribute to the late Wes Pue, under whose broad vision, extraordinary leadership, and unwavering commitment to socio-legal studies our Law and Society Series was established and rose to prominence.

The Law and Society Series explores law as a socially embedded phenomenon. It is premised on the understanding that the conventional division of law from society creates false dichotomies in thinking, scholarship, educational practice, and social life. Books in the series treat law and society as mutually constitutive and seek to bridge scholarship emerging from interdisciplinary engagement of law with disciplines such as politics, social theory, history, political economy, and gender studies.

Recent books in the series:

For a complete list of the titles in the series, see the UBC Press website, www.ubcpress.ca.

Ancillary Police Powers in Canada

A Critical Reassessment

John W. Burchill, Richard Jochelson,
Akwasi Owusu-Bempah,
and Terry Skolnik

UBCPress · Vancouver

Printed in Canada on FSC-certified ancient-forest-free paper (100% post-consumer recycled) that is processed chlorine- and acid-free.

UBC Press is a Benetech Global Certified Accessible™ publisher. The epub version of this book meets stringent accessibility standards, ensuring it is available to people with diverse needs.

Library and Archives Canada Cataloguing in Publication

Title: Ancillary police powers in Canada : a critical reassessment / John W. Burchill, Richard Jochelson, Akwasi Owusu-Bempah, and Terry Skolnik.

Names: Burchill, John W., author. | Jochelson, Richard, author. | Owusu-Bempah, Akwasi, author. | Skolnik, Terry, author.

Series: Law and society series (Vancouver, B.C.)

Description: Series statement: Law and society series | Includes bibliographical references and index.

Identifiers: Canadiana (print) 20240391950 | Canadiana (ebook) 20240392019 | ISBN 9780774871051 (hardcover) | ISBN 9780774871068 (softcover) | ISBN 9780774871082 (EPUB) | ISBN 9780774871075 (PDF)

Subjects: LCSH: Police — Canada. | LCSH: Law enforcement — Canada.

Classification: LCC KE5006 .B87 2024 | DDC 344.7105/2 — dc23

Canada Council   Conseil des arts
for the Arts   du Canada

Canadä

BRITISH COLUMBIA
ARTS COUNCIL

BRITISH
COLUMBIA

UBC Press gratefully acknowledges the financial support for our publishing program of the Government of Canada, the Canada Council for the Arts, and the British Columbia Arts Council.

This book has been published with the help of a grant from the Canadian Federation for the Humanities and Social Sciences, through the Scholarly Book Awards, using funds provided by the Social Sciences and Humanities Research Council of Canada.

UBC Press is situated on the traditional, ancestral, and unceded territory of the xʷməθkʷəy̓əm (Musqueam) people. This land has always been a place of learning for the xʷməθkʷəy̓əm, who have passed on their culture, history, and traditions for millennia, from one generation to the next.

UBC Press
The University of British Columbia
www.ubcpress.ca

Contents

Part 3: Critiquing Police Powers

Figures and Tables

Acknowledgments

We acknowledge our families and friends. Special thanks to Lauren Gowler for her editing work and to Judge David Ireland for his formative contributions. We thank the Legal Research Institute at Robson Hall, Faculty of Law, University of Manitoba for funding student assistants during this project.

Ancillary Police Powers
in Canada

Introduction
Judicial Oversight of Police Powers in Canada

This book explores police powers from varying perspectives and viewpoints. Specifically, we interrogate the powers conferred to police by Canadian courts. While there is a real need for police to protect the public and prevent crime, the way in which they do so must be carefully circumscribed to protect our rights and freedoms. That is to say, the police do not have limitless power in Canada. When investigating crime, searching, detaining, or arresting individuals, police are always required to obey the law. While many laws controlling state powers are defined by the legislature through statute, laws relating to state powers also exist in the legal decisions written by judges. This book explains how common law police powers came to be, what the powers are, how and when Canadian courts have generated and deployed these powers, and the potential dangers of expanding these powers further.

Our collective of authors has assembled a text that surveys the history, current application, and future development of these judge-made police powers in Canada. The generation, deployment, and legality of police powers is a complex area of legal study that requires nuanced review and analysis. Thus, we have approached this book from a multidisciplinary standpoint informed by varied theoretical perspectives. By blending our expertise in historical perspectives, critical legal theories, and empirical analysis, we offer the reader a unique and thought-provoking journey into the essence of policing in Canada.

From our provincial and territorial trial courts, through provincial superior and appellate courts, all the way to the Supreme Court of Canada, judges in Canada make law every day. Their decisions interpret statutory law (as enacted by Parliament and the provincial legislatures), and while our perspectives are intentionally diverse, the authors have written this book with two goals in mind. First, we want the reader to understand what the police are permitted to do and why. Where do the police derive their significant powers to investigate and prevent crime? What are the limits of police powers, and how can our citizens better understand their rights when they come into contact with the police? The courts have bestowed the police with many powers to stop, search, and otherwise investigate us in the pursuit of public safety and crime prevention. We can therefore all benefit from an increased understanding of these powers. In essence then, the following chapters seek to build a picture of common law police powers that is both accessible and thorough.

Second, and perhaps most importantly, we want the reader to think critically about the powers of our policing agencies. We examine not simply what the law is but also why the law exists and, indeed, whether the law is justifiable. To this end, we offer critiques of how and why courts have continued to distribute powers to the police. We suggest that unquestioning acceptance of police powers paves the road to unjust oppression and that Canadians can, and should, demand their elected representatives direct the apparatus of the state to benefit its ordinary citizens. The open-minded reader will be asked to seriously consider the propriety of common law police powers in Canada.

In the recent jurisprudence, the Supreme Court of Canada has noted that a new common law police power requires, first, that a *prima facie* interference with the liberty of a person takes place at the hands of the police; once established, a court needs to consider if the purported police power falls within the general scope of the duties of preserving the peace, preventing crime, and protecting life and property; and, last, a court must consider whether the police power used is reasonably necessary: "In determining the boundaries of police powers, caution is required to ensure the proper balance between preventing excessive intrusions on an individual's liberty and privacy, and enabling the police to do what is reasonably necessary to perform their duties in protecting the public."[1]

Certainly, support for the creation and use of common law police powers remains popular for police services. In the context of initial jurisprudential static for the use of sniffer dogs as a common law power, Tom Stamatakis,

vice-president of the Canadian Police Association in 2008, infamously expressed his dissatisfaction, noting: "We're no longer going to be able to
show up and randomly search."[2] As we will learn in the upcoming chapters, the ancillary powers doctrine, a calculus originally deployed in a British
case, was ultimately applied in the Canadian context, perhaps most famously in *Dedman and the Queen*.[3] The use of the test in the concoction of
new police powers in Canada, rather than its original use as an element of
establishing offences against police acting in the course of their duties, is a
frequent critique; the transmogrification turned the ancillary powers test
in Canada into a net-widening exercise rather than the UK approach that
considered the test an element of a discrete offence committed against police
officers.[4]

Whatever the utility of ensuring crime prevention, public peace, safety,
and the preservation of evidence, an early critique in the Canadian context
has been that the basic tenets of the rule of law have been compromised by
frequent use of the test:

> James Stribopoulos describes the Court's use of the ancillary power
> doctrine as movement away from the Diceyan notion of the rule of law
> in which "the absolute supremacy or predominance of regular law"
> supersedes "wide discretionary authority." Steadfast adherence to the rule
> of law would support the principle of legality – the notion that liberty
> is residual and that everything not expressly forbidden is permitted.
> The use of the ancillary powers doctrine, in Stribopoulos' view, has al-
> lowed the Court to drift from "its historic role of standing firm between
> the individual and the state, insisting on adherence to the principle of
> legality, and refusing to make up for shortcomings in police powers." In
> this sense, Stribopoulos argues that the Court has moved away from its
> "long-established role" and toward a function "traditionally reserved for
> Parliament."[5]

Indeed, if the Court is creating police powers through judicial decisions,
there are analogies between the concoction of police powers that invoke
the critique of the judiciary as activist and intruding on the purview of the
legislature, since discrete proliferations of police powers could arguably
be better left to the parliamentarian.[6] This sort of activism is contestable
since the calculation for raising an activism critique is usually understood
as a judicial end-run against legislatures. However, it is certainly possible to
argue that the use of the ancillary powers test is activist in a broader sense

when one considers the dialogue that occurs in a constitutional democracy between the courts and Parliament:

> If we take a broader view of dialogical models, we can elucidate further consequences of the Court's development of the ancillary powers test. Some have preferred to situate a fuller articulation of dialogue in the assessment of post-decision dynamics. For instance, Margit Cohn and Mordechai Kremnitzer argue that legislative, administrative, public and subsequent judicial responses to the originating judicial decisions all provide useful indicia of the degree of a court's activism – the more subsequent post-decision approval that occurs in these other spheres, the less activist the decision.[7]

As we shall see in the upcoming chapters, the ancillary powers test has been powerfully promulgated in recent years, with a seemingly recent re-traction the endurance of which will only be determined in the fullness of time. There is little doubt that in the last forty years, as the jurisprudence has disseminated, the Supreme Court of Canada has attempted to articulate new ancillary powers in a way that respects constitutional principles. Nonetheless, the dynamic raises the issue of who will question the Court's deployment of these powers if the Court drafts the powers while policing the boundaries of those same powers. In earlier work, this conundrum was described as pre-emptive deference:

> [T]he Court's use of deferential utilitarianism (in the form of preemptive deference) to retrospectively evaluate split-second police decision making and justify the creation of new, constitutionally impervious, common law police powers effectively stunts the Court's ability to advocate for rights or to effectively engage in a dialogue with Parliament. This seems to be rejection of the Court's traditional role as a defender of individual liberties. In this context, deferential utilitarianism is abandonment of first principles in a rights culture – the belief that when "courts uphold core values" they are not being activist.[8]

There are certainly alternatives to court creation of common law police powers. Some have advocated for a legislative solution like the British *Police and Criminal Evidence Act*.[9] Such approaches are capable of being critiqued for a lack of flexibility and responsiveness to novel policing situations. These approaches, though, do preserve the abilities of courts to challenge the constitutionality of police conduct in the consequence of existing legislation. The benefits include fair notice to citizenry and preservation of the constitutional guardianship of courts. The detriments include that police officers might feel unduly reined in during emergent situations for fear of court sanction. Legislation is a complex process involving an investment of resources and deep study – an expensive proposition.

Yet when courts take on the role of police power creation, they do so in a limited context between only an accused and a police officer – should courts be asked to make broad policing pronouncements on the basis of limited scope, expertise, and evidence? On the other hand, no two police-citizen encounters are the same, and the common law approach allows context and real-time events to influence the lawfulness of the encounter. The tension between legislated police powers mirrors the age-old tension between crime control and due process concerns.[10]

In the expanse of scholarly discourse on the law and society, the profound challenges surrounding the representation of Indigenous communities have predominantly found their place in discussions of incarceration and charging rates, as explored by Patricia Monture in 2014.[11] However, a noticeable lacuna persists within the existing literature – an oversight that extends to the treatment meted out to Indigenous individuals during detention or arrest, as illuminated by the Aboriginal Justice Inquiry (AJI).[12] Indeed, the AJI called for a comprehensive overhaul of the justice system to meet the requirements, needs, and rights of Indigenous persons.[13] Curiously less common in the Canadian scholarly treatment is appropriate attention directed toward the experiences of Indigenous persons upon detention or arrest. There exists in the literature robust discussion that suggests ancillary powers provide disconcerting moments for arbitrary police discretion to enter the state-citizen equation – for example, some contend that common law police powers provide the police officers with authority to engage in racial profiling under the guise of a random stop.[14] It is relatively uncontroversial to note that police stop Indigenous and racialized persons more frequently, creating an inference that common law police power creation might suffer from the same deficiency.[15] Certainly, some empirical evidence supports this proposition in the context of Indigenous persons, even as racial profiling in the context of Black detainees is more extensively studied.[16]

Some scholars contend that delving into the intricacies of participation within the Canadian justice system is fraught with the shadows of colonial coercion, a compelling narrative that, perhaps, has stifled the pursuit of comprehensive inquiry. Alternatively, it could be posited that the academic spotlight has been fixated on the more conspicuous realms of criminal trial or sentencing, inadvertently sidelining the critical nuances embedded within police encounters, as articulated by the AJI. The absence of a fully developed literature addressing the systemic issues inherent in police encounters (in the context of common law police power articulations) with Indigenous individuals is a palpable gap that must be bridged. An important first step is understanding the issues that manifest in the creation of police powers by courts.

In recent years, there are further examples of how lived experiences affect those being policed, a matter that we explore in the chapters below. While many see the police as an essential component of a just and safe society, there are significant groups in society that have had, and continue to have, troubled relationships with law enforcement. A Statistics Canada study by Adam Cotter notes that

> according to the 2020 General Social Survey (GSS) on Social Identity, one in five Black (21%) and Indigenous (22%) people have little or no confidence in police, double the proportion among those who were neither Indigenous nor a visible minority (11%) ... Relative to the overall population, Black people and Indigenous people had particularly negative perceptions of the ability of police to treat people fairly and be approachable and easy to talk to.[17]

Historical state racism and the over-policing of marginalized, racialized, and Indigenous communities have perpetuated environments of social harm in Canada. Many communities across Canada have been impacted by violence, and some of this violence has been caused by state institutions and policing. This too is reflected in Cotter's report:

> Perceptions of the police and other institutions were more negative among Black and Indigenous people. Black and Indigenous people were about twice as likely as non-Indigenous, non-visible minority people to state that they had little or no confidence in police. Linked to this, Black and Indigenous people more commonly felt that police were performing poorly in at least one part of their job.[18]

The unjustified state killing of citizenry has led to social movements such as Defund the Police and Black Lives Matter. These movements capture the public disapprobation of police violence and, by extension, police powers.[19]

Our critical analysis of the generation and deployment of police powers is therefore informed by the wider social framework of a concerned citizenry committed to safer communities.

Over and above what is granted to the police by statute, the common law recognizes that police have a general duty to preserve the peace, protect life and property, and prevent crime. Courts have used this general duty to generate and deploy specific police powers to detain, search, and investigate the public. In the chapters that follow, we suggest that police powers must not be uncritically accepted as an imperative to this general duty of policing. If we simply acquiesce to the continued expansion of common law police powers, we risk diminishing the rights of individuals to live free from state intrusions into their private lives. This is particularly troubling in the context of the constitutional rights conferred to us all under the *Canadian Charter of Rights and Freedoms*.[20]

We have divided our discussion of judge-made police powers into three parts. Chapters 1 and 2 introduce the reader to the history of common law police powers in Canada. Here, we explore the history of police powers and offer a detailed examination of how these powers took hold in Canadian jurisprudence. Chapters 3 and 4 look at the judicial expansion of police powers by detailing specific powers and explaining how courts have constitutionalized and expanded these powers over time. Chapters 5, 6, and 7 offer a critique of police powers through a theoretical examination of state domination and an in-depth analysis of the specific problem of over-policing Black Canadians through the abuse of stop-and-frisk powers.

Part 1: History and Context

Chapter 1: The Common Law Constable

Chapter 1 explores and examines the origins, traditions, and purpose of policing. The author investigates the history of policing, starting in the ancient world. By examining the long history of policing, the reader has a better understanding of its role in the era of judge-made common law police powers. This chapter traces the origin of the word "police" from ancient Athens, through to continental Europe, and into the Anglo-Saxon lexicography. From there, we engage with the development of police and the authority they held in England up until the Norman conquest.

Once we have explored the roots of the word "police," we will shift focus toward the role of the constable. We pay heed to the "authority," "duty," and "powers" that emanate from the role of a constable. By analyzing the early modern understandings of the role of a constable, we build the groundwork for an in-depth discussion of police powers that are derived from statute. Research indicates that guidance on the duties and powers of police can be traced to legislation from the Middle Ages, such as the *Ordinance for the Preservation of the Peace* in 1242 and the *Statute of Winchester*.[21] Thereafter, the discussion moves to the early modern period up until the industrial age to engage with texts that have developed the conception of police duties and powers. Here, we look at jurisprudence from the nineteenth century that shaped the limits and boundaries of police powers in that period. Courts of the era developed the principle that officers had a duty to preserve the peace and could encroach justifiably on individual rights to do so.

Once Chapter 1 builds a broader understanding of how the duties of police officers are intimately connected with common law powers, we pivot to the Canadian context to connect the Canadian model to that of the English model that developed over the course of centuries. In the early years of the Confederation and the *Constitution Act, 1867 (British North America Act)*, we can see that Canadian legislators were keen on adopting the English justice system in Canada, with Newfoundland taking the lead pursuant to the *Royal Proclamation* of 1729.[22] Gradually, other provinces and cities began to create the bedrock of what would become modern-day policing in Canada. This examination of the Canadian historical perspective inevitably leads us to the Canadian common law adoption of the *Waterfield* test, which is the nub of this book and the central test that has facilitated the expansion of police powers in the Canadian common law.[23]

Chapter 2: The Supreme Court's Embrace of the Ancillary Powers Doctrine
In Chapter 2, we delve deeper into the *Waterfield* test or what is now more commonly known as the ancillary powers doctrine, which truly takes on a life of its own in the case of *Dedman v The Queen*.[24] More specifically, we present and analyze the most notable ancillary powers cases over the last thirty-five years that have impacted policing in Canada. Shortly after the enactment of the *Canadian Charter of Rights and Freedoms*, the Supreme Court of Canada had the tall task of interpreting this newly minted constitutional document. Sections 7–14 of the *Charter* were enacted to protect individuals from the encroachment of the state on civil liberties. Thus, it was incumbent upon the Supreme Court justices to interpret and develop the common law principles that were to become first principles of *Charter* jurisprudence with respect to the criminal law and policing.

In the wake of the *Charter, Dedman* came before the Supreme Court, a case centred on a roadside detention at a police check point, and it gave the majority of the Court an opportunity to articulate and apply the *Waterfield* test to an unregulated policing practice. Thus, *Dedman* signifies the beginning of a vast expansion of powers when novel or unregulated police conduct falls before a court. From *Dedman*, Chapter 2 moves to consider *R v Orbanski* and *R v Elias* and the right to counsel at roadside stops. We then examine the seminal case of *R v Godoy* that recognized police entry into the home in response to an emergency call as a valid police power under the common law.[25]

Chapter 2 highlights how these seminal cases have helped to expand and shape police powers and, thus, protect certain police conduct from *Charter* scrutiny. Post-*Dedman*, courts took it upon themselves to develop search-and-seizure jurisprudence under the *Waterfield/Dedman* test. Cases such as *R v MacDonald* provided future decisions with expanded criteria for a reviewing judge to determine whether a police search and seizure was lawful.[26] Close to twenty years after *Dedman*, the Supreme Court of Canada recognized the powers of investigative detention and search incident to detention in *R v Mann*.[27] *Mann* developed the reasonable suspicion standard as the test to determine whether police justifiably detained a suspect in an investigation.

Moreover, Chapter 2 engages with the sniffer dog cases of *R v Kang-Brown* and *R v A.M.* as well as *R v Clayton*, which detail the examination of the scope of roadblocks and safety searches.[28] We endeavour to present how the Supreme Court's articulation of the *Waterfield* test developed as the decades rolled on into the new century. We end the chapter with consideration of a key recent decision by the Supreme Court – *Fleming v Ontario* – where the Court decided against recognizing the power to arrest an individual, who was acting lawfully to prevent a breach of the peace.

Part 2: Judicial Expansion of Police Powers

Chapter 3: Search Incident to Arrest

Chapter 3 centres on the police power of search incident to arrest, formalized under the common law in *Cloutier v Langlois*.[29] Search incident to arrest has since been developed extensively in Supreme Court jurisprudence in the past several decades since *Cloutier*. Chapter 3 provides insight into the scope and refinement of this power. The chapter first acknowledges and discusses the unique and critical question of whether the right to search a person who has been lawfully arrested arises incidental to the arrest. Then, the chapter tracks the language in *Cloutier* to illuminate how such a search is minimally intrusive on the person in custody.

After a discussion of *Cloutier*, Chapter 3 explicates the Supreme Court of Canada's development of search incident to arrest in several high-profile cases. In the wake of *Cloutier*, *R v Golden* examines whether the common law authorized police to perform a strip-search incident to arrest.[30] This invasive technique led to the establishment of preconditions that must be satisfied before police can conduct a strip-search of the arrestee. Further, the chapter examines the majority's reasoning as to how strip-searches must be conducted in a manner that does not infringe section 8 of the *Charter*.

As well, Chapter 3 engages with a highly intrusive form of search incident to arrest that produces bodily samples from the individual under custody. The first of these cases discussed – *R v Stillman* – provides us with limitations on the extraction of samples subsequent to arrest.[31] In *Stillman*, the justices determined that police actions were abusive and that the power itself was limited to deter *carte blanche* conduct. The second of these "bodily sample" cases reviewed in this chapter – *R v Saeed* – focuses the discussion on the use of penile swabs to retrieve a complainant's DNA.[32] In *Saeed*, the majority of the Supreme Court found that DNA taken from the arrestee's penis did not breach his section 8 rights. The majority maintained that the accused did not have a significant privacy interest in the complainant's DNA and, thus, could not avail themselves of section 8 protections.

Chapter 3 segues from bodily samples and DNA to searches of property incident to arrest. Naturally, where one is domiciled, one's vehicle, and one's personal smart phone attract varying levels of section 8 protection under the common law. Here, we look at *R v Caslake* and *R v Fearon* to determine whether search incident to arrest has any readily ascertainable limits on its scope.[33] As far back as *Cloutier*, the Supreme Court has maintained that search incident to arrest could expand to include premises and property. This notion was realized in *Caslake*. In *Caslake*, we see a Supreme Court majority posit that the "need for law enforcement authorities to gain control of things or information" outweighs an individual's privacy rights that are protected under section 8 of the *Charter*.

The Supreme Court continued its expansion of the scope of search incident to arrest in *Fearon* to include cell phones. In *Fearon*, the Supreme Court was divided as to how searches of cell phones should be reviewed by a court. The dissenting opinion of Justice Andromache Karakatsanis identified the majority's approach as impractical and that the digital revolution created a new, intensely private, and personal sphere for Canadians that should not be trammelled.

Chapter 4: An Empirical Analysis of Ancillary Powers Generation and Deployment

In Chapter 4, we turn to empirical data that has been retrieved by our researchers that shows how common law police powers have expanded at the hands of the ancillary powers doctrine. While the *Charter* imbues the judiciary with the role and responsibility of protecting constitutional rights and freedoms, it has also been used by the judiciary to limit and restrict rights and freedoms. As such, Chapter 4 examines hard evidence in the Canadian common law that shows how rapidly the expansion and application of police powers has taken place in the *Charter* era. We infer from our findings that the ancillary powers doctrine has had a vastly disproportionate effect on racialized minorities and Indigenous people in Canada.

We return to the case of *R v Mann* as an example of how the recognition of powers such as investigative detention and search incident to detention has had a negative impact on certain populations over others. We identify that the absence of race-based discussions in *Mann* to limit the scope of investigations on predominantly racialized neighbourhoods was a missed opportunity by the Supreme Court of Canada, especially when considering the proliferation of street checks across the country in the wake of *Mann*.

After revisiting *Mann*, we turn to more recent case law to propose that the current iteration of the Supreme Court appears to be signalling a more cautious approach to recognizing new police powers, primarily in *Fleming v Ontario*.[34] Our discussion of *Fleming* flanks the presentation and analysis of the empirical data that is central to Chapter 4. We use the methodology of generation cases where a new power is created, and the deployment (application) of those powers as tools is used to assist in measuring and categorizing powers into discreet units. Our findings are grouped by levels of court and types of power and time frames. The data that has been extrapolated from various legal databases uncovers the proliferation of these powers since *Dedman* and shows a steady rise in generation and deployment cases in the several decades that have been analyzed. Our most recent data is given particular attention when determining whether the Supreme Court's decision in *Fleming* marks a turning point in the jurisprudence.

After our analysis of the empirical data, we assess three appellate-level cases that have been released since the ruling in *Fleming* to identify nuances in the decisions and to highlight the complexity within which the ancillary powers doctrine generates and deploys novel and unregulated police powers in the common law.

Part 3: Critiquing Police Powers

Chapter 5: The Doctrine's Proportionality Problem

Chapter 5 looks at some of the proportionality constraints imposed by the *Waterfield* test. Courts only authorize ancillary police powers that are reasonably necessary to fulfill law enforcement duties. As part of the proportionality analysis, courts evaluate the importance of an ancillary police power, its impact on liberty, and whether it is necessary for officers to restrict liberty to fulfill a police duty. The ancillary powers doctrine's proportionality analysis is similar to the analysis under section 1 of the *Charter*. However, in Chapter 5, we argue that the ancillary powers doctrine's proportionality test is flawed in many respects and employs a weaker proportionality framework compared to section 1 of the *Charter*. For example, when applying the ancillary powers doctrine, judges may not consider how common law police powers can result in selective enforcement and racial profiling, which will be further discussed in Chapter 6.

Chapter 5 argues that the ancillary powers doctrine's proportionality framework has fundamental problems that undermine the legitimacy of common law police powers. It advances the following three arguments. First, the ancillary powers doctrine's proportionality analysis fails to consider three types of harms: collective, non-egalitarian, and repetitive. Yet these types of harms can justify stronger transparency and oversight mechanisms for a particular common law police power or militate against the creation of a new ancillary police power altogether. Second, the ancillary powers doctrine's proportionality analysis is inaccurate due to information failures. When applying the *Waterfield* test, courts authorize common law police powers that apply to the future. For this reason, judges tend to lack information about how police officers have exercised – and will exercise – this power. Years later, empirical studies may reveal that officers have enforced a particular police power disparately or selectively. Third and interrelatedly, there is the judiciary's inability to conduct accurate proportionality analysis, which undermines the ancillary powers doctrine's justifiability. Inaccurate proportionality assessments erode the validity of such justifications and ultimately corrode the ancillary powers doctrine's legitimacy.

Chapter 6: Ancillary Police Powers and the Black Experience in Canada

Chapter 6 explores the tenuous relationship between Black communities and police stop and search in Canada. We explore this relationship through a historical lens and provide further contextualization by examining public perceptions of police bias. The chapter engages with both official and unofficial sources of data to investigate the disproportionality of police stop-and-search practices on Black communities. Our analysis begins by focusing on the latter part of the twentieth century when Canada's Black population experienced rapid growth, and many Black immigrants settled in the Greater Toronto Area. Several high-profile killings of Black males by police officers sparked community mobilization in Toronto in the 1970s. These incidents were followed by more shootings involving Black men in the 1980s, prompting further turmoil and mobilization in the community. These events prompted a review of police practices in the province and, ultimately, the creation of new oversight mechanisms, such as Ontario's Special Investigations Unit.

Chapter 6 then explores significant events and related activism in the 1990s and 2000s where public concern about relations between the police and Black communities shifted to focus on the frequency and nature of police contacts with Black people. Amid this persistent issue, the *Toronto Star* published the first of a series of profiles on the relationship between the police and Toronto's Black communities. We identify the *Toronto Star*'s work as pivotal in shining a light on racial profiling in policing and raising public consciousness about the issue.

We then move into a discussion of the public perceptions of police bias through an examination of various large-scale surveys that were administered in the last several decades to gain a sense of the perception of how Black individuals are treated by police. The discussion then pivots to a look at the difficulty of gaining access to official sources of data about the stop and search of citizens that are disaggregated by race. We identify how, slowly, researchers are gaining access to police stop-and-search data. Through this data, researchers have drawn findings that support the conclusions drawn from Black communities that Black individuals are more likely to have police encounters than other races. Chapter 6 moves to consider the consequences of such police activity on Black communities. We examine how undue police encounters detrimentally impact the mental health of racialized individuals and contribute to their criminalization. Furthermore, Chapter 6 engages with how these systematic stops of racialized minorities negatively impacts the functioning of the criminal justice system.

Chapter 7: The Doctrine as a One-Way Ratchet

Chapter 7 argues that judicially created police powers result in a one-way ratchet in criminal procedure, especially in the context of street-level policing. The term "one-way ratchet" implies that courts have expanded police powers but have not broadened the scope of fundamental rights and remedies for police misconduct commensurately. The opening parts of Chapter 7 discuss the three prominent critiques of the ancillary powers doctrine. First, in criminal procedure, the Supreme Court of Canada's role has evolved from guardian of constitutional rights to a creator of police powers that endangers these rights. Second, the ancillary powers doctrine is inconsistent with the rule of law because courts authorize new common law police powers retro-actively. As a result, police officers and individuals cannot know the scope of law enforcement powers. Third, courts tend to ignore how a novel common law police power can contribute to racial profiling and discrimination.

Chapter 7 then demonstrates how and why ancillary police powers pro-duce a one-way ratchet in criminal procedure. It shows how courts have created new law enforcement powers but have not expanded the scope of individual rights or legal remedies commensurately. Despite the growth of police powers, remedies such as *Charter* damages and tort law have largely failed to prevent and counteract unlawful police action. This chapter ex-plains how the ancillary powers doctrine creates perverse institutional incen-tives that contribute to these tendencies. The judicial creation of police powers discourages lawmakers from enacting new police powers or restrict-ing existing ones and encourages judges to act as legislators in the domain of criminal procedure.

Drawing on the republican conception of freedom as non-domination, Chapter 7 explains how the ancillary powers doctrine subjects individuals to unilateral and uncontrolled threats of interference. It discusses how low-visibility ancillary police powers, such as traffic stops, frisk searches, and investigative detentions, can breed distrust that discourages cooperation with law enforcement. As a result, ancillary police powers can undermine the very law enforcement objectives that justify their existence: preventing crime, protecting people and property from harm, and maintaining public order. The concept of a one-way ratchet explains why the ancillary powers doctrine can contribute to greater domination, especially for racialized and Indigenous persons.

The concluding part of this chapter describes why individuals seek to protect themselves against domination that flows from ancillary police powers. Individuals resort to certain forms of self-help, such as counter-surveillance and cop watching, because they cannot rely on courts to protect their fundamental rights and interests adequately. Ultimately, this chapter deepens our understanding of why the ancillary powers doctrine is objectionable for reasons that are typically overlooked.

In conclusion, our exploration traverses the historical origins of policing, evolving through the development of police powers in England and subsequently altering the Canadian legal approach to common law policing. We examine the Canadian context, with a focus on the Supreme Court's embrace of the ancillary powers doctrine, exemplified by the influential *Waterfield* test. We place the approach under empirical scrutiny, unravelling the proportionality challenges within the ancillary powers framework, exploring its impact on the policing of Black people in Canada, and noting that the doctrine operates as a one-way ratchet in criminal procedure. This holistic examination not only sheds light on the historical and legal intricacies surrounding police powers but also highlights the consequences of their expansion, urging a nuanced revaluation of the delicate balance between law enforcement necessities and individual rights in the Canadian justice system.

PART 1
History and Context

The Common Law Constable 1

> Police forces exist in municipal, provincial, and federal jurisdictions to exercise powers designed to promote the order, safety, health, morals, and general welfare of society ... [Their duties] stem not only from the relevant statutes to which reference has been made, but from the common law, which recognizes the existence of a broad conventional or customary duty in the established constabulary as an arm of the State to protect the life, limb and property of the subject.
>
> — *O'ROURKE V SCHACHT*, DECIDED 19 DECEMBER 1974

It is fair to assume that most Canadians want to live their lives in a peaceful and safe manner. Daily, we do not want to have to worry about others stealing or vandalizing our personal property, invading our homes, or inflicting harm or injury to ourselves, our friends, and our family. If we have been wronged, we do not want to have to resort to taking "justice" into our own hands to make things right. We expect to live in an ordered, civilized society, not one overrun by chaos. This is a need we hold today and one that society's past has upheld. The "police" – in various forms – have long been enlisted to uphold the law, to protect life, liberty, property, and to preserve public order.

Police are most recognized for their role in fighting crime. However, over the centuries, the police's duties, responsibilities, and functions have varied and become multifaceted, extending beyond the scope of mere crime control. Early Canadian police forces were responsible for fighting fires, conducting inspections of food, operating ambulances, catching stray dogs, and lighting streetlamps. These tasks and responsibilities arose organically as they have served the public interest. This is the very essence of the role that police play in society. It is expected that they are employed to protect the well-being of individuals, foster feelings of security within the community, and aid where needed.

In Winnipeg, for example, the police responded to 234,212 calls for service in 2022. However, only 30 percent of those calls (72,059) involved criminal offences.[1] Of these, there were 16,590 "domestic event" calls; however, less than 15 percent resulted in criminal charges.[2] Another 20,342 calls were to "check on the well-being" of an individual. These statistics are representative of most police departments, where many of the activities performed by the police are related to social behaviour or environmental issues not related to crime control. Responsibilities include looking into missing persons cases, following up with noise complaints and other disturbances, and responding to instances of public drunkenness, mental health issues, vehicle accidents, malfunctioning traffic lights, and animal complaints, to name a few.[3]

The Origins of Policing: Tracing the Development of Policing from Ancient Greece to Victorian England

Unsurprisingly, the concept of "policing" arose before there was ever a formal police force or institution put in place. To understand the full importance and early origins of policing, it is perhaps best to start with the etymology of the word. "Police" comes from the Latinization of the ancient Greek word *polītia,* which draws on both *polītēs* (citizen) and *polis* (city). From the ancient roots of the word, there is an importance being placed on the administration of public order and civility within the city as well as the regulation of citizens' interactions with each other and with their government.[4] Indeed, in Athens during the fifth century BC, magistrates were responsible for maintaining order in the markets, overseeing honest measuring standards and public hygiene, protecting morals, surveying foreigners, and preventing accidents such as fires.[5] In carrying out the "policy" of the government, magistrates used Scythian slaves or "rod-bearers" to help achieve some of these tasks.

As with most things, the Romans followed suit. Emperor Caesar Augustus (63 BC–14 AD) divided the city into regions and precincts (*vici*) that were overseen by *vicomagistri*. Like the Greeks, the vicomagistri utilized *vigiles* (watchmen) to patrol the streets at night, be on the lookout for fires, apprehend thieves and robbers, guard the baths, and maintain general public order in the city.[6] This early concept of policing quickly proliferated across Europe in the subsequent centuries: "police," "policei," "pollicei," "policey," "pollicey," "pollizey," "pollizei," "politzey," "pollucey," and "pullucey" – while the spelling varied, the meaning encompassed similar ideas of citizenship, administration, government, civil polity, and public order.

The earliest policing system in England was community based and implied collective responsibility. The system hinged on the Anglo-Saxon *frankpledge*. This was a promise, which every adult male undertook, and required each individual to be responsible for the conduct of the men in their community and for the group's overall protection. To formalize the obligation, the men were organized into *tithings* (groups of ten) headed by a *tithingman* (also referred to as a *borsholder*). Each tithing, in turn, was grouped into a hundred, which was headed by a hundredman, who served as both administrator and judge. Each hundred was grouped into a shire and was placed under the supervision of the shire-reeve, a position that eventually developed into the modern office of the county sheriff.[7]

If one of the men in the tithing engaged in wrongful behaviour, the other nine would ensure that the wrongdoer would appear in court or would bear the collective responsibility or burden for what he had done. However, the law gave the tithingman (the leader of each tithing) a "certain *special authority over and above* his general obligations as a member of the tithing." Legal scholar Phillip Stenning notes that chief among the tithingman's responsibilities was that of organizing the "hue and cry." This was essentially a "sounding of the alarm" that required every able-bodied man to join in the search and pursuit of the fleeing wrongdoer, who had evaded or escaped from custody. The tithingman was also responsible for the wrongdoer while he was in custody and would generally "place him in the local stocks until he could be brought before a 'court' for bail." The law also accorded the tithingman a "special authority to intervene to prevent or terminate breaches of the peace."[8]

This frankpledge method of policing continued unchanged until England's conquest by the Normans in 1066, who added the office of constable. The word "constable" comes from the Old French term *"conestable,"* which at first simply designated a person holding a public office.[9] In a more general capacity, the constable adopted the earlier office of the tithingman, its frankpledge obligations, and the legally prescribed responsibilities. Scholars and historians generally agree that the office of the constable and his accompanying duties represent the foundation of contemporary policing.

The Constable's Unique Historical Position: Deriving Powers from Both Statute and Common Law

Before tracing the historical role of the constable, it is important to clearly distinguish between the terms "authority," "duties," and "powers." Police duties are often seen as the larger "goals" and "objectives" that officers are legally obligated – by virtue of their occupation – to pursue and achieve. "To preserve the peace" and "to protect life and property" – duties that have long been entrenched in the constable's office – have been recognized by the common law courts and codified in police service legislation. However, police duties have traditionally been expressed in very broad, rather non-specific language. What does it mean to "prevent crime"? This duty could encompass a lot of different types of actions. Perhaps this broad wording purposefully leaves questions about what police officers are legally and practically allowed to do unanswered and, thus, open to interpretation and flexibility.

Police powers are the specific tasks, actions, and conduct that the police are authorized to perform to achieve their larger duties. A straightforward example would be the power of arrest. This is an exceptional power. It is a power that individual citizens do not possess and, in ordinary circumstances, are forbidden by law from performing. Yet when an officer arrests someone, they are interfering with that individual's physical person and restricting their liberty to move around freely. If the law was blind to the distinction between actions performed by a police officer and those performed by a normal citizen, it would most certainly condemn this type of intrusive action as assault or trespass. As such, the law would impose an appropriate punishment. For this reason, the law has developed rules for justifying police powers (such as arrest, searches, and seizures) and has afforded police officers protection in the form of specially created exceptions to the general prohibitory rules of criminal law or torts.

But who authorizes which powers the police are entitled to use? Early societies recognized, as we do today, that for a constable to lawfully exercise their powers – especially those that interfere with the rights of others – those powers must rest on the authority of law and not on the will or whims of an individual or group. Thus, the assorted powers that the constable came to possess during a millennium of service arose from two distinct sources of authority: from statute and from common law. An early iteration of the powers that are authorized by statute and the common law are found in *The Complete Constable,* an early written source that was published in 1692. The text of *The Complete Constable* recognized that the constable's powers were derived from both the common law and statute: "[I]n some things acting of himself, without any command from others [the constable] is said to be *ex officio* and in other things [he is] not to act without a Commandment, Warrant, or Precept from another person." While *The Complete Constable* reiterated the three functions of the constable in preserving the king's peace, the text sets out some of the general tasks that a constable was sworn by his oath to pursue:

1 In general, to serve the King and Queen [and if in a Leet, the Lord of the Mannor] in the Office of a Constable: This extends to his whole Office.

2 In particular, to see the King and Queen's peace to be kept and preserved.

3 To arrest such persons as shall in their presence ride or go offensively Arm'd, or commit any Riot or Affray, &c.

4 Upon Complaint, to apprehend all Felons, Barretors, Rioters, &c. and upon resistance to levy Hue and Cry, and pursue them.

5 To see the Watch be duly kept in the Town.

6 To see that the Statute for punishment of Rogues, Vagabonds, Idle persons, and Night-Walkers be duly put in execution.

7 To have a watchful Eye upon persons keeping unlawful Gaming houses, and such as frequent the same, and use any unlawful Games and Plays there, or elsewhere.

8 At the Assizes, Sessions, or Leet, to present the Offences of Tipling, Drunkenness, and profane Swearing; against which the Statutes have provided.

9 To present all Bloodshedding, Affrays, Outcries, Rescues, &c.

10 To execute truly all Precepts and Warrants to them directed from the Justices and others in Authority.

The rest of the instructions are in general: to do and execute all other things belonging to the office of a constable, to the best of his power, knowledge, and ability, and this again extends to his whole office.[10]

Police Powers Derived from Statute

Deriving powers from statute is something that we are more familiar with today. Through statutes and acts, lawmakers delineate the scope and limits of police behaviour. For example, a statute, like the *Criminal Code*, aims to clearly define police powers as well as lay out the various requirements that must be met to use those powers.[11] Certain authorizations are broad in scope, giving officers more discretion. Other powers are narrowly tailored to apply in specific circumstances for limited purposes. The legislative process today often involves debate among lawmakers, input from the public, and studies commissioned and consulted, alongside discussions with police forces and administration. The law is refined until it gives clear guidance on what the police are authorized or not authorized to do. Through these statutes and acts, police acquire executive powers.

This practice extends back to the early days of the constable's office, as seen in thirteenth-century pieces of legislation, which sought to describe this rapidly expanding position. As mentioned previously, while constables were appointed to keep the peace, they were also being given functions other than detecting or preventing violence. The *Ordinance for the Preservation of the Peace* of 1242 identified one function of constables as keeping watch at the city gates during the night and arresting any suspicious foreigners who passed by.[12] The *Statute of Winchester*, in 1285,[13] further elaborated on this "ancient custom" by establishing the "watch-and-ward" system. The duties of the constable expanded to provide security for travelling justices, lighting streetlamps, calling time, watching for fires, and reporting other conditions. This statute also commanded that the woods, ditches, and hedges on either side of the highways be cleared for two hundred feet so that "no men can hide near the road with evil intent."[14] This effort to reduce the incidence of highway robbery was aimed not only at maintaining peace but also at preventing crime.

Through the authority of other written laws, the constable took on assorted tasks that made him an aid or agent to quasi-judicial officers, such as the justices of the peace, the coroner, and the sheriff. In his treatise, *On the Laws and Customs in England* from 1235, Henry de Bracton describes the constable's identity as the "keepers of the Court's senses."[15] While the constable himself lacked the authority to act as "judge," the constable took note of what he saw, heard, felt, smelled, and tasted on the streets and in the community for the court's benefit and record. Of course, the constable also acted as the "strong arm," executing court orders and bodily arrests.[16]

Police Powers Derived from Common Law

Yet the focus of this book lies with the other unique source of authority from which constables draw their powers. "Common law" police powers are powers that are recognized and articulated by judges in the court setting on a case-by-case basis. Since these powers are not created via the legislative process but, rather, through court decisions, they are sometimes described as "ancillary" powers – those that run alongside the powers prescribed by lawmakers.[17]

Here, it is important to clarify a key point. The courts are not technically creating new police powers. The judges are articulating powers that the police have always possessed but have never previously been proscribed by the legislature or the courts. There are several police practices and customs that pre-date the inception of the English common law tradition and are described as powers that are "original" and "inherent" to the constable's office and duties. These ancient powers perhaps arose from royal command or community custom and, after centuries of continual use, found themselves rooted firmly in the constable's toolkit. Thus, over the centuries, the courts have used their special authority to recognize in law the powers and duties already possessed by the constable by virtue of their office. As touched upon earlier, these are generally seen as fitting within the larger "goals" of the constable: "the preservation of peace, the prevention of crime, and the protection of life and property."[18] In the following discussion, we will build on these theories by looking at Irish and British jurisprudence where common law police powers really began to take shape and solidify.

"Preserving the Peace": Early Irish/British Jurisprudence

Examining the constable's common law duty to "conserve the peace," William Lambard, a sixteenth-century legal writer and historian, found that this duty was accompanied by three distinct tasks: prevent, pacify, and punish. He stated that the constable should first foresee and prevent anything that "tendeth, either directlye, or by meanes, to the breach of the peace." Second, the constable should quiet or pacify those "that are occupied in the breach of the peace" by restoring order during the commission of an offence. Third, the constable should "punish" those who have already broken the peace, by bringing the wrongdoers before the courts, where the full punitive powers of the law would be applied. For good measure, Lambard even strove to define what a "breach of the peace" was. He suggested that the definition not only included fighting or violence but also could include any felony, public disturbances, or even infliction of fear: "[W]hether it be by unlawful wearing of armour, or by assembling of people to do any unlawful act, are taken to be disturbances or breaches of the Peace."[19]

For constables in the sixteenth century or for police officers today, preserving the peace involves dealing with a wide and varied list of unexpected and often uncontrollable forces. On the one hand, it could mean addressing noise disturbances or calming down a heated squabble between neighbours. On the other hand, it could involve breaking up violent fistfights in the streets. However, most of the early cases that examine the constable's duty to "preserve the peace" involve the police trying to stop individuals from going about their lawful behaviour or attempting to disperse public meetings because the officers believe, based on experience or prior knowledge, that the situation will likely escalate into violence. In the sampling of cases that follow, we clearly see the conflict of interests: the individual's desire to remain undisturbed in their lawful conduct and the state's duty to take actions to prevent violence or riotous behaviour from occurring.

The 1864 Irish case of *Humphries v Connor* involved a police officer removing an orange lily from the buttonhole of a woman's jacket.[20] Wearing a flower on one's lapel was not in itself an unlawful activity, neither was the woman's decision to walk through a crowd of devout Roman Catholics wearing the flower as a symbol of her Protestant pride.[21] However, with tensions running high between the two religious groups, a number of Catholics started following the woman making a "great noise and disturbance." In trying to calm the situation, Officer Daniel Connor asked the woman (Anne Humphries) to remove the flower from her jacket, a request she adamantly declined. When the Catholic pursuers threatened to start throwing punches, Officer Connor "gently and quietly" removed the emblem from the woman's person to prevent violence from being inflicted.

While the officer had not physically harmed her in the process of removing the flower, the woman brought legal action against the officer, arguing that he had committed a trespass upon her person and had interfered with her inherently lawful conduct. The question before the Court rested on whether a constable was entitled to interfere with an individual who was not about to breach the peace or commit an illegal act – but was likely to be "an object of insult or injury" by other persons who intended to breach the peace. Ultimately, the Court of Queen's Bench found that Officer Connor's conduct was an unavoidable action that was necessary to prevent a breach of the peace. Thus, the charge against the officer was dismissed. Justice O'Brien held that it is a constable's duty to prevent offences from occurring when it appears to him that the circumstances justify it. When considering if some direction should be given to the police in how they should exercise their discretion in the future so as not to abuse it, O'Brien J stated that the law "would not protect a Constable from any unnecessary, excessive, or improper exercise of such power in other cases."[22]

   In support of this conclusion O'Brien J considered several cases including *Cooke v Nethercote*,[23] *R v Browne*,[24] *Ingle v Bell*,[25] and *R v Hogan*,[26] where the duty of the police to keep the peace interfered with individual rights, even where the activity might be lawful. Justice Hayes, while concurring with O'Brien J, added that a constable by his very appointment is charged with the solemn duty of seeing that the peace is preserved.[27] He continued, saying that while the law had not ventured to lay down with precise measures all the facts that call for a constable's interference, "he is not only at liberty, *but is bound,* to see that the peace is preserved and that he is to do everything that is necessary for that purpose."[28] Thus, from this case, it arose that if there were no other means of restoring the peace, an officer was permitted by the common law to interfere with an individual's lawful conduct. More specifically, a police officer was entitled to remove a personal object on a person that is a provocation to others and may incite a breach of the peace.

   Twenty years later, in 1882, the courts considered this principle again in another Irish case, *O'Kelly v Harvey*.[29] What actions could an officer take against an individual who was not doing anything inherently unlawful to prevent a breach of the peace? In this case, O'Kelly was organizing a public demonstration for the Land League, with the objective of persuading tenants not to pay their rent. However, the police received tips from informants that many Orangemen, members of the opposing political party, were preparing to "assemble by the thousands" and perform a counter-demonstration. When O'Kelly refused the officer's request to disperse the Land League's meeting, Officer Harvey laid his hands on "the plaintiff in order to separate and disperse the meeting, using no more violence than was necessary for that purpose." O'Kelly subsequently brought an action for assault and battery, arguing that he had been doing nothing wrong and that he had the right to assemble lawfully and unmolested. Yet the officer argued that in forcibly dispersing the meeting he "believed, and had reasonable and probable grounds for believing, that a breach of the peace would occur if said meeting were allowed to be held and continued, and that the public peace and tranquillity could not otherwise be preserved than by separating and dispersing" the meeting. If there was no other way in which the breach of the peace could be avoided but by stopping and dispersing the plaintiff's meeting, was the defendant justified in taking the necessary steps to stop and disperse it? In the opinion of the Exchequer Division and in the Irish Court of Appeal, the officer was justified in doing what he did. In his judgment, Chief Baron Christopher Palles stated that

> under such circumstances the Defendant was not to defer action until a breach of the peace had actually been committed. His paramount duty was to *preserve the peace unbroken,* and that, by whatever means were available for the purpose ... he is, of course, entitled, and in fact bound, to intervene the moment he is in reasonable apprehension of a breach of the peace being imminent; and, therefore, he must in such cases necessarily act on his own *reasonable* and *bona fide belief* as to what is *likely* to occur.[30]

The courts in England gave an indication of their willingness to accept these broader police powers established in the Irish cases. In *Thomas v Sawkins* in 1935, the Divisional Court concluded that police officers were entitled to "enter and remain at public meetings on private premises" if they had reasonable grounds for believing that if they were not present, an offence or breach of the peace would occur.[31] In this case, Alun Clydwyn Thomas had rented out the local library hall and had organized a public meeting to protest a controversial bill before Parliament and demand the dismissal of the local chief constable. Having heard the topics up for discussion, three police officers presented themselves for admission to the meeting. Even though the doorkeepers had been instructed not to admit the police, the officers nevertheless entered the hall and seated themselves in the front row. After filing a complaint with the police station, Thomas demanded that the officers leave the meeting. The officers refused, believing that if they left a breach of the peace was likely to occur. They argued that their belief was based on their experience and knowledge of similar previous meetings. When Thomas attempted to eject the police from the hall, Constable James Sawkins pushed his arm away, which resulted in Thomas filing an action for assault and trespass.

Relying on *Humphries* and other cases, the Court found that "the powers and duties of the police are directed, not to the interests of the police, but to the protection and welfare of the public." Chief Justice Lord Hewart maintained that where "reasonable grounds for believing that an offence is imminent or is likely to be committed," an officer has authority under the common law to intervene. This was echoed by Justice Avory, who justified the police conduct of entering the hall as necessary to prevent a breach of the peace under the common law. There was no need for express statutory authority for the officers' actions because the officers had reasonable grounds to enter the premises.

Six months afterwards, the Divisional Court released its decision in *Duncan v Jones*.[32] Not unlike *Sawkins*, but without reference to that decision, the Court deemed that the police were in the execution of their duty to "preserve the peace" when they prevented the plaintiff from holding a public meeting. Ms. Katherine Duncan was planning to hold a public meeting on a busy street in New Cross in the city of London to adamantly defend the "right of free speech and public meetings." Before the meeting commenced, Inspector William Jones told her that she could not have her meeting there for fear that her speech would create a breach of the peace. However, he suggested that she relocate and hold her meeting on another street, 175 yards away. She refused the officer's request and began to address her audience. Moments into her speech, she was arrested and convicted of wilfully obstructing the officer in the execution of his duty.

The Court concluded that the circumstances of the case gave the officer authority under the common law to prevent a breach of the peace. The facts indicated that a year prior to the matter at hand, the appellant was involved in a similar meeting, which led to a disturbance. The Court established that there was a causal connection between the previous meeting and the subsequent disturbance. As a result, the officer in question had "reasonably apprehended a breach of the peace" in the present circumstances. Thus, a lawful authority arises from which an officer may interfere with one's liberty or property rights to prevent the breach.

"Protecting Lives and Property": *Haynes v Harwood*

Police officers, alongside the fire department or ambulances (which until more recent times were overseen by the police), are often summoned by the public to respond to emergencies. They risk their lives to aid others and try to de-escalate dangerous situations whether they are in the home or on the streets. This could involve carefully handling individuals who pose a danger to the public or securing the area of an accident and ensuring public safety. In the case of *Haynes v Harwood* in 1935, the Court of King's Bench found that under the police's common law duty to protect life and property, the police are expected to chase after rogue horses running down the street.[33] In this case, the defendant's servant, while conducting business at the wharf, left the defendant's two-horse carriage unattended on a busy street. Two boys started throwing stones, which caused the horses to jolt, breaking the chain. The horses, still attached to the carriage, started running down the busy town street toward a group of children and elderly ladies.

Constable Thomas John Haynes, who witnessed this incident from inside the police station, raced outside to stop the horses. He was able to wrangle the runaway horses before anyone else was hurt but sustained injuries while doing so. Constable Haynes sought damages from the defendant for the injuries he sustained from stopping the horses. The Court of King's Bench ruled in favour of the officer, but the defendant appealed to the English Court of Appeal. Nevertheless, the Court of Appeal found that the officer had not "voluntarily" taken the risk but was legally obligated to stop the horses, pursuant to his general duty "to protect life and property." The constable's actions and his injuries were a direct consequence of the defendant's negligence, and the defendant was required to pay damages.

"Preventing Crime": Police Power of Search Incident to Arrest

Police officers are most often associated with their duty of "preventing crime" and catching criminals. The power of arrest has traditionally been statutorily ascribed to officers. Yet the ability of police to search a prisoner and seize their property has not been explicitly laid out in legislation historically. However, these types of searches were simply seen as proper, routine practice. From the fifteenth to the eighteenth century, there was more tolerance for intrusive and violent acts committed toward persons arrested and accused of crimes. As well, most objects seized upon arrest, such as bags of coins or weapons, could be found without any lengthy or extensive search of the person.[34] The court understood a constable's motivation to search a prisoner's body for concealed weapons and to seize stolen property in order not only to put an end to criminal activity but also to ensure safety.

Entick v Carrington, a seminal English case from 1765, is an important decision to analyze for two reasons.[35] First, it is an example of a common law court recognizing a constable's power of seizure but also trying to limit this power by asserting that "the State was not entitled to seize items for purely evidentiary reasons."[36] While this position was later overturned in Canada with the codification of the *Criminal Code* in 1892, it remained vital both in the United States and in Great Britain for a good deal longer.[37] Second, perhaps more far-reaching in its impact, the Court articulated that the government and the prerogative powers they held were not above the law of the land. If a state agent acted without the authorization of law or exceeded the powers given to them by the law, they would still be subject to the same charge of trespass or assault as would be the case for any individual. Thus, government officials, acting in their executive capacity, could not exercise public power unless such exercise was authorized by the rule of law, either by statute or common law. Lord Camden famously stated:

> By the laws of England, every invasion of private property, be it ever so minute, is a trespass. No man can set his foot upon my ground without my licence, but he is liable to an action, though the damage be nothing, which is proved by every declaration in trespass, where the defendant is called upon to answer for bruising the grass and even treading upon the soil. If he admits the fact, he is bound to shew by way of justification, that *some positive law has empowered or excused him*. The justification is submitted to the judges, who are to look into the books; and see if such a justification can be maintained by the text of the statute law, or by the principles of common law. If no such excuse can be found or produced, the silence of the books is an authority against the defendant, and the plaintiff must have judgment.[38]

Many of the early "search-and-seizure" cases focused not upon the legality of whether the search should take place but, rather, upon the prisoner's property that was seized by the police. In *R v Barnett* in 1829[39] and in *R v O'Donnell* in 1835,[40] the courts acknowledged that the police were allowed to search prisoners upon arrest and seize property that was materially related to the offence charged. However, with these cases, the judges criticized the police practice of depriving the prisoners of money found on their persons that was not connected with the offence:

> Generally speaking, it is not right that a man's money should be taken away from him, unless it is connected in some way with the property stolen. If it is connected with the robbery, it is quite proper that it should be taken. But unless it is, it is not a fair thing to take away his money, which he might use for his defence. I believe constables are too much in the habit of taking away everything they find upon a prisoner, which is certainly not right. And this is a rule which ought to be observed by all policemen and other peace officers.[41]

Here, Edward Barnett was charged with murder, while Daniel O'Donnell was charged with stealing silver spoons from his mistress's house. Both defendants argued that by seizing the money found upon them, the constables had deprived them of the means of affording lawyers and making a proper case in court. In both instances, the judges agreed that the money was unrelated to the charges and ordered it returned to the defendants.

These cases implicitly recognized that a constable had the right to seize property that was related to the offence charge and that those objects could be used as evidence. This was more expressly acknowledged in the Irish case of *Dillon v O'Brien and Davis* in 1887[42] and slightly later by the British courts in *R v Lushington* in 1894.[43] Within the latter case, Justice Wright in the Court of Queen's Bench stated that "[i]n this country I take it is undoubted law that it is *within the power of,* and is *the duty of,* constables to retain for use in Court things which may be evidence of crime, and which have come into the possession of the constable without wrong on their part."[44] However, one of the first cases that contested the actual search of an arrested individual was the influential decision of *Bessell v Wilson* in 1853.[45]

In his judgment, Chief Justice Lord Campbell revealed that he was not concerned with the existence of this type of police search power but, rather, critical of the police's decision to search the plaintiff given the facts of the situation. In this case, Bessell, the plaintiff, was a tradesman and was arrested for having failed to pay a court-issued fine related to a copyright complaint. Lord Campbell CJ argued that there was little foundation for the police to believe that the plaintiff might have been concealing a weapon and found that the search was unjustified given the circumstances. Lord Campbell CJ stated that such searches needed circumstantial justification to intrude on an accused's person:

> It is often the duty of an officer to search a prisoner. If for instance, a man is taken in the commission of a felony, he may be searched to see whether the stolen articles are in his possession, or whether he has any instruments of violence about him, and, in like manner, if he be taken on a charge of arson, he may be searched to see whether he has any fire-boxes or matches about his person ... It may be highly satisfactory, and indeed necessary that the prisoner should be searched.[46]

This approach was adopted later that same year in *Leigh v Cole.*[47] This case examined an assault action brought against the police superintendent, who had allegedly apprehended, beaten, searched, and locked the plaintiff in a prison cell overnight for making a public drunken disturbance. In his charge to the jury on the legality of the search, Justice Williams made the following comments about this common law police power:

> With respect to searching a prisoner, there is no doubt that a man when in custody may so conduct himself, by reason of violence of language or conduct, that a police officer may reasonably think it prudent and right to search him, in order *to ascertain whether he has any weapon with which he might do mischief to the person or commit a breach of the peace;* but at the same time it is quite wrong to suppose that any general rule can be applied to such a case. Even when a man is confined for being drunk and disorderly, it is not correct to say that he must submit to the degradation of being searched, as the searching of such a person must depend upon all the circumstances of the case.[48]

Bessell and *Leigh* marked the starting point of judges grappling to give guidance and definition to this search power. In this era, courts were beginning to recognize the balance that needed to be struck between the necessary tools and practices that the police require to do their job and the interests and liberties held by individuals accused of criminal activity.

Codification of Common Law Powers

Many of the police powers recognized by the common law courts of Britain and Ireland ultimately made their way into legislation. Beginning in the 1600s and 1700s, there were efforts in England to move away from the church's canon law and the customary laws of post-feudal landlords and to centralize the common law by entering it into parliamentary statute.[49] Thus, many of a constable's common law powers, which the courts had recognized or given effect to, were eventually written down in legislation.[50] However, the practice of judges recognizing a constable's powers continued to occur in the common law courts.

During the same time, the constable's role grew exponentially, taking on a wide assortment of "collateral" community tasks in addition to crime control. This is no more evident than in the long list of duties assigned to constables in Jacob Giles's 1729 edition of *A New Law-Dictionary*. Duties included identifying "all defects of highways and bridges, and the names of those who ought to repair them; scavengers who neglect their duty; and all common nuisances in streets and highways; bakers who sell bread underweight; brewers selling beer to unlicensed ale-houses; forestallers, regrators, ingrossers."[51] The Crown relied on constables to fill in where needed and pursue tasks that were required to maintain civil order within quickly growing communities. Policing, thus, came to include public health, hygiene, food and drink, morals and manners, clothing, the maintenance of roads, bridges and town buildings, public security especially from fires, the regulation of the market, the performance of trades and occupations, religious observances, dealings between innkeepers and guests, and the behaviour of servants toward their masters.

When the London Metropolitan Police became institutionalized in 1829, the original title of the legislation was *An Act for Improving the Police in and near the Metropolis*.[52] In the 1800s, London was experiencing a dramatic influx in its urban population. The Industrial Revolution was ramping up trade and commerce, progress in medicine, and improvements in agricultural methods. These immense social and economic changes led to the relocation of rural populations to towns and cities in search of work. London's constables and night watchmen were insufficient and inefficient in dealing with the growing size and population of the city as well as its corresponding increase in disorder. Thus, institutionalizing "the police" was one attempt to regulate life in London. As noted by Patrick Colquhoun in his *Treatise on the Police of the Metropolis*, published in 1796, there were also various acts of Parliament enacted to regulate the comfort and convenience of the inhabitants of London, featuring regulations about paving; watching, lighting, cleansing, and removing nuisances; furnishing water; building houses; extinguishing fires; and hackney coaches, carts, and other carriages – to which he later added the sewage system and signs and signposts, among others.[53]

In the general orders and instructions given to the London Metropolitan Police, Joint Commissioner Sir Richard Mayne wrote that "the primary object of an efficient police is the prevention of crime: then next that of detection and punishment of offenders if crime is committed. To these ends all the efforts of police must be directed. The protection of life and property, the preservation of public tranquillity, and the absence of crime, will alone prove whether those efforts have been successful and whether the objects for which the police were appointed have been attained."[54] Thus, the success of the police as an institution was measured by how well they accomplished and brought about these objectives. The statements made by Sir Richard in 1829 are still very relevant today. The efficiency and success of the police depends on the approval and cooperation of the public. Public opinion has long determined, to varying degrees, the esteem and respect to which the police are held. One of the key principles of modern policing in England was that the police sought to work with the community and as part of the community.

Early Policing in Canada: Modelling Canadian Police Forces after the English

During the nineteenth century, there was also a significant number of people migrating from the British Isles to the North American colonies. To deal with the mass of immigrants that were beginning to settle, the colonies replicated the systems of England to help establish order and structure. As such, the essential features of a constable's office, which had been established to administer criminal justice in England, were reproduced in all material respects in the British North American colonies. When the *Constitution Act, 1867 (British North American Act)* was enacted, the constitutional document contained no express language that suggested eliminating or altering the powers and functions of pre-Confederation police officers or constables.[55] To the contrary, the preamble of the *Constitution Act, 1867* explicitly states its intention to implement a legal structure "similar in principle" to that of the United Kingdom.[56] As a consequence, the arrangements made by early colonial administrators to the police in the Canadian territories were no exception to this general rule. Public police officials and forces established in the late eighteenth and early nineteenth centuries were explicitly modelled on their English constable counterparts. Thus, the Canadian police officers continued the British tradition of deriving their powers from both statute and the common law.

The first colony to incorporate the essential elements of the English justice system was Newfoundland, which appointed justices of the peace and constables pursuant to the *Royal Proclamation* in 1729.[57] The other maritime colonies quickly followed. In 1749, Nova Scotia required all settlers to assemble in smaller companies and select a constable, who would then be sworn in by the justices of the peace. This selection process continued until the *Town Officers Act* was passed, whereby constables were then nominated by a grand jury and formally appointed by a justice of the peace.[58] Since the powers, duties, or responsibilities of a constable were not laid out in the statutes of these maritime jurisdictions, it was concluded that the office provided for was the common law office of constable. Thus, in addition to the general duties of preserving peace, preventing crime, and protecting life, officers were directed to carry out any other tasks assigned to them by the justices who appointed them.

Similar developments occurred in the remaining provinces and territories. After five years of military rule in Quebec, during which policing functions were discharged by the militia, civilian rule was introduced in 1764. However, this policing structure was gradually replaced by the constable or bailiff of England.[59] Soon after the English common law was officially received by the province of Upper Canada, the Legislative Assembly enacted the *Parish and Town Officers Act*.[60] This act provided that justices of the peace were responsible for appointing a high constable and group of constables for every "parish, township, reputed township, or place." A similar provision was contained in the *Laws of Assiniboia* for the Hudson Bay territory, which was passed by the governor and council of the Red River Settlement in 1862.[61] As a result, the "office of the constable," in all its capacities – a local peace officer, salaried and subject to the direction of the local magistrates to maintain the public peace and security – had become firmly established as part of the government structures of pre-Confederation Canada.

This system included a continued reliance on Canadian constables to carry out "collateral services." In future Canadian cities, like Calgary, early constables were initially responsible for inspecting buildings, roads, fresh fruits, vegetables, and meats; issuing licences; and maintaining an animal pound. In Sudbury, they were tax collectors, sanitary inspectors, truant officers, and firemen. In Regina, the duties of the first constables included firefighter, sanitation inspector, and dog catcher.[62] Early constables in Winnipeg were gunpowder inspectors, licence inspectors, water (aqueduct) inspectors, bailiffs, jailors, court security officers, dog catchers, and parks and bicycle path inspectors. In fact, the police in the Winnipeg metropolitan area also ran the public ambulance service until 1975 and oversaw the local fire departments during the same time.[63] In smaller Manitoban towns, like Deloraine and Winkler, constables were responsible for ringing the town bell, firefighting, lighting and putting out the street lamps, taking care of the town hall and fire engine, staffing the local jail, attending to dog licences, fixing and maintaining sidewalks and roads, directing traffic, enforcing the town curfew, acting as the local weed inspector, building inspector, licence inspector, and, later, testing for drivers licences.[64]

The reason that these collateral services remained central to early police work lies in the fact that the Canadian legislation establishing the police was not a prescriptive plan with specified duties but, rather, an enabling measure. Legislators assigned a general "catch-all" function to the constable in lieu of creating new agencies or professionals. This was especially important in the early days before Confederation when there was a lack of governmental resources and manpower. The constable was expected to help where needed to maintain civil society. Gradually, however, such collateral services were assigned to other departments or agencies of government. During the late nineteenth and early twentieth centuries, functions and activities previously undertaken by the police – animal welfare, licensing, fire prevention, food safety, sidewalk repair – were separated from the institution of police. While this could be viewed as "narrowing" the police function, it was the provisioning of policing powers to other areas of government, which were dedicated to ordering those aspects of society. Yet the original enabling legislation, which established the Canadian police, continued to remain broadly construed.

Indeed, when the *Canadian Constables' Assistant* was first published in 1852, Judge James Robert Gowan stated that

> [t]he office of constable, in Canada, is co-incident with the introduction into the Province of the Criminal Law of England. It is of great antiquity ... The authority of Constables is general and special; the office partaking of the nature of both. The general authority accrues by virtue of their own right as officers – the special authority accrues by the right of someone else. *All* constables are *conservators of the peace by right* of their office, and are also *the immediate and proper officers of Justices of the Peace*. Under these two heads the subject matter may be for the most part collected and arranged.[65]

Judge Gowan continued:

> Constables by virtue of their inherent powers may act without warrant in the prevention of crime, and for the arrest of offenders. As the immediate and proper officers of Justices of the Peace, constables act under, and are bound to obey the lawful mandates of the Magistrates of their County ... [While] it is always safer for a constable to act under the warrant of a Justice of the Peace; and, where circumstances permit delay, he should take care to arm himself with one; but immediate interference is frequently necessary, and, as a constable, is in most cases, liable to punishment, for neglecting to act when the law permits him to do so, the nature and extent of his powers should be rightly understood, that on an emergency, he may with promptness and decision do what the law requires of him.[66]

Confederation did not disturb the reliance upon the office of constable as the basis of policing in Canada. The first significant influence upon the future of policing in Canada was the enactment in 1868 of the *Police of Canada Act*, which created a dominion police force to administer criminal and other federal laws. The act was short and provided the officers "with all the powers, rights and responsibilities which belong by law to constables duly appointed."[67] Various provincial acts followed in Manitoba and Quebec, which established province-wide police forces of their own in 1870.[68]

Little has changed in the intervening 150 years since Confederation. Section 42(3) of the 1990 *Police Services Act* (section 82(3) of the *Community Safety and Policing Act*, when it was proclaimed in force) outlines the modern duties of a police officer:

> 82(1) The duties of a police officer include,
>
> > (a) preserving the peace.
> > (b) preventing crimes and other offences and providing assistance and encouragement to other persons in their prevention.
> > (c) assisting victims of crime.
> > (d) apprehending criminals and other offenders and others who may lawfully be taken into custody.
> > (e) laying charges and participating in prosecutions.
> > (f) executing warrants that are to be executed by police officers and performing related duties.
> > (g) performing the lawful duties that the chief of police assigns.
> > (h) completing training required by this Act or the regulations.
> > (i) complying with the prescribed code of conduct; and
> > (j) performing such other duties as are assigned to him or her by or under this or any other Act, including any prescribed duties.
>
> ...
>
> (3) *A police officer has the powers and duties ascribed to a constable at common law.*[69]

These broad, undefined duties of a constable "at common law" appear in most Canadian *Police Acts* today.[70] In addition, the duties assigned to the police in all provinces and territories include the duty to "preserve the peace." This is to be distinguished from the duty to prevent crimes and offences, apprehend offenders, maintain law and order, execute warrants, and assist victims, which are all separately enumerated.[71] The essence of a police officer's duties, as stated by the Supreme Court of Canada, is wide and varied and not easily compiled into an exhaustive list. In fact, many police duties are "totally divorced from the detection, investigation, or acquisition of evidence relating to the violation of a criminal statute."[72] These duties have included:

- entering a house to abate a noise nuisance[73]
- stopping a water tap that is overflowing[74]
- dousing a fire or checking for explosive chemicals[75]
- responding to the sound of an alarm[76]
- checking on property that has been vandalized[77]
- helping the blind and infirm, to direct people who have lost their way
- pull down a galloping horse to prevent an accident from occurring[78]
- aiding those in distress, combating actual hazards, preventing potential hazards from materializing, and providing an infinite variety of services to preserve and protect community safety[79]
- stopping fights and preventing the commission of crime[80]
- keeping the peace and preventing that which might cause serious injury to someone or even to many people or to property[81]
- protecting the safety of animals that are in need of immediate welfare and care.[82]

Adopting the British Common Law Practices: The *Waterfield* Test

As can be evidenced, statutory law regarding police powers and duties is widespread in Canada. The British influence on Canadian policing duties and powers under statutory law is also observable. Canadian law, however, began to deviate from the British model in the twentieth century. One such deviation in the common law – the *Waterfield* test – has its roots in the British common law but has taken on a uniquely Canadian character.[83] The next section will tease out this phenomenon and analyze how judge-made law, by way of the *Waterfield* test, has served as a gap-filling measure when statutory law falls short in providing guidance to courts on novel police conduct.

To appreciate the impact of the *Waterfield* test on police powers in Canada, we must return once again to the British common law where its namesake, *R v Waterfield*, is found. The *Waterfield* case involved two friends, Eli Waterfield and Geoffrey Lynn. Earlier on the day in question, Lynn had been driving Waterfield's car and had crashed it into a brick wall after an altercation with a few other men. This incident prompted the police to start a dangerous driving investigation and to seek evidence from the car that had been in the collision. While on patrol, two constables spotted Lynn sitting in the car at a local marketplace. They approached the vehicle, requesting that Lynn keep the car where it was and that they perform a search. Not fond of this idea, Lynn asked who was going to stop him if he wanted to leave. Seeing this interaction between the police and his friend, Waterfield quickly arrived on the scene. Trying to prevent the officers from impounding his car, Waterfield told Lynn to drive away. The officers surrounded the vehicle, but, at Waterfield's further urging, Lynn drove forward toward one of the officers, requiring him to dive out of the way of the car's path.

Charges were laid against both men: Lynn for dangerous driving and for assaulting an officer in the execution of his duties and Waterfield for having counselled, procured, and commanded Lynn to do the illegal behaviour. However, the charges against Waterfield and Lynn depended upon whether the assault had occurred during the execution of the constable's official duties. This led to an examination of whether the police, themselves, had been acting lawfully when they surrounded Waterfield's vehicle and attempted to detain the men for questioning. Did their actions fall within the scope of what they were legally authorized to do?

For the UK Court of Criminal Appeal to answer this question, Justice Ashworth enunciated what would become known as the *"Waterfield* test." The purpose of this test was to determine whether, at the time of the offence, the constables had been acting according to either their statutory or common law duties. Instead of listing the constable's various powers, Ashworth J suggested that it would be more convenient to examine what "the police constable was actually doing" at the time of the assault. More specifically, the test aimed to determine if the constable's conduct was *prima facie* interference with the person's right to liberty or property. If it was not, the officer was likely in the right. However, if the officer was interfering with the individual's rights, Ashworth J proposed a consideration of two factors. First, the Court had to examine whether the officer's conduct fell "within the general scope of *any duty* imposed by statute or recognised at common law." If satisfied that the officer's conduct fell under such a purview, the Court then needed to examine whether the actions involved an *unjustified* use of power to achieve that duty.[84]

In the eyes of the Court, it was plain to see that the constables, in preventing Lynn and Waterfield from taking the car away, were thereby "interfering with them" and their property. Having passed this initial threshold, the Court moved on to analyze the first step of the test: Did the police's actions fall within the scope of any duty? Here, the Court found that the police actions were not authorized under statute and, after a review of the British jurisprudence, did not fall within the scope and extent of any common law duties. The Crown raised an argument that the two constables had been acting out of "a duty to preserve for use in court evidence of crime." While the Court agreed, it found that "the execution of that duty did not, in the view of this court, authorize them to prevent removal of the car in the circumstances."[85] Even though the officers were acting in pursuit of an admirable duty, they were acting outside the scope of what their duties authorized and, thus, were beyond the protection of the law.

In his concluding remarks, Ashworth J stated that "while it is no doubt right to say in general terms that police constables have a duty to prevent crime and a duty, when crime is committed, to bring the offender to justice, it is also clear from the decided cases that when the execution of these general duties involves interference with the person or property of a private person, the powers of constables are not unlimited."[86] This case lays down the principle that the police are not permitted to execute their duties in a manner that interferes with an individual's right of property or liberty in the absence of statutory or common law authorization. The test, articulated in this case, was used and created to determine the criminal liability of the accused. In the following two cases, we shall see that the Canadian courts have adopted this British test and used it for its initially designed purpose. However, as we will continue to explore in the next chapter, the purpose of the *Waterfield* test was quickly transformed by the Canadian courts to allow them to create new common law police powers.

R v Stenning, which was delivered in 1970, was the first instance where the Supreme Court of Canada applied the *Waterfield* test in Canada.[87] In this case, two police officers arrived at the property of a car dealership to investigate a reported gunshot fired earlier that evening. When they arrived at the business, they found a man outside beaten and bleeding. They also noticed someone moving around inside the building. Even though they did not have a warrant or statutory authorization that would permit them access, the officers entered the building through a window to continue their investigation. While searching the premises, the officers found two individuals pretending to sleep. The officers shook them awake and questioned them on their reasons for being on the premises. The respondent, Michael Anthony Stenning, was reluctant and evasive in answering. When the officers stated that they would arrest him if he did not disclose his identity,

Stenning suddenly jumped up and struck one of the officers in the face, breaking his nose and injuring his eye.

The main question before the Court was remarkably like the question considered in *R v Waterfield*. The charge against the respondent – assaulting a police officer under section 232(2) of the *Criminal Code* – required that the officer had been acting within the scope of his duties at the time of the assault.[88] However, this question was complicated by the fact that the officers had technically been trespassing. The *Police Act* did not expressly authorize the actions that the officers took to continue their investigation.[89] Since they had not obtained the consent of the owner or a search warrant but had opted for entering the building through a window, the officers were technically operating outside the strict letter of the law.

However, to the Supreme Court of Canada, this did not seem to matter. Whether the officers had been trespassing or not, the Court found that the officers had been engaged in the execution of their duties. The Court was satisfied that they had been fulfilling the broader common law duty to investigate occurrences or the statutory duty of preserving the peace, preventing robberies and other crimes, and apprehending offenders under section 47 of the *Police Act*. Yet, for the Supreme Court, the real clincher was that there had been no unlawful interference with either the liberty or the property of the respondent. Thus, the analysis failed to pass the *Waterfield* test's initial threshold. Even though Stenning was the son of the property owner and was entitled to be there, the Court found that there was "no evidence that, prior to his assault on [Constable] Wilkinson, he advised Wilkinson as to this, that he questioned Wilkinson's right to be there, or that he asked him to leave."

The first prong of *Waterfield* – whether there was a *prima facie* interference with one's liberty or property – is not engaged in *Stenning*. Four years after *Stenning*, the Supreme Court returned to the nascent *Waterfield* test in *R v Knowlton*.[90] The facts in *Knowlton* may remind the reader of earlier British common law cases where preservation of the peace and the accused's wilful obstruction of an officer exercising their duty was the central focus. *Knowlton* serves as a reminder of the broad and fluid powers of an officer in novel circumstances. In *Knowlton*, the accused was a photographer who wanted to photograph Soviet premier Alexei Kosygin during his time in Edmonton. Fearing a recurrence of an earlier incident in Ottawa, the police created a security zone around the hotel that the premier was staying at to control who was entering the building. Refusing to heed the police's warnings, E.J.N. (Edgar John Neil) Knowlton pushed past the officers and the barricade to gain a better position for taking pictures. He was arrested for obstruction.

At issue was whether the accused had unlawfully and wilfully obstructed a peace officer in the execution of his duty, thereby committing an offence under section 118(a) of the *Criminal Code*.[91] As the police were not explicitly enforcing any law at the time, Knowlton argued he could not be guilty of obstructing them in their duties. The Supreme Court of Canada disagreed. While accepting that the police had interfered with the liberty of the appellant, including his undoubted legal right to circulate freely on a public street, the Court upheld the police action pursuant to a constable's common law duty to preserve the peace and prevent crime. Considering the earlier assault on the Soviet premier, the Court thought it reasonable for the police to seek to guard against any further disturbance. Chief Justice Fauteux, for a unanimous Court, explained that the conduct of the police clearly fell within the general scope of the duties imposed upon them.[92] When the Supreme Court heard the case, it reiterated the *Waterfield* calculus to determine "(i) whether such conduct of the police falls within the general scope of any duty imposed by statute or recognized at common law and (ii) whether such conduct, albeit within the general scope of such a duty involved an unjustified use of powers associated with the duty." The Court found that the officers were acting pursuant to their duties and that Knowlton had committed an offence.

What these early cases show is that the *Waterfield* test provided courts with a flexible approach to determining whether state incursion on one's liberty or property was justified. *Knowlton* foreshadows further experimentation and exploration by the Supreme Court of Canada of *Waterfield*'s potential to delineate and delimit police conduct within the common law.

Conclusion

This chapter has highlighted the roots of police powers and their lineages and iterations in the statutory and common laws of Britain and Canada. Importantly, the common law and statutory law regarding police duties and powers have existed symbiotically within common law legal systems. Yet we can also see the historical connection between the police and the community they serve. Over the course of centuries, this relationship has been reimagined and revised by the changing needs and ideals of society. Society's need to preserve the peace, protect lives and property, and prevent crime gave rise to the officer's duties and powers that were recognized and authorized by legislators and judges.

Undeniably, early Canadian policing was inherently linked to policing practices found in the British common law. In its infancy, Canada strove to model its police forces after the British model. Canada's rapidly developing and expanding infrastructure appears to have adopted a tried and tested model to continue this expansion. We see that Canadian statutory guidance as to the limits of policing have changed very little since Confederation. Where the Canadian approach has truly deviated from Britain is with respect to the *Waterfield* test.[93] At each step of the way, courts have grappled with the balance between the exercise of police duties and the citizen's right to be free from state interference with their liberty or property. Many of the cases that have been discussed in this chapter have pointed to the friction between these two prevailing needs. Historically, judicial review of police conduct has recognized that any police conduct must be authorized by law. Judges have also developed the common law to address circumstances that do not dovetail with statutorily recognized powers and duties.

The Supreme Court's Embrace of the Ancillary Powers Doctrine

2

with Lauren Gowler

Waterfield/Dedman and Their Progeny: Policing in the *Charter* Era

The *Canadian Charter of Rights and Freedoms*, enacted in 1982, was aspirational legislation.[1] It was an effort to reconstruct Canada's Constitution to better meet the needs of all Canadians. The *Charter* articulated and guaranteed a set of rights and freedoms that Canadian citizens believed were necessary in a free and democratic society – such worthy values as the "right to equality," "freedom of expression," the "right to live and work anywhere in Canada," and "the right to life, liberty and security of the person." The ideal scenario was to create predictability for all Canadians – citizens and state agents alike.

In the area of criminal procedure, the *Charter* stimulated the courts and the legislature to redraw the boundaries of legitimate policing by bringing Canadian laws, such as the *Criminal Code*, in line with the values and rights promised in this new constitutional document. This task involved striking a delicate balance between what the state needed in its efforts to maintain a safe ordered society and serving the interests of Canadian citizens, who hoped to live their lives with minimal government intrusions. Sections 7–14 of the *Charter* afforded legal rights to Canadians when they interacted with law enforcement and the justice system. However, these theoretical liberties required legislative guidance and judicial interpretation to be effective in the real world. What was an "unreasonable" search? What was the definition of "detainment"? What legal standard would the police need to attain before arresting a suspect? These were questions to which both law enforcement and citizens wanted answers.

The *Charter* provided the individual with an instrument to keep government and state officers accountable. In the contexts of police investigations – searches, detentions, and arrests – it became possible to challenge every single piece of behaviour conducted by police officers with a simple question: "Did they have the authority to do that?" Meanwhile, the *Charter* also gave the state an opportunity to defend perceived breaches of the *Charter*, if it could prove that the infringing action was "justifiable in a free and democratic society." Early post-*Charter* cases, like *Hunter v Southam*, showcased the Supreme Court of Canada's efforts to give pragmatic meaning to *Charter* rights – setting out high legal standards for police discretion, detailed requirements for searches, and prior authorization for state actions.[2] In wishing to respect the individual's rights while also addressing the powers that police required to go about their duties, the Court hoped that these rules and restrictions would provide better predictability when it came to police-citizen interactions and would prevent *Charter* breaches from occurring in the first place.

Nevertheless, in the aftermath of the *Charter*, scholars thought that Parliament would be the principal actor in addressing, refining, and articulating the scope of police powers. It seemed like a reasonable premise given the inherently democratic function of government and the inevitable need for reconciliation between the pre-*Charter* laws governing criminal procedure and the rights and freedoms guaranteed in Canada's new *Charter*. However, the government of the time, and subsequent administrations, did not rise to this challenge. Rather, politicians and legislators alike preferred to leave this daunting responsibility to the judiciary, which began addressing and dealing with these gaps in the law as they were brought before the courts. While this strategy was piecemeal in fashion, the courts, as we will come to see, rose to the challenge.

The tool that was handpicked by the courts for this important task was the *Waterfield* test, a British legal test that had arrived on Canadian shores to little fanfare in the 1970s.[3] As we saw in the historical survey of Chapter 1, the *Waterfield* test had been seldom applied in Canada. When it was applied, in the pre-*Charter* cases of *Stenning* and *Knowlton*, the test was only a dispositive of the narrow question: Had the police officer been acting in the course of his duties as a peace officer at the time of the given police-citizen encounter?[4] In its homeland, the *Waterfield* test maintained this narrow scope and only squeaked out a modest existence, which was partly due to the active role that the British Parliament had played in defining police powers rather than leaving it to the courts.[5] As we will come to see, in Canada, the *Waterfield* test has been everything but modest. It has served as a lodestar for the Supreme Court of Canada in its journey of methodically expanding common law police powers.

This chapter provides a survey of the most notable ancillary powers cases – *Waterfield/Dedman* and their progeny – over the last thirty-five years.[6] We examine common law police powers related to roadside stops, in the home, and during investigative detentions, searches, and arrest. The aim of this chapter is to present the reader with an overview of the jurisprudence, explaining how the Supreme Court applied and modified the test set out in *Waterfield* and highlighting the judicial commentary surrounding this legal doctrine. In doing so, we will create a foundational base for later discussions on the advantages and concerns of the ancillary powers doctrine and the Court's role in recognizing and creating common law police powers. In the early cases of *Stenning* and *Knowlton,* the Supreme Court had not licensed police actions generally, nor had it proposed any new free-standing common law powers under the charge of *Waterfield*. All of this was soon to change in 1985 with the case of *Dedman v The Queen*.[7] In *Dedman,* the Court concretized the ancillary powers doctrine into police powers that had never before been seen or authorized.

Dedman: The Supreme Court's Transformation of *Waterfield*

Robert Dedman was driving down the highway when a police officer pulled him over.[8] There had been nothing improper or erratic about his driving that would arouse police suspicion, nor had Dedman broken any highway traffic laws.[9] The stop was part of a check stop program, known as RIDE, which stands for reduce impaired driving everywhere. The program was designed as an exercise to catch impaired drivers at locations where the police believed there was a high incidence of impaired driving, and, on a random basis, they would signal motorists to pull over in order to assess the driver's level of sobriety.[10] The officers would strike up a conversation by asking for a valid driver's licence and proof of car insurance, but their main goal was to detect the otherwise "undetectable drinking driver."[11]

When the officer checked Dedman's licence, he smelled a strong odour of alcohol on the accused's breath. The officer requested that Dedman supply a breath sample in a roadside screening device. Despite repeated attempts, the accused failed to provide a sample of breath that was sufficient for a proper reading. Thus, Dedman was charged with failing to comply, without reasonable excuse, with the officer's demand to supply a breath sample, pursuant to section 234.1(2) of the *Criminal Code*.[12]

At trial, the accused argued that he had been arbitrarily detained and that the police lacked the proper legal authority to conduct roadside investigations like this. If the police's actions – in stopping Dedman's vehicle – were found to be unauthorized and, hence, unlawful, the officer's subsequent demand for a breath sample would also be unlawful. When the Supreme Court of Canada heard the case, it was asked to determine whether the police officer possessed the statutory or common law police power to stop Dedman's vehicle and to question him. To determine the validity of the roadside stop, the highest court in Canada relied on the seldom used and largely ignored *Waterfield* test. This test, as enunciated by Justice Ashworth of the British Court of Criminal Appeal, begins with a threshold question: Was the police conduct an interference with the person's liberty or property?

In this instance, the police were stopping motorists on an arbitrary basis to question them and determine sobriety. Did this police action constitute an interference with Dedman's rights? Both the Supreme Court majority and dissent said "yes." The random vehicle stop was a *prima facie* interference with Dedman's liberty, specifically his right to circulate freely on the public highway. While the majority noted that this liberty was technically exercised in the context of a licensed activity, which was more readily subject to regulation and oversight, it was nonetheless interfered with by the police officer.[13] In his dissenting opinion, Chief Justice Brian Dickson was steadfast in reminding the Court of the individual's right "to be left alone" from the government.[14] Canadians should be free from private or public restraint, except where the law provides otherwise.

Once an interference with liberty is established, one moves on to consider the more analytical branch of the *Waterfield* test: Does the conduct fall within the general scope of any police duty imposed by statute or recognized at common law?[15] As introduced in the previous chapter, the police can only interfere with the liberty or property of an individual when their actions are authorized by law – whether that be by a statute or by the common law. Otherwise, their conduct is illegal. Police officers are not above the rule of law: "No one is entitled to impose any physical restraint upon the citizen except as authorized by law, and this principle applies as much to police officers as to anyone else."[16] The only plausible reason that a police officer can interfere with a citizen – an action that would generally be seen as criminal or tortious – is because the law authorizes that action.

In the case at bar, the Supreme Court was unable to find statutory authority, under the *Criminal Code* or the Ontario *Highway Traffic Act*, that authorized police to randomly stop vehicles as part of the RIDE program.[17] The Court therefore turned to exploring the common law. Speaking for the majority, Justice Le Dain stated that this power to stop motorists fell within the general scope of two common law police duties: to prevent crime and to protect life and property.[18] The majority found that the RIDE program was intended to improve the deterrence and detection of impaired driving – an offence under the *Criminal Code* – and that impaired driving was, as described by the Court, a "notorious cause of injury and death."[19] Therefore, the majority found that the first branch of the *Waterfield* test was easily satisfied.

The Supreme Court of Canada then turned to a consideration of the second branch of the test: whether such conduct, albeit within the general scope of such a duty, involved an unjustified use of powers associated with the duty.[20] Finding that neither *Waterfield* nor the cases that had applied the test up to this point had articulated the criteria for this stage, Le Dain J relied on the words "reasonably necessary" from *Johnson v Phillips* to compose some semblance of criteria.[21] He found that the police's actions, which interfered with an individual's liberty, "must be necessary for the carrying out of the particular police duty and it must be reasonable of the public purpose served by the interference" in order to be considered justifiable.[22] This second branch of the test, and the criteria articulated by Le Dain J, ultimately shapes and modifies how the Court uses and applies the *Waterfield* test in subsequent cases.

Using these criteria, the majority engaged in a makeshift cost-benefit analysis of what was "reasonably necessary" to determine the justifiability of the police officer's action. The majority relied on the following factors as the apparent benefits of the program and the officer's actions: that impaired driving is a serious societal problem; that driving is a licensed activity that the state has the power to regulate; that the program had been widely publicized, thus minimizing the adverse psychological effect upon drivers; and, finally, that the inconvenience suffered by those detained would be marginal given the short duration of the detention.[23] While considering the costs, the majority found the arbitrary nature of the detention, the unpleasant psychological effects experienced by innocent drivers, and the ultimate erosion of an individual's liberty to circulate undisturbed to be onerous.

Ultimately, however, the majority found that the benefits derived from this program outweighed any of the negative impacts that might arise from police arbitrarily stopping drivers. Addressing a serious social problem, like drunk driving, was an important enough public purpose that they were willing to recognize this type of police action as reasonably necessary to carry out this program. As a result, the Court held that the police possessed the power at common law to randomly stop and detain motorists in their vehicles for the purposes of evaluating their sobriety.[24] The majority concluded that the use of police powers in this context was justifiable under the second branch of the *Waterfield* test. In his dissent, Dickson CJ vehemently disagreed. Accompanied by Justices Jean Beetz and Julien Chouinard, Dickson CJ sharply criticized the majority's adoption and interpretation of the *Waterfield* test.

Dickson CJ started his judgment by drawing a clear distinction between the duties of a police officer and the power, or lawful authority, the police possess to achieve those duties. He found that simply because a police officer possessed a general common law duty – to prevent crime, protect life, or preserve peace – did not mean that the officer could do everything or anything in their means to achieve that duty.[25] The existence of a common law duty did not, in itself, necessitate, imply, or automatically create police powers, especially powers that interfered with Canadians' liberties:

> The fact that police officers could be described as acting within the general scope of their duties to investigate crime cannot empower them to violate the law whenever such conduct could be justified by the public interest in law enforcement. Any such principle would be nothing short of a fiat for illegality on the part of the police whenever the benefit of police action appeared to outweigh the infringement of an individual's rights.[26]

Police and governmental agents are not above the rule of law. Dickson CJ adamantly opined that an officer needed to have been granted lawful authority, by statute or by the common law, to perform any actions that interfered with the property or liberty of an individual. While Dickson CJ acknowledged the desirable objective of the RIDE program, he warned that its important public purpose should not obscure or sway the Court's analysis and scrutiny of the police powers being exercised in this case:

> In striving to achieve one desirable objective, the reduction of death and injury that occurs each year from impaired driving, we must ensure that

other, equally important, social values are not sacrificed. Individual freedom from interference by the state, no matter how laudable the motive
of the police, must be guarded zealously against intrusion. Ultimately,
this freedom is the measure of everyone's liberty and one of the corner-
stones of the quality of life in our democratic society.[27]

To Dickson CJ, the action of arbitrarily stopping and questioning motorists was unjustifiable. These random stops of motorists – where the police
had "no reason to believe, prior to the stop, that the motorist had committed, or was committing a criminal offence" – were unlawful, unauthorized,
interferences with liberty interests.[28] Since police lacked the general common
law authority to detain a person for investigative questioning, Dickson CJ
asserted that he was "unable to find any basis for the power to stop and
detain motorists."[29]

Further, Dickson criticized the majority's use of *Waterfield* as a generative
test, strongly encouraging that the authorization of new police powers –
those not yet contemplated by the common law or articulated in statute – was
a matter best left to the legislature, not the courts.[30] He warned that each
time the Court undertook this modified *Waterfield* test, it would be placing
itself in the perilous situation "of limiting liberty, routinely infringing on
privacy, and embodying a crime-control and policing-centric ethic."[31] The
chief justice was "clearly striking a warning bell against the courts becoming
an originating locus of police powers":

> With respect, the majority of the Court departs firm ground for a slippery
> slope when they authorize an otherwise unlawful interference with in-
> dividual liberty by the police, solely on the basis that it is reasonably
> necessary to carry out general police duties. The objection to a random
> stop made without any grounds for suspicion or belief that the particular
> driver has committed or is committing an offence goes far beyond the
> unpleasant psychological effects produced for the innocent driver. Even
> if these would tend to be minimized by the well-publicized nature of
> the ... program, the erosion of individual liberty with its ultimately
> detrimental effect on the freedom of all members of society would
> remain.[32]

In *Dedman*, the Supreme Court of Canada transformed the British *Waterfield* test into a convenient tool, one that could fill perceived gaps in the law
of criminal procedure by expanding or creating new police powers on a

ANCILLARY POWERS DOCTRINE

Common law police powers are powers that are recognized and articulated by judges, in the court setting, on a case-by-case basis. Since these powers are not created via the legislative process but, rather, through court decisions, they are sometimes described as "ancillary" powers -- those that run alongside the powers prescribed by lawmakers.

THE *WATERFIELD* & *DEDMAN* TEST

The Ancillary Powers Doctrine has repeatedly been applied by Canadian courts to determine whether — and in what circumstances — a particular police power exists at common law. This doctrine arose from a test established in the UK case of *R. v. Waterfield* (1963) and developed through the Canadian courts since *R. v. Dedman* (1985).

IN EACH CASE, THE COURT HAS ENDEAVOURED TO:

1 DEFINE THE COMMON LAW POWER
IDENTIFY the police power at issue and clearly SPECIFY the particular conditions and parameters for its use.

2 CONSIDER THE SITUATION
EVALUATE whether the police in this situation acted in accordance with that common law police power?

THRESHOLD CONSIDERATION

Starting Point: Court must define the police power or action that is being asserted and the liberty interests that are at stake. The Ancillary Powers Doctrine only comes into play where the power at issue involves a *prima facie* interference with liberty.

DEFINE POLICE ACTION

ASK:
What were the police doing in this situation?

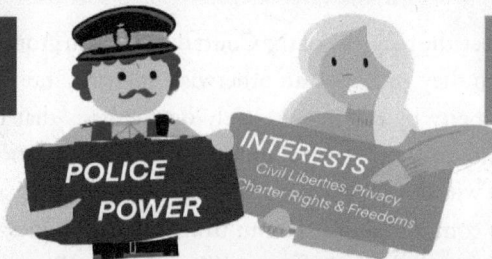

POLICE POWER

INTERESTS
Civil Liberties, Privacy,
Charter Rights & Freedoms

IDENTIFY LIBERTY INTEREST

ASK:
Did the police's action interfere with a person's liberty or property?

Conducting a Roadside Sobriety Stop	*INTERFERING WITH*	Ability to drive about freely
Performing a Pat-Down Search	*INTERFERING WITH*	Individual's physical autonomy & privacy
Searching a cellphone	*INTERFERING WITH*	Individual's property & private information

WAS THERE AN INTERFERENCE? ▬▬▬ **IF YES, PROCEED** ▬▬▬▶

FIGURE 1 Ancillary Powers Doctrine

THE ANALYSIS PROCEEDS IN TWO STAGES ➡

FIRST STAGE

ASK: Does this conduct fall within the scope of the police's...

COMMON LAW DUTIES

PREVENTING	PROTECTING	PRESERVING
CRIME	**LIFE**	**PEACE**

OR

STATUTORY DUTIES

Criminal Code
Highway Traffic Act
Police Services Act

If the action falls within the scope of the police's common law duties, the Court proceeds...

SECOND STAGE

ASK: Does the police action at issue involve a justifiable exercise of police powers associated with that common law duty?

"TO BE JUSTIFIED, the power must be REASONABLY NECESSARY"

JUSTICE LE DAIN:

"Police actions, which interfere with an individual's liberty, must be **necessary** for the carrying out of the particular police duty, and it must be **reasonable** of the public purpose served by the interference in order to be considered justifiable."

from *DEDMAN* (1985)

*This stage requires the court to balance the **need for the power** against the **intrusion on the individual's rights**. Weighing the following three factors:*

1 IMPORTANCE OF THE DUTY TO THE PUBLIC GOOD
* What's the larger objective (duty) that the police are pursuing with their actions? How important is that duty to the public good?

2 THE EXTENT OF THE INTERFERENCE WITH THE LIBERTY
* How serious was the interference with the individual's liberty?
* What are the consequences arising from the interference?

3 NECESSITY OF THE INTERFERENCE WITH THE INDIVIDUAL'S LIBERTY FOR PERFORMANCE OF THE DUTY
* Were there less intrusive measures available to police in this circumstance?

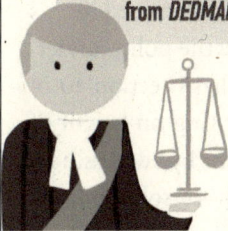

FIGURE 2 The Analysis Proceeds in Two Stages

case-by-case basis where police conduct was ultimately deemed justifiable (see Figures 1 and 2).

The Right to Counsel at Roadside Stops: *R v Orbanksi* and *R v Elias*

The jointly heard cases of *R v Orbanski* and *R v Elias* in 2005 revisited the *Waterfield* test in the context of roadside stops and police investigations of impaired driving.[33] *Dedman* had established that the police had the general common law power to arbitrarily stop drivers for a sobriety check but had largely remained silent on what the police could lawfully do once they pulled the driver over. The cases of *Orbanski* and *Elias* delved into the finer details, asking whether the police had the legal authority to question drivers about their prior alcohol consumption and request that a driver perform a sobriety test without first advising the driver of their right to counsel.

In the *Orbanski* case, the police had stopped the accused because of erratic driving behaviour. After disregarding a stop sign and swerving across the road, the police stopped him and requested that he perform a series of roadside sobriety tests – recite the alphabet, walk a straight line heel to toe, and follow the officer's finger with his eyes. Orbanski was unable to perform these tests and was arrested for impaired driving. In the *Elias* case, Elias was pulled over at a random roadside stop whereby it was requested that he provide a breath sample via an approved screening device, and he failed. Elias was charged with, and arrested for, impaired driving. In both cases, the officers had reported smelling alcohol on the men, and both Orbanski and Elias admitted to having been drinking previously when asked.

The argument presented by Orbanski and Elias was that the police should have provided them with their right to counsel before the officers took any steps to assess their sobriety. The critical question that was examined in this appeal was whether, for that brief detention period while the police undertook screening measures for sobriety, Orbanski's and Elias's section 10(b) *Charter* rights were justifiably limited or suspended. Writing on behalf of the majority, Justice Louise Charron started her judgment by addressing a few of the difficulties that police face when assessing drivers' sobriety:

> The challenge arises from the fact that drinking and driving is not in and of itself illegal. It is only driving with an impermissible amount of alcohol in one's body, or driving when one's faculties are impaired that is criminalized. The line between the permissible and the impermissible is not always easy to discern, and the necessary screening can only be achieved through "field" enforcement by police officers. It follows that these of-

ficers must be equipped to conduct this screening, though with minimal intrusion on the individual motorist's *Charter* rights.[34]

Charron J asserted that requiring police to advise motorists of their section 10(b) rights as soon as the driver rolls down their window would undoubtedly lead to "longer and often unnecessary" detentions.[35] Proper screening of drivers, she opined, requires a certain degree of interaction between the police and the motorist. However, given the diverse situations that officers find themselves in at roadside stops, she asserted that it is "both impossible to predict all the aspects of such encounters and impractical to legislate exhaustive details as to how they must be conducted."[36]

Although the screening measures utilized by the police in these cases were not expressly authorized by the statute – namely, Manitoba's *Highway Traffic Act* – the majority chose to broaden the statutory interpretation by finding that the limit on the detained drivers' rights was "necessarily implicit" in Manitoba's *Highway Traffic Act*'s operating requirements.[37] While statutory provisions can provide the police and citizens with more guidance and certainty regarding investigatory measures, Charron J argued that "many of the powers set out in the amendments are implicit" in the existing Manitoba legislation.[38] In fact, she suggested that common law could be used to flesh out the full scope and meaning of the police's statutorily authorized powers:

> The recognition of these powers is not carved out of whole cloth from common law principles to suit the occasion – these powers are part of the longstanding statutory scheme that permits police officers to stop drivers and check their sobriety. The scope of justifiable police conduct will not always be defined by express wording found in a statute but, rather, according to the purpose of the police power in question and by the particular circumstances in which it is exercised. Hence, it is inevitable that common law principles will need to be invoked to determine the scope of permissible police action under any statute. In this context, it becomes particularly important to keep in mind that any enforcement scheme must allow sufficient flexibility to be effective. The police power to check sobriety, as any other power, is not without its limits: it is circumscribed, in the words of the majority of this Court in *Dedman* by that which is "necessary for the carrying out of the particular duty and it must be reasonable, having regard to the nature of the liberty interfered with and the importance of the public purpose served by the interference."[39]

Agreeing with the trial judge, the majority also found that the officers had common law authority for their actions. Deploying the *Waterfield/ Dedman* test, they decided that the officers were acting in accordance with their duties to protect life and prevent crime. Charron J found that the roadside screening measures, which the police took to assess Orbanski's and Elias's sobriety, were reasonable and necessary steps in fulfilling their duties, satisfying the second branch of the *Waterfield/Dedman* test. The Court found that the investigative questions posed by the police officer were "relevant, involved minimal intrusion, and did not go beyond what was necessary" for the officer to carry out his duty.[40] In the case of Orbanski and the sobriety field tests, the majority agreed with the trial judge's reasoning that "[t]he police constable suspected that the appellant had been driving while his ability to drive was impaired by alcohol. However, he did not think that he had reasonable and probable grounds to demand that the appellant take a breathalyzer test. He requested the sobriety test in order to see whether his suspicions were well founded."[41] The majority found that both the provincial legislative scheme and the common law granted the police the authority to detain the motorists for this investigation. Charron J concluded her judgment with a section 1 analysis, determining that the limit on Orbanski's and Elias's section 10(b) rights were ultimately justified. She reasoned that

> [t]he objective of reducing the carnage caused by impaired driving constitutes a compelling state objective; the use of reasonable screening methods is rationally connected to the objective; the infringement of the right to counsel was no more than necessary to meet the objective; and, in light of the limited use that can be made of the compelled evidence collected during the screening process, there was proportionality between the deleterious and salutary effects of the screening measures.[42]

Justices Louis LeBel and Morris Fish disagreed with the approach taken by their Supreme Court colleagues. Asserting that the majority had made a crucial misstep in its utilization of the *Waterfield* test, LeBel J called the majority's judgment "a strained legal interpretation to sidestep inconvenient *Charter* rights for the greater good."[43] The innocent driver, in experiencing police action, is dubious of where the law stands and what rights and obligations they possess. The dissent argued that this lack of knowledge puts the citizen in a position of disadvantage relative to the state. Not only is this person experiencing a deprivation of liberty in being detained, but they may be at risk of incriminating themselves. LeBel J asserted that the right to counsel is the "main safeguard to the citizen that his or her other rights will be respected."[44] The legal advice, which arises from section 10(b), ensures that detainees are "informed about their rights and obligations," are provided "adequate information as to how to exercise those rights or fulfill those obligations," and receive assistance in "regaining his or her liberty."[45]

Drivers are under no obligation to "perform the tests or to answer the questions of police, for the sake of investigative efficiency."[46] However, the dissent asserted that the majority's stance and the actions of the police in this case suggest that randomly stopped drivers, such as Orbanski and Elias, should "not be reminded of their constitutional rights" lest they choose to actually exercise those rights and make police work more toilsome. In this manner, the dissent suggested, "effective law enforcement would come to depend on individual's ignorance of their legal rights."[47] The dissent asserted that "the power to request sobriety tests or to put questions to the driver regarding his or her consumption is found nowhere in the statutes, not even implicitly or by giving them broad interpretation."[48] The two justices held that "the operational requirement argument [argued by the majority] seems to relate more to the justification for a limit than to the existence of the limit. Because it is necessary, the courts will then create it."[49] LeBel J disparaged the majority's tactic:

> Most respectfully, this argument is essentially a utilitarian one based on expediency rather than legal principles. Drunk driving is evil. Drunk driving is dangerous. Drunk driving must be swiftly taken off the road. If there is something missing in the statute, let us read in the necessary powers. Failing that, let us go to the common law and find or create something there.[50]

The majority's decision demonstrated the Court's willingness to invoke common law police powers to help "fill gaps" in legislation and provide the police with the necessary investigatory powers and measures that they require on a case-specific basis. The dissent saw this as a huge problem:

> The adoption of a rule limiting *Charter* rights on the basis of what amounts to a utilitarian argument in favour of meeting the needs of police investigations through the development of common law police powers would tend to give a potentially uncontrollable scope to the doctrine developed in the *Waterfield/Dedman* line of cases ... The doctrine would now be encapsulated in the principle that what the police need, the police get,

by judicial fiat if all else fails or if the legislature finds the adoption of legislation to be unnecessary or unwarranted. The courts would limit *Charter* rights to the full extent necessary to achieve the purpose of meeting the needs of the police. The creation of and justification for the limit would arise out of an initiative of the courts. In the context of cases such as those we are considering here, this kind of judicial intervention would preempt any serious Charter review of the limits, as the limits would arise out of initiatives of the courts themselves.[51]

LeBel J echoed the warnings of Dickson CJ's dissent in *Dedman* – namely, that it should be the legislature, not the courts, that should be granting powers to the police and placing carefully tailored limits on citizens' rights. The courts should then return to the traditional task of addressing and reviewing challenges arising from these statutorily prescribed limits on individual rights and freedoms that are enshrined in the *Charter*.

Entry into the Home in Response to Emergency Calls: *R v Godoy*

The home has long attracted a special kind of privacy and protection for the individual. The seminal judgment of *Semayne's Case* in 1604 pronounced that "the house of everyone is to him as a castle and fortress" and that if the king's sheriff wished to enter, he "ought to signify the cause of his coming and to make requests to open doors."[52] The age-old rule is that police require a warrant – prior permission from a judge – in order to intrude into someone's domestic space. In *R v Godoy*, this principle was challenged; the sanctity of the home was called into question by overarching concerns for public safety.[53] This case concerned the scope of common law police powers in response to emergency calls. Writing for a unanimous Court, Chief Justice Lamer upheld the Ontario Court of Appeal's decision that the police possess both a common law duty to investigate 911 calls and the power to forcibly enter an individual's home to locate the 911 caller.

In *Godoy*, officers received instruction from radio dispatch to investigate an "unknown trouble call" originating from the appellant's apartment.[54] The 911 call had been disconnected before the caller was able to communicate what was wrong. Calls such as this are deemed to be a "high priority" given that an individual was trying to seek immediate assistance, but the situation was complicated by the fact that the identity, situation, and trouble faced by the caller was unknown. Thus, protocol required that the officers treat these situations with extreme caution since the exact circumstances and potential danger were unclear. When the officers arrived at the home of Godoy, the appellant answered with the door only slightly ajar. The officers expressed their concern and desire to enter the apartment to investigate the 911 call. The appellant responded that everything was fine and attempted to close his door. In response, the officers forcibly entered the apartment without Godoy's consent and against his protests. Once inside, the officers heard crying from the bedroom where they found the appellant's wife curled on the floor sobbing with evidence of trauma to her head and face. She indicated that her husband, the appellant, had hit her. In the struggle to arrest a resisting Godoy, an officer was injured, resulting in a further charge of assaulting a police officer.

The questions before the Supreme Court prompted a return to the *Waterfield* calculus in order to determine whether the police were acting in the execution of their duties when they forcibly entered Godoy's apartment in response to the 911 call. There was no question that the forcible entry into the dwelling constituted a *prima facie* interference with Godoy's liberty and property.[55] The home has long been recognized as a special haven for the citizen where only a judicially issued warrant could legally allow for a police intrusion. Despite the virtuous motive behind the action, the officers' conduct was still technically trespassing. Hence, the Court moved to the first branch of the *Waterfield* test: Did the police action fall within the general scope of any duty imposed by statute or recognized at common law? The Court agreed that officers have a general duty to protect life, whether that was through the *Police Services Act*'s statutory duty of "assisting victims of crime"[56] or the general common law duties "ascribed to a constable at common law."[57]

This finding led to the second branch of the *Waterfield* test. What can the police do in order to fulfill this duty, and does the conduct in question involve an unjustified use of police powers? At the time of this hearing, the Supreme Court relied on the judgment of Justice Doherty in the case of *R v Simpson* to shed some light on what was "justifiable" or "reasonably necessary" police behaviour: "[T]he justifiability of an officer's conduct depends on a number of factors including the duty being performed, the extent to which some interference with individual liberty is necessitated in order to perform that duty, the importance of that duty to the public good, the liberty being interfered with, and the nature and extent of the interference."[58]

The Court ruled that one's privacy interests "cannot trump the safety of all members of the household," especially when those individuals may be the victims of domestic abuse.[59] Lamer CJ reasoned that the police might be sceptical of the individual who answers the door. In fact, Lamer CJ proposed that the person answering the door might well be the cause for the 911 call. Obviously, if a caller is in such danger that they are unable to either communicate with the 911 dispatcher or answer the door upon the police's arrival, the caller's only hope is that the police will physically locate them within the dwelling. In these circumstances, entering is deemed a necessity in the interest of public safety. However, the judgment was narrow in scope, carefully limiting the extent of the intrusion to the safety of the 911 caller. The Court found that the importance of the police's duty to protect life warrants and justifies a forced entry into a dwelling by police in order to "ascertain the health and safety of a 911 caller." Lamer CJ reasoned that if police do not have the authority to locate the caller, the admirable purposes of an emergency response system are rendered pointless.

Search Powers

In the *Charter* era, the standards that courts have used to justify police searches have been articulated by the Supreme Court of Canada in several key decisions. Section 8 states that "[e]veryone has the right to be secure against unreasonable search or seizure." Thus, section 8 is intimately tied to an individual's property rights and the seizure of property located on one's person, or in one's house, vehicle, or possessions, such as computers or cell phones. To provide some context, we will briefly elaborate on principles that courts have developed out of the fundamental rights that are protected under section 8 of the *Charter*. After this brief introduction to search and seizure, we will shift to considering how the *Waterfield* calculus has affected the way in which courts review police conduct that infringes section 8 rights.

The seminal case of *Hunter v Southam* was the first instance of the Supreme Court engaging with section 8 and the *Charter* in a meaningful way.[60] This decision was released in 1984, a year before *Waterfield* took on new life in *Dedman*. In *Hunter*, the Supreme Court, led by Dickson CJ, found that the appropriate standard that a reviewing judge must apply in a section 8 application is "reasonable and probable grounds, established upon oath, to believe that an offence has been committed."[61] Along with this standard, and other shifting standards that have been elucidated by the courts over the years, one must have "a reasonable expectation of privacy" for section 8 rights to be invoked.[62] In other words, section 8 may only be engaged if the individual had a reasonable expectation of privacy in the property that was searched.[63] To determine whether an individual has a reasonable expectation of privacy in a given case, a judge must look at the totality of the circumstances. The

Supreme Court has relied on US jurisprudence in determining the factors to be considered in such an analysis:

- presence at the time of the search
- possession or control of the property or place searched
- ownership of the property or place
- historical use of the property or item
- the ability to regulate access, including the right to admit or exclude others from the place
- the existence of a subjective expectation of privacy
- the objective reasonableness of the expectation.[64]

Approximately three years after *Hunter,* the Supreme Court of Canada had another opportunity to engage with searches under section 8 of the *Charter.* In *R v Collins,* a majority of justices gave three necessary conditions to satisfy the requirements under section 8: "A search will be reasonable if it is authorized by law, if the law itself is reasonable and if the manner in which the search was carried out is reasonable."[65] These principles that have been espoused by the Supreme Court have been accentuated by the *Waterfield* doctrine. As critics have noted, while *Hunter* brought forth "bright-line standards and a method for balancing circumstances that would erode the values of privacy and dignity that run through the core of section 8," *Waterfield* engendered uncertainty and unpredictability.[66] Thus, we will now turn to cases where the *Waterfield* test was applied to circumstances of search and seizure to better understand its impact on section 8 rights.

Entry into the Home and Safety Searches: *R v MacDonald*

The incursions of police into the home continued in *R v MacDonald* in 2014 in the context of police safety searches on one's doorstep.[67] In this case, two police officers responded to a noise complaint of loud music emanating from the accused's apartment. Before the police's arrival and involvement, MacDonald, who was hosting a party with a few co-workers, had rudely refused numerous requests from neighbours and the concierge to turn down his music. When MacDonald finally answered the police's knocking, he only partially opened the door, allowing the officers to see his face and the right side of his body. However, the police spotted that the accused was hiding something "black and shiny" behind his leg. When the officer repeatedly asked the accused what he was holding, MacDonald refused to answer. Suspecting that the accused was holding a weapon, the officer pushed the door open a few inches further to discover that MacDonald was holding a handgun. The officer forced his way past the door and into the apartment, struggling with MacDonald until he was able to disarm him.

The main issue presented to the Supreme Court was whether the officer's action of pushing the door open further constituted a "search" under the *Charter* and whether such a search was authorized by common law, relying once again on the *Waterfield* test. The Court found that the officer's action of pushing open the door and reaching inside went beyond the "implied license to knock on the door" and constituted an interference with MacDonald's reasonable expectation of privacy within his home.[68] However, as the Court ultimately found, safety searches fall within the general scope of the common law duty to protect life and safety. For a safety search to be reasonably necessary, under the second stage of *Waterfield*, the Court weighed the factors articulated in police powers jurisprudence, such as "the importance of the performance of the duty to the public good," "the necessity of the interference with individual liberty for the performance of the duty," and "the extent of the interference with individual liberty."[69]

Similar to its findings in *Godoy,* the Supreme Court of Canada found that the duty to protect life and safety was of "utmost importance to the public good" and that in some circumstances, "interferences with individual liberty" would be necessary to carry out that duty.[70] When an officer was required to interact with an individual who they believed may be armed or dangerous, the Court found that a safety search would be a reasonable means of eliminating the threat of concealed weapons, even if the search imposed an infringement on the individual's liberty. The Court explained that these types of safety searches would generally be conducted by police as a "reactionary measure" in response to a "dangerous situation created by individuals, to which the police must react on the sudden."[71]

Yet the majority was mindful of the risks of abuse this search power posed, especially on the doorstep of the home. The Supreme Court explained that "even though all Officer Boyd did was push the door open slightly further, this had the potential to reveal to the officer any number of things about MacDonald, as they could now see more of the interior of the unit."[72] Searches conducted in the context of one's home could reveal a considerable amount of "very sensitive personal information" and had the possibility of severely threatening the privacy of the appellant. In response to this concern, the Court insisted that a safety search would be authorized by law only if the officer had "reasonable and probable grounds" that their safety (or that of the public) was at stake. Limiting the extent of the interference, the Court placed more restrictions on the scope of the search:

> Although the specific manner (be it a pat-down, the shining of a flashlight or, as in this case, the further opening of a door) in which a safety search is conducted will vary from case to case, such a search will be lawful only if all aspects of the search serve a protective function. In other words, the authority for the search runs out at the point at which the search for weapons is finished.[73]

Having found that the police action constituted a search and that the safety search fell under the police's authorized common law powers, the Supreme Court turned to determining whether the search itself was unreasonable and violated the rights afforded to MacDonald under section 8 of the *Charter*. To do this, the Court looked to a test set out in *Collins*, which states that warrantless searches are deemed reasonable if 1) they are authorized by law; 2) the law itself is reasonable; and 3) the manner in which the search was carried out was also reasonable.[74] By conducting the *Waterfield/ Dedman* test and coming to the conclusion that safety searches are authorized under common law, the Court satisfied the first two requirements of the *Collins* test. The third requirement – on whether the search was carried out in a reasonable manner – also ties into the *Waterfield* analysis of whether the police's action was "reasonably necessary."

With respect to the third requirement, the Court agreed with the trial judge's findings that the officer, in pushing open the door further into MacDonald's unit, did what was necessary to eliminate a possible threat to the police's or public's safety and nothing more. The officer had twice questioned MacDonald as to what he held in his hand but received no answer. In these circumstances, the trial judge held, it would be hard to imagine a less invasive way of determining whether MacDonald was concealing a weapon (and thereby eliminating any threat in that regard) than the actions taken by Officer Boyd.[75] In upholding that the officer's actions constituted a reasonable search and that there was no violation of MacDonald's section 8 rights, the majority solidified the safety search in the officer's arsenal of authorized powers at common law.[76]

The dissent, while disagreeing with the standard set forth by the majority for enabling police to conduct these safety searches, poignantly expressed the need for police to have these types of search powers:

> Every day, throughout this country, police officers put their lives and safety at risk in order to preserve and protect the lives and safety of others. In return, they are entitled to know that when potentially dangerous situations arise, the law permits them to conduct minimally intrusive safety searches to alleviate the risks they face. That is the fundamental bargain we, as a society, have struck with the police – and it is a fundamental commitment upon which the police are entitled to rely.[77]

Once again, the general duties of the police provided the Supreme Court of Canada with the fertile earth from which to produce a new, and very real, power of the police to enter homes. But what of state-citizen interactions on the street? How would the ancillary powers doctrine inform and control what happens when an officer meets an individual on the street? We now turn our attention to investigative detentions and the law of search and seizure.

Investigative Detentions and Searches

The cases of *Godoy* and *MacDonald* make it clear that courts were willing to expand police powers to enter a home where specific safety concerns existed. But what of a more typical interaction between an officer and a citizen on the street? Canadian courts would have to determine the scope of police powers to stop, detain, and search an individual where no grounds to arrest were yet apparent. These situations would engage the *Charter* protections of the right to not be arbitrarily detained (section 9) and the right to be free from unreasonable search and seizure (section 8).

Investigative Detention: *R v Mann*

In December 2000, shortly before midnight, two police officers received a radio dispatch to check out a reported break and enter occurring in downtown Winnipeg. As the officers were approaching the scene of the crime, they noticed an individual walking along the sidewalk who purportedly closely matched the description of the suspect. Officers stopped the individual – Phillip Mann – and asked him to identify himself. Even though his name did not match the suspect's name, the officers requested a pat-down safety search of his person to look for concealed weapons. Mann consented and during the pat-down search, one officer felt a soft object in the pocket of Mann's sweater. Without asking for further consent or questioning the appellant about the contents of his pocket, the officer reached in and retrieved a small bag of marijuana. The officer then reached into another pocket and found several small plastic bags, two Valium pills, and a treaty card confirming the appellant's identity. In a poor turn of circumstances for Mann, who was not the suspect the officers were searching for, he was arrested and charged with possession of drugs for the purposes of trafficking.

At trial and on appeal, Mann maintained that this search and seizure violated his section 8 *Charter* rights to be free from "unreasonable search and seizure." However, in order to decide on the constitutionality of the search, the Supreme Court first had to deal with the legality of the stop. Were the police authorized to stop Mann, detain him for investigative purposes, and request a search of his person? The answers to these questions would help determine whether the police were justified to search inside Mann's pocket and whether the evidence found would be excluded, thus acquitting the appellant. The majority judgment, penned by Justice Frank Iacobucci, began with a rationalization for why the judiciary – as "custodians of the common law"[78] – should use the courts as the "proper forum for the recognition and ordering of further development" of police powers absent legislative intervention: "[T]he unregulated use of investigative detentions in policing, their uncertain legal status, and the potential for abuse inherent in such low-visibility exercises of discretionary power" were reasons that spurred the majority to intervene in this area of criminal procedure. Thus, the Court applied the *Waterfield* test to determine whether the police had the common law power to 1) detain Mann for investigative purposes; and 2) perform a pat-down search of Mann and seize drugs from his pocket.

The majority started with investigative detention, largely affirming Justice Twaddle's application of *Waterfield* at the Manitoba Court of Appeal. The actions in question passed the threshold inquiry; the police stopping and detaining the accused for questioning was considered a *prima facie* interference with Mann's self-autonomy and freedom of movement. In considering the first prong of the test, the majority agreed with the Court of Appeal's ruling; the action fell within the general scope of the police's common law duties to prevent crime and protect life and property. In considering the second prong of the test, the majority found that the officers' decision and action of detaining Mann for investigative purposes was a justified use of their common law power. In applying the second stage of the *Waterfield* test, the Court clarified some of the developments regarding how the courts should determine "reasonable necessity" or go about justifying the police's conduct at this stage of the test. Drawing on past jurisprudence – such as

Dedman and *Cloutier v Langlois* – the majority articulated three factors that should be considered. Was the police action, which invaded the rights of the individual,

- necessary in order for the peace officer to perform their duty,[79]
- reasonable in light of the public purpose served,[80] and
- reasonable in light of the nature of the liberty interfered with?[81]

In the specific context of investigative detention, Doherty JA helped add a "further gloss to this second stage of the *Waterfield* test" in *Simpson*.[82] Inspired by US jurisprudence, Doherty JA held that investigative detentions could only be justified at common law "if the detaining officer has some *articulable cause*."[83] To stop someone for questioning, the detaining officer had to have "reasonable cause to suspect" that the person, whom the police wished to detain, was criminally implicated or involved in the activities under their investigation.[84] The officer's articulable cause – or equivalent standards of "reasonable cause to suspect" – had to be based on the assessment of evidence and objective-discernible facts pertaining to the circumstances. An officer's mere "hunch based on intuition gained by experience" would not be satisfactory.[85] The courts described this standard as lower than "reasonable and probable grounds," a standard used to deploy arrest powers, but still one that required objective and subjective reasoning.[86]

In *Mann*, however, the Supreme Court majority articulated its preference for the term "reasonable grounds to detain" over "articulable cause," largely due to the long history and familiarity of the Canadian courts with this phrase. Addressing the slight tweaks made to the *Waterfield* test and the *Simpson* articulable cause requirement, the majority laid out what should be considered in the second stage of the test when it came to evaluating the power of police to detain citizens:

> The detention must be viewed as reasonably necessary on an objective view of the totality of the circumstances, informing the officer's suspicion that there is a clear nexus between the individual to be detained and a recent or on-going criminal offence. The overall reasonableness of the decision to detain, however, must further be assessed against all of the circumstances, most notably the extent to which the interference with individual liberty is necessary to perform the officer's duty, the liberty interfered with, and the nature and extent of that interference, in order to meet the second prong of the *Waterfield* test.[87]

When applying these principles to the facts of *Mann*, the majority held that the officer had reasonable grounds to detain the accused on the downtown streets of Winnipeg. Iacobucci J stated that the accused "closely matched the description of the suspect given by radio dispatch, and was only two to three blocks from the scene of the reported crime."[88] The justice, echoing the findings of the lower courts, continued to find that these factors led the officers "to *reasonably suspect* that the appellant was involved in criminal activity, and at the very least ought to be investigated further."[89] The legality of the stop was confirmed and consequently resulted in the common law police power to detain individuals for investigative purposes.

The majority then moved on to contemplate the legality of the search, deploying the *Waterfield* test once again. In the Supreme Court's view, the pat-down search was another interference with Mann, specifically an intrusion of his physical autonomy. However, the Court felt that the search fell within the police's common law duty to protect life – specifically, in this case, the officers' lives. The Court finally considered the second branch of the *Waterfield* test: Was the police's search a reasonably necessary action for the performance of this duty? Before rendering its opinion on the facts, the Court attempted to delineate the scope and contours of this search power against the search power that arose incidentally to arrest. The Court asserted that this type of search power, which was associated with investigative detentions, did not exist as a "matter of course."[90] Unlike searches that were incident to arrest, which could be used to preserve and discover evidence on the body of the arrestee, the search incident to detention could only be used as a protective search for concealed weapons. The officer had to believe, on reasonable grounds, that their safety, or the safety of others, was at risk. The officer's decision to search must also be reasonably necessary considering the totality of the circumstances.[91] The decision to perform a safety search could not be justified based on a "vague or non-existent concern for safety," nor could it be premised upon "hunches or mere intuition."[92]

The majority found that there were reasonable grounds for a protective search of the appellant. The officers wanted to perform a pat-down of the outer surface of Mann's clothing in order to feel for any weapons that he may potentially have concealed. There was a logical possibility that Mann, suspected on reasonable grounds of having recently committed a break and enter, could have been in the possession of break-and-enter tools, which could have been used as weapons. The officers wanted to ensure that the appellant was not armed with weapons that could unexpectedly and fatally be used against them. The search itself was supposed to be brief and minimally intrusive. The Court found on the balance of these factors; the officer was justified in conducting a pat-down search for protective purposes. The problem that arose was that the officer was not authorized to go beyond the initial pat-down and reach into the appellant's pocket. This more intrusive part of the search – going beyond the outer layer of Mann's clothing and fishing around in his pockets – was considered an unreasonable violation of the appellant's reasonable expectation of privacy.

The majority agreed with the trial judge's finding that "there was nothing from which [the officer could] infer that was reasonable to proceed beyond a pat down search for security reasons."[93] The majority asserted that in these types of safety searches, the officers must confine their search strictly to what was minimally necessary to learn whether the appellant was armed or whether the officer would need to disarm if he discovered weapons. The small soft baggie was highly unlikely to be a weapon. The Court articulated that searches incidental to investigative detention were not licences for a general power to explore the suspect's person for whatever evidence of criminal activity the officer might stumble upon. Even though Iacobucci J recognized that the power of search incidental to investigative detention existed at common law, the Court found that the manner of this search was unreasonable and contravened the appellant's section 8 rights. The evidence was excluded, and Mann was acquitted.

Roadblocks: *R v Clayton*

Further to the police's common law powers of investigative detainment and safety searches established in *Mann*, the Supreme Court of Canada continued to examine the scope of these powers in *R v Clayton* in 2007 when the police set up a roadblock in response to a "gun call." In September 1999, late one evening, the police received a 911 call from an agitated caller who reported that he could see four of about ten "black guys" holding handguns in front of a strip club. The caller also identified the make and model of four vehicles in the parking lot, which had their headlights on. Within minutes of the call being made, the police arrived at the scene and blocked both entrances to the parking lot. Almost immediately after the police set up this perimeter, a car approached the back exit, prompting the two officers to stop the vehicle. The officers informed the occupants that there had been a "gun call" and requested that they step outside the car and comply with a safety search. Even though the car was not one of the vehicles identified by the 911 caller, the officers premised their request for a search as both occupants, Clayton and Farmer, met the general description of the suspects being "black men."

Farmer protested at this idea, but, after the officer's repeated attempts to make him exit, he eventually exited the vehicle. Clayton, the passenger, refused to make eye contact with the police and gave evasive answers when questioned. The officer noted that Clayton was wearing black gloves even though it was not "glove weather." A nervous Clayton eventually exited the car but was reluctant to move away from the door of the car. When the officer sought to relocate him to the rear of the car, Clayton pushed the officer over and ran away toward the club. Officers, positioned at the front entrance, tackled Clayton to the ground. In searching him, the officers found a loaded semi-automatic handgun in Clayton's trouser pocket. Alerted to the discovery of this handgun, the officer arrested Farmer for possession of the gun found on Clayton. When searching Farmer, the officer also found a loaded handgun under Farmer's jacket. Both faced charges of possession of prohibited firearms under the *Criminal Code*.

At trial, Clayton and Farmer argued that the detention and the search had violated their sections 8 and 9 rights under the *Charter* and questioned the legality of the police's tactic to erect a roadblock. The courts faced the question of whether the police conduct was authorized by law. Justice Rosalie Abella, writing for the majority, broke her analysis into two parts: first considering the initial stop of the vehicle made by police, followed by an examination of whether the police were authorized to continue detaining and searching the respondents. Undertaking an assessment of this initial detention, the majority found that the police conduct met the threshold and first question of the *Waterfield* test. There was no statutory provision under the *Police Services Act* that expressly authorized this initial stop.[94] However, Abella J found that the police were "clearly acting in the course of their duty to investigate and prevent crime." The Court fundamentally disagreed with the appeal court's conclusions on the second stage of the test. Doherty JA had found that the police had not used their powers in a justifiable manner, and he was troubled by the police's failure to tailor their detention, noting that the respondent's "sporty Jaguar" did not match the reported vehicle description. Ultimately, the majority preferred to side with the trial judge's findings that the police were justified to stop all vehicles leaving the parking lot: "Had they sat by and watched vehicles leave," the police would have "been derelict in their duties."[95]

The majority used the criteria articulated by the Court in *Mann* to argue that the police were justified in stopping the respondents. Abella J submitted that the police needed to consider the larger context of the situation or the "totality of the circumstances." The presence of firearms led to a high-risk situation, where members of the public could potentially be harmed. Thus, the police were motivated to act swiftly and sought to only detain vehicles leaving from the club's vicinity. Law enforcement believed that stopping cars that were leaving from the parking lot could either help them "apprehend individuals in possession of dangerous weapons" or gain more information concerning the offence being investigated. The majority found that further detaining the car and its occupants was prudent given that the respondents were "black males" and that they were leaving the parking lot moments after the police had arrived. These factors led the officers to reasonably suspect that Clayton and Farmer were in possession of firearms and could pose a threat to the safety of the officers and the public. Borrowing the reasons laid out in *Mann*, the Court found that it was a justifiable course of action for the officers to conduct a safety search – incidental to their investigative detention – to determine if the detainees had concealed weapons and eliminate the threat if they did. The Court found that the "search was necessarily incidental to the lawful investigative detention and, consequently, there was no violation of section 8."

Although concurring with the majority's ultimate decision on the issues, dissenting Justice Ian Binnie critiqued how they arrived there and proposed a new analytical approach for how common law police powers should be assessed against *Charter* rights. He submitted that the "reasonably necessary" test, found at the second stage of *Waterfield*, is not a *Charter* test and should not be "an adequate substitute for proper Charter scrutiny." The common law is "no more immune from *Charter* scrutiny than is statute law."[96] The dissent argued that any common law police powers, if they are to be legally authorized, had to be subjected to explicit *Charter* analysis under section 1:

> It seems to me problematic in a case like this, however, to say the authorizing law is subject to *Charter* scrutiny without in fact subjecting the authorizing law to any recognizable *Charter* scrutiny. My preference is to conduct "*Charter* scrutiny" using our usual *Charter* framework of analysis rather than calling in aid a British case like *Waterfield* decided almost 20 years before the *Canadian Charter* came into existence. No reason is given by my colleague for creating a different scheme of *Charter* scrutiny for common law police powers from that which the courts have developed for statute law (and applied, as will be seen, to other areas of the common law). The *Oakes* test, unlike *Waterfield*, is based on the wording of the

Charter itself. Moreover, common law police powers illustrate a serious difficulty, I believe, with my colleague's approach. On occasion an Attorney General will argue (as here) that a common law which authorizes police conduct that infringes individual *Charter* freedoms may be justified in the larger interest of society. In a number of cases we have held that a common law power may infringe a *Charter* right but nevertheless be upheld under s. 1, or as it is sometimes put, we have found a *Charter* infringement but not a *Charter* violation. Conflating in a *Waterfield*-type analysis the consideration of the individual's ss. 8 and 9 rights and society's s. 1 interests can only add to the problematic elasticity of common law police powers, and sidestep the real policy debate in which competing individual and societal interests are required to be clearly articulated in the established framework of *Charter* analysis.[97]

The dissent articulated that the *Waterfield* test and the *Oakes* test are not duplicative of one another, the latter carrying with it a high standard and a principled approach for justifying rights violations in the "larger interests of society."[98] The dissent posited that it was possible that a common law police power could survive the two-pronged *Waterfield* test – by being deemed "reasonably necessary" for the police to achieve their duty – but still fail an *Oakes* analysis. The dissent was insistent that the *Waterfield/Dedman* test "should not provide an end run around *Oakes*." LeBel J acknowledged that "the common law famously adapts itself to the evolution of society. A balance that might have tilted the law in favour of civil liberties in a society less infected with an urban gun problem now tips the other way." Despite this reality, LeBel J asserted that "such claims to common law police authority should still be subject to more structured Charter review."

Criticism was given that the determination to restrict the common law power only to "serious firearm offences" would provide insufficient "guidance" for future police conduct. In response, Binnie J stated:

> General guidance is a matter for Parliament. Courts are required to adjudicate specific fact situations. Common law develops by the accumulation of a variety of precedents before (if at all) more generalised principles can be deduced ... Parliament, on the other hand, can take a much broader view of what is required, and it is to be hoped that legislators in this country will address the issue of police powers in a comprehensive way, as has been done in many other common law jurisdictions.

The dissent also addressed the comments of Doherty JA regarding the "systemic failings" of police training. Binnie J stated that the common law does not hand the police a simple "rule" that can be applied:

> I am struck by the failure of their training to address in any way the limits of the ancillary power doctrine. This court, and others including the Supreme Court of Canada, have endeavoured over at least the last decade to articulate the ancillary power doctrine in a way that is consistent with both the principles protected by the *Charter* and in the community need for effective law enforcement. In interpreting that doctrine, the courts have recognized the difficulties inherent in policing, where officers face an infinite variety of fact situations and often must make quick decisions. The case-specific approach developed in these authorities has not penetrated the training of the officers involved in this case. The testimony of these officers strongly suggests that their police force has made no effort to embed the approach to the ancillary power doctrine adopted by the courts into police training. This systemic failure would suggest that the court must deliver its message in a more emphatic way.[99]

Sniffer Dogs: *R v Kang-Brown; R v A.M.*

The companion cases of *R v Kang-Brown* and *R v A.M.* in 2008 mark the Supreme Court of Canada's next major milestone in the consideration of the ancillary powers doctrine. Both cases concerned the police's use of drug-detection dogs for warrantless sniff searches of the appellants' personal belongings. The search conducted in *A.M.* was of a student's backpack in a high school gymnasium. The police had been granted an open invitation by the school's principal to search for drugs with their dogs, even though there had been no specific suggestion or complaint that drugs were present at the school. However, the officers were tipped off by a positive alert from their dog and discovered a bag of drugs on further inspection of the student's backpack. *Kang-Brown* concerned a plain-clothed Royal Canadian Mounted Police officer, who was positioned at the Calgary bus terminal and observed Kang-Brown, a South Asian man, disembarking with a bag from a Greyhound bus. Kang-Brown's prolonged stare and uneasy posturing led the officer to engage him in conversation. When the officer asked if he could look inside the appellant's bag, Kang-Brown set the bag on the floor and proceeded to unzip it, appearing as though he was consenting to the search. However, when the officer went to touch the bag, the accused pulled it away, looking nervous. The officer called over another officer with a drug-detection dog to provide assistance. The dog indicated the presence of drugs in Kang-Brown's bag. Based on the dog's positive alert, the officers arrested him and subsequently searched the bag to discover two bags of cocaine and a container of heroin.

The Supreme Court's judgment in these cases is convoluted, somewhat complicated, and, at times, difficult to follow. The Court splintered into multiple different opinions on a number of sub-issues: 1) whether police possessed a common law power to search using a sniffer dog; 2) whether a drug-detection dog's sniff amounted to a search under section 8 of the *Charter;* 3) if it was considered a search, whether the search in this case violated the accused's section 8 *Charter* rights; and 4) what standard should be used to deploy a sniffer dog. It is a lot to sift through. Of the eight sets of reasons cumulatively penned for these twin cases, two are of particular importance to our current survey – those of Binnie and LeBel JJ, both found in *Kang-Brown*. In that case, all the justices found that the dog's sniff of the accused's bag at the bus station amounted to a search. Both groups of justices agreed to the fact that there was no statutory authority that allowed police to perform sniffer-dog searches for such criminal investigations. However, the Court came to polarizing opinions on whether the police held the authority at common law to conduct sniffer-dog searches and what the Court's role should be in formulating common law police powers.

A cobbled-together majority of four, led by Binnie J, eventually ruled that the common law did grant the police the authority to conduct warrantless sniffer-dog searches of Canadians and their personal belongings if an officer held a reasonable suspicion that the individual was possibly involved in criminal activity. Yet a larger majority of six found that the sniffer-dog searches of both appellants were ultimately unreasonable and violated the section 8 *Charter* rights of each defendant. Thus, the evidence discovered by the police with the help of their dogs was excused in both instances. However, the complexity of the judgment arises in how each of the justices came to this conclusion, and it is worthwhile to examine the divergent positions assumed by LeBel and Binnie JJ.

LeBel J refused to acknowledge the existence of the police power at common law. In *Kang-Brown,* he argued that the police held no reasonable and probable grounds to believe that the accused had drugs in his possession or that he had committed an offence at the time they performed a sniffer-dog search. LeBel J stated that without the positive results of the sniffer-dog search, the police would have had no reason to arrest Kang-Brown or further search his bag. LeBel J was concerned by the majority's efforts to lower the triggering standard for a warrantless sniffer-dog search from the "reasonable and probable grounds" set out in *Hunter* to a lower standard of "reasonable suspicion" similar to that established in *Mann* and *Clayton* for investigative detentions.[100] He argued that the warrantless search was unreasonable in that it lacked authorization by law, failing the *Collins* test in the absence of prior judicial authorization and reasonable and probable cause.

Continuing to examine LeBel J's judgment, we find an attempt to revive Dickson CJ's plea from the *Dedman* dissent, one that urged that Parliament should be responsible for expanding the law concerning police investigative powers, not the courts. LeBel J was not concerned with whether the courts possess law-making powers but, rather, with how and when it is appropriate for the courts to exercise their law-making power. While the Court's recent precedents in *Mann* and *Clayton* demonstrated the Court's willingness to articulate and develop new common law police powers, LeBel J warned that this did "not mean that the Court should always expand common law rules, in order to address perceived gaps in police powers or apprehend inaction by Parliament, especially when rights and interests as fundamental as personal privacy and autonomy are at stake."[101] LeBel J reminded his fellow jurists that the "court must remain alive and sensitive to the fact that they are ultimately the guardians of constitutional rules, principles and values."[102] In expanding the common law police powers, the courts, rather than the legislature, are the ones eroding individual's constitutional rights and freedoms through their own judicial decisions. Concerned by the difficult position this put the Supreme Court in, LeBel J called for a proper dialogue between the courts and the legislature:

> A requirement that Parliament act first would put the courts in a better position to address the competing interests at play and would ensure that the justification process meets constitutional standards. The extension of the common law police powers [by the Court] as proposed in this case would shortcut the justification process and leave the Court to frame the common law rule itself without the full benefit of the dialogue and discussion that would have taken place had Parliament acted and been required to justify its action.[103]

LeBel J recognized that the courts are also ill-equipped to develop an adequate legal framework for the use of police dogs, given that the judiciary knows little about the investigative techniques and accuracy of sniffer dogs. To LeBel J, it seemed ridiculous that the Supreme Court was being asked to curtail *Charter* rights "for fear of leaving a void in the law and interfering with the use of a fairly widespread police investigative technique."[104] The Court, he submitted, would create a new common law rule on the basis of little more than unverified and unverifiable assumptions. For these reasons, LeBel J and his small minority refrained from discovering or articulating a common law police power that would allow the police to use sniffer dogs to investigate potential suspects.[105]

However, Binnie J penned the prevailing judgment, finding varying levels of support from Chief Justice Beverley McLachlin and Justices Marie Deschamps, Marshall Rothstein, and Michel Bastarache. This assembly of justices willingly declared that the police possessed a common law power to use sniffer dogs for investigative searches; however, they differed on the requisite standard that had to be met before a dog-sniffer search could be executed. Binnie J acknowledged and welcomed LeBel J's call for parliament-ary intervention, similar to how he did in *Clayton;* however, he asserted that the Supreme Court should not favour an approach that "effectively renders sniffer dogs useless," waiting around for Parliament to enact legislation.[106] Binnie J, alongside McLachlin CJ, asserted that a sniffer dog is an "investiga-tive tool" similar to devices such as "binoculars, flashlights and night vision goggles" and not a "police power" like the powers to detain or to arrest.[107] Thus, to the justices, it seemed unnecessary and burdensome to require the police to pester Parliament for authority every time they want to use tools that are deployed in full public view, like sniffer dogs.[108]

Binnie J also remarked on the lack of predictability a potential litigant would face if the Supreme Court refused to continue its approach:

> In fairness to litigants, the Court ought not ... to waver unpredictably between the willingness of the Court to explore adjustments in the com-mon law of detention or search and seizure based on reasonable suspicion ... and the "hands off" or "leave it to Parliament" attitude my colleague advocates in this case. How are litigants to anticipate whether they will find the Court in a "can do" mode or a "leave it to Parliament" mode? In my view, *Mann* and *Clayton* resolved the Court's attitude to this par-ticular area of common law police powers in favour of the former. We have crossed the Rubicon.[109]

Building on this statement, Binnie J advocated that the "Court should pro-ceed incrementally with the *Waterfield/Dedman* analysis of common law police powers rather than try to re-cross the Rubicon to retrieve the fallen flag of the *Dedman* dissent" and wait for Parliament to step in.[110] To clarify the Court's commitment to the ancillary powers doctrine, Binnie J asserted that the outcome of future cases will not "always or even generally be in favour of the existence of a police power"; rather, "where a court concludes, after analysis, that the police do not have the power they claim, it will be up to Parliament to decide what law, if any, it wishes to enact on the subject."[111]

For this particular common law power, however, Deschamps J's reasons appear to provide the closest thing to a *Waterfield/Dedman* analysis.[112] She began with defining the purported power – the police's use of well-trained and highly accurate sniffer dogs as an investigative tool – and the appellant's interest being interfered with – namely, their privacy. At the first stage, she acknowledged that "investigating ongoing narcotics trafficking" would ultimately fall under the police's common law duty to investigate and prevent crime.[113] At the second stage, she turned to consider whether this power is reasonably necessary to the performance of that duty, relying on the factors articulated and clarified in *Dedman*, *Mann*, and, later, in *MacDonald*. Considering that the trafficking of drugs is a serious offence, she found that "taking proactive steps to intercept narcotics along drug routes and prosecute drug couriers who facilitate the movement of drugs" is a worthy public objective.[114] Examining the method employed, she commented that the sniffing of the drug-detection dogs is minimally intrusive – the dog briefly sniffs the object in question and indicates the positive presence of drugs by sitting down. The high accuracy rate of the dog in *Kang-Brown* led the officers to believe that the positive signal was a pretty likely indicator of the presence of drugs in the accused's bag.

However, as mentioned, there was disagreement between the members of the majority on what standard an officer would need to possess before employing a drug-detection dog. The critique of a higher standard of "reasonable and probable grounds" was that in passing that threshold, the officers could engage in activities that were more intrusive than the use of sniffer dogs. In possessing reasonable grounds, they could already perform a search of the bag or even arrest the accused. However, the Court suggested that the lower standard of "reasonable suspicion" allowed the officer to possess a suspicion, supported by objectively discernible facts, that the individual in question was possibly involved in criminality. Although a "mere hunch" or educated guess would not satisfy the reasonable suspicion standard, the majority was wary of making the triggering standard too difficult or demanding for officers to satisfy.[115] After pronouncing the pre-conditions of this common law power, a slim majority, spearheaded by LeBel J,[116] found that the officer in *Kang-Brown* based the deployment of the sniffer dog on speculation rather than on "objectively verifiable evidence supporting reasonable suspicion." With the absence of reasonable suspicion, the search was not authorized by the common law (or statute) and failed to satisfy the first requirement of the *Collins* test for a reasonable warrantless search.

In summary, the Supreme Court of Canada expanded common law police powers to allow for home entries, investigative detentions, and safety searches on the street, the power to block roads and search suspects, and the power to use sniffer dogs even in the absence of reasonable and probable grounds to believe evidence of an offence would be found. This uninterrupted trajectory of power expansion seemed to pave the way for an unlimited amount of police powers to flow from their general duties to protect the citizenry and prevent crime. The runaway powers train was picking up speed. What then would happen when the police detained a man not for any wrongdoing but, rather, to pre-emptively prevent a breach of the peace. Would the Court finally curtail the expansion of common law police powers?

The Court's Refusal to Affirm a Common Law Police Power:
Fleming v Ontario

Randy Fleming was walking along the shoulder of the road carrying a large Canadian flag. He was on his way to a counterprotest flag rally, which was being organized in response to the occupation of a First Nations group on Crown land. Given previous clashes that had occurred in the past between the protest groups, the police had developed a plan to keep the peace by ordering that counterprotesters would not be allowed on the occupied property. However, Fleming was unaware of the police's mandate. In order to avoid a passing police vehicle coming down the road, Fleming stepped off the shoulder and onto the Crown land. When the police noticed where Fleming was standing, they turned their vehicle around and started yelling at him to return to the road. Meanwhile, nearby protestors, noticing the commotion made by the police, began moving toward Fleming. Even though the approaching protestors were not carrying weapons or uttering threats, the police officers – uneasy of the situation that could unfold – told Fleming that he was under arrest and led him off the property. Confused with what was happening, Fleming refused the officer's request to drop the flag he was carrying. The officers forced him to the ground, took his flag, and handcuffed him. Police took him to the police station where they released him a few hours later.

Fleming was charged with obstructing a peace officer in resisting arrest. However, the crucial question was whether the police had the lawful authority to even arrest the appellant. Fleming was doing nothing wrong in walking along the road, entering the occupied property, or standing there with his Canadian flag: "He had committed no crime. He had broken no law. He was not about to commit any offence, harm anyone, or breach the peace."[117] However, the police argued that their actions – of arresting Fleming for his own protection – were authorized under the common law. Thus, Fleming successfully appealed this case to the Supreme Court of Canada, asking the justices to clarify the existence and scope of this common law power: Do the police have the authority at common law "to arrest someone, who is acting lawfully, in order to prevent an apprehended breach of the peace"?[118]

In a rare instance, the Supreme Court found that the power claimed by police did not exist at common law.[119] This meant that the actions of the police were not lawfully authorized and that the arrest of Fleming was illegal. This stance marks one of the first instances of the Court refusing when asked to recognize and expand the police's powers at common law. Justice Suzanne Côté, writing for the Court, provided an excellent overview of the *Waterfield/Dedman* test, preferring to use the terminology of the "ancillary powers doctrine." She also reiterated the idea that the Court must "tread lightly" in considering proposed common law police powers but, at the same time, "cannot abdicate their role of incrementally adapting common law rules where legislative gaps exist."[120] Following the *Waterfield/ Dedman* test, Côté J began the preliminary stage by defining the proposed power and acknowledging the interests being impacted. The power, she stated, targets individuals who are acting lawfully, those who have "not committed, and are not about to commit, either an indictable offence or breach of the peace."[121] Relying on case law and scholarly commentary, she clarified that an act that seeks to "breach [of] the peace" must involve some level of violence or risk of harm.

It is in facing this serious risk of harm that the common law has granted the state the ability to lawfully interfere with an individual's liberty. Historically, at common law, the police have possessed the power to arrest or detain a person who is about to commit a breach of the peace.[122] In fact, this common law power has been codified and can be found under section 31(1) of the *Criminal Code*. However, this power is markedly distinct from the one being proposed by the police in this case. Côté J remarked that "the power at issue would target individuals who are not suspected of being about to break any law or to initiate any violence themselves, in situations in which the police nonetheless believe that arresting the individuals in question will prevent a breach from occurring." She found that there is a difference between having the power "to arrest someone who is personally about to breach the peace" and the "power to arrest someone whose lawful conduct may provoke others to breach the peace."[123]

Côté J also examined the impact that this interference has on the appellant. Arrest is one of the most extreme powers available to police, "an action which completely restricts the person's ability to move about in society free from state coercion."[124] Due to the serious limitations placed on an individual's rights, the police are required to possess reasonable and probable grounds to believe that the individual they seek to arrest committed, is committing, or will commit a crime. Yet the police were proposing the power to "preventatively" arrest a law-abiding citizen. Côté J remarked that this "purported power would directly impact on a constellation of rights that are fundamental to individual freedom in our society" – namely, freedom from arbitrary arrest and detainment under section 9, the general liberty interest in being free from the exercise of force by the state under section 7, and the right to express one's self, even if that expression may provoke or enrage others, under section 2(b) of the *Charter*. At the first stage of the test, Côté J acknowledged that the proposed police power – as an action that seeks to prevent a hypothetical breach of the peace – still fell within the general scope of the police's common law duties of preserving the peace, preventing crime, and protecting life and property.

The real scrutiny of the power arises in the second stage of the test, when it is asked whether the power is reasonably necessary for fulfilling the police's duty. Côté J remarked that the purported power of arrest was particularly difficult to justify at this second stage of the analysis. She explained that the "characteristics of the power, and in particular its impact on law-abiding individuals, its preventative nature, and the fact that it would be evasive of review, all mean that it will be more difficult to justify as reasonably necessary compared to other common law powers. The bar is higher."[125] With respect to the "preventative" nature of this power, she continued to explain that

> where such preventative actions do not interfere with individual liberty, the police do of course have broad latitude. Once invasive police actions do intrude upon individual liberty, however, the courts must be very cautious about authorizing them merely because an unlawful or disruptive act could occur in the future. Vague or overly permissive standards in

such situations would sanction profound intrusions on liberty with little societal benefits.[126]

At the third stage, the exercise of the respondents' purported power would be evasive of review. Since this power of arrest would generally not result in the laying of charges, the affected individuals would often have no forum to challenge the legality of the arrest outside of a costly civil suit.

With these considerations in mind, Côté J walked through the second stage of the analysis following the three factors laid out in *MacDonald*. Since "breaches of the peace can threaten the safety and lives of individuals" as well as "erode the public's sense of security," Côté J agreed that preserving the peace and protecting people are immensely important police duties.[127] While she found that a power as drastic as arrest cannot be justified under common law, she did acknowledge that there may be "exceptional circumstances" in which interference with liberty is required to prevent a breach of the peace.[128] However, in her view, the statutory power of arrest that the police possess – which, for example, can be exercised if an individual resists or obstructs an officer taking other, less intrusive means – should be sufficient. She found that "any additional common law power of arrest would be unnecessary."[129] Further, the mere fact that a police action was "effective" cannot be relied upon to justify its lawfulness in interfering with an individual's liberty. The result does not justify the means. Côté J remarked:

> If the police can reasonably attain the same result by taking an action which intrudes less on liberty, a more intrusive measure will not be reasonably necessary no matter how effective it may be. An intrusion on liberty should be a measure of last resort, not a first option. To conclude otherwise would be generally to sanction actions that infringe the freedom of individuals significantly as long as they are effective. That is a recipe for a police state, not a free and democratic state.[130]

Turning more to the details of the case, Côté J doubted the argument that Fleming's arrest was effective in preventing violence, given that the trial judge's findings stated that there was not a real risk of such violence. In addition, the policy that the police had established, whereby counter-protesters were not allowed to enter the occupied property, did not have "special status at law." Thus, the Supreme Court agreed with Justice Huscroft of the Ontario Court of Appeal that "[t]he lawfulness of Mr. Fleming's arrest did not depend on whether it complied with police policy."[131]

Conclusion

The application of the ancillary powers doctrine is an example of how the *Charter*'s jurisprudence is non-linear. In other words, the growth of the *Waterfield* test in Canadian criminal law has shaped *Charter* jurisprudence in unexpected ways, as we have seen in the seminal cases that have been reviewed in this chapter. When *Dedman* was decided, the courts created and applied a flexible, gap-filling tool to address instances where legislation fell short of delineating police powers. This gap-filling measure was utilized in cases that essentially expanded police powers by subsuming unregulated and novel powers into the common law canon. However, this expansion did not occur without concern over the use of *Waterfield* to address legislative gaps. Beginning with Dickson CJ in *Dedman* and continuting with LeBel and Fish JJ in *Orbanski*, there have been stark dissenting opinions about the way in which *Waterfield* was co-opted to undermine *Charter* protections.

The cases that have been highlighted in this chapter are examples of how viewing police powers through the lens of *Waterfield* may expand powers in areas of private life that are sacred, such as one's own home. Thus, dissenting warnings about the use of *Waterfield* to expand powers that are generally under the purview of the legislature are and have been key sticking points in the use of this test. For instance, cases such as *MacDonald* and *Mann* have engaged with the tension between police safety searches and the protection of liberty and privacy. The balancing act that judges must perform while applying *Waterfield* is difficult since these two needs may often be unreconcilable upon review. As the Supreme Court ramped up its use of *Waterfield*, it recognized over time that the test may be difficult to rein in. The Supreme Court has acknowledged that its use of *Waterfield* has led to judicial intervention when it comes to uncertainty in police powers legislation. In *Kang-Brown*, Binnie J saw the Court's position as one that required an interventionist approach in matters where the legislature had been silent. By recognizing sniffer dogs in *Kang-Brown*, Binnie J argued that the Court remains resolute in its use of the *Waterfield* test and must remain consistent in its gap-filling role. This moment in police power history is an example of a divided Court's hesitancy in pulling the reins on *Waterfield*.

When we fast-forward to *Fleming*, we can observe the latent hesitancy espoused by Dickson CJ and LeBel J coming full circle. The Court in *Fleming* refused to recognize a very serious power to arrest someone who is acting lawfully. According to a unanimous Court, it did not meet the ancillary powers doctrine because it was not reasonably necessary and would have had a profound impact on law-abiding citizens. As we discussed in Chapter 1, apprehended breaches of the peace have been used as a reason to condone police action that interferes with seemingly law-abiding conduct by individuals. Thus, *Fleming* marks a turning point in the police powers jurisprudence to date. It also represents a lineage of cases dating back to the earliest conceptions of police powers whose residual effects still play out in Canadian courts.

In its infancy, the *Charter* was an attempt by legislators to balance the scales of justice and to carve out fundamental rights that may not be so easily trammelled by state incursions. However, tests, such as *Waterfield* and *Oakes*, that came shortly after the decision in *Dedman*, are tools to measure and weigh state activity that infringes on our private lives. As well, in prior eras, the Supreme Court has maintained that judges are the guardians of the Constitution. Where police conduct is unjustifiable or unauthorized by law, it is *prima facie* unconstitutional. But the *Waterfield* test appears to circumvent the protections afforded by the *Charter*. This, in turn, has left the judiciary with more reason to intervene than not. Indeed, *Waterfield* has asked us to reimagine the role of judges in the criminal justice system. The question that arises is whether judicial activism in the era of *Waterfield* has unburdened the legislative impetus to address gaps in the law. A corollary to this is whether *Waterfield* is the best approach to addressing unregulated and unrecognized police conduct.

PART 2
Judicial Expansion of Police Powers

Search Incident to Arrest

with Lauren Gowler

3

Introduction

Search incident to arrest is a fundamental police power that grants law enforcement officers the authority to conduct a warrantless search of an individual and their immediate surroundings following a lawful arrest. This chapter explores the historical origins and development of search incident to arrest, delving into its deep roots in the common law and its evolution through landmark legal cases. Despite the influence of the *Waterfield* test and other balancing approaches, search incident to arrest holds historical significance that dates back over two centuries.[1] Understanding its historical context is crucial to comprehending the delicate balance between law enforcement interests and individual privacy rights.[2]

Preceding the *Waterfield* Test: The Common Law Foundation

The recognition of search incident to arrest can be traced back to early common law cases that established the rationale behind this police power.[3] One such case is *Dillon v O'Brien* in 1887, which acknowledged the interests justifying searches incident to arrest.[4] The Court highlighted the significance of preserving evidence and ensuring the appearance of the accused before the Court. These early precedents laid the groundwork for the establishment of search incident to arrest as a police power deeply embedded in the English and Canadian legal systems.

Establishing Search Incident to Arrest: *Cloutier v Langlois*

The *Cloutier v Langlois* case played a pivotal role in defining search incident to arrest as a police power. Although it did not directly cite the *Waterfield* test, *Cloutier* indirectly linked search incident to arrest to the common law, primarily citing the *Dedman* case.[5] The *Dedman* case introduced justificatory questions that involved weighing law enforcement needs against individual freedoms. This approach tailored the common law power to search incident to arrest, defining its limits and justifications.[6] *Cloutier* established search incident to arrest as a police power prior to the development of the *Waterfield* calculus. The use of the *Waterfield* precedent for searches incident to arrest functions solely as a confirmatory device to tailor limits and meet concerns about these types of searches, rendering their use justifiable. In other words, searches incident to arrest, while touching on and informed by the balancing calculus of *Waterfield,* have deep roots that preceded the advent of ancillary powers in England and Canada. Indeed, without invoking the *Dedman* and *Waterfield* test, the Court in *Cloutier* found multiple Canadian authorities for the warrantless search of an arrested person, authorities from 1895, 1921, 1932, 1946, 1949, 1955, 1972, 1984, 1985, 1987, 1988, and 1989.[7]

The *Cloutier* Court used these precedents to conclude that

> [t]he common law has consistently allowed searches of the person incident to arrest where the arresting person has reasonable grounds to believe that the suspect may have concealed upon his person articles which may afford evidence with respect to an offence, weapons, or other objects which may enable the suspect to commit acts of violence or effect an escape.[8]

The *Waterfield* test, known for its balancing approach in determining the reasonableness of searches, has had an impact on various search powers, including searches incident to arrest. However, it is essential to recognize that search incident to arrest already existed as a police power before the importation of the *Waterfield* test into Canadian law. *Cloutier* and other cases used *Waterfield* as a confirmatory device, reinforcing the limits and justifications for searches incident to arrest, balancing privacy interests. In this regard, the search incident to arrest power, in its modern form, could be seen as a hybrid successor of early common law arrest powers and *Waterfield* analyses.

The significance of privacy rights at the core of section 8 protection, as elucidated in *Hunter v Southam* in 1984,[9] has been acknowledged by the courts. Searches incident to arrest are often assessed in the context of the balance between security, safety, and privacy. Indeed, the common law has always sought to grant police powers consistent with the protection of individual rights. Hence, the Court in *Cloutier* and subsequent cases recognized the permissibility of frisk searches incident to arrest but set well-defined contours and limitations for these searches. The delicate balance between effective law enforcement and the protection of individual privacy rights is a recurring theme in the development of search incident to arrest.

The Ongoing Significance of Historical Precedents

The historical acceptance of searches incident to arrest is reinforced by numerous Canadian authorities predating *Waterfield*. *Cloutier* cited several precedents from different time periods, dating back to the late nineteenth century, supporting the warrantless search of an arrested person.[10] These historical precedents have had a significant impact on modern interpretations and continue to shape contemporary legal frameworks surrounding search incident to arrest. The historical evolution of search incident to arrest highlights its deep roots in the common law and its development through landmark legal cases. From its early recognition in *Dillon* to its establishment as a police power in *Cloutier,* search incident to arrest has undergone significant refinement to strike a delicate balance between law enforcement interests and individual privacy rights. While the *Waterfield* test and other balancing approaches have influenced its modern application, the historical context emphasizes that search incident to arrest has deep historical significance that predates these frameworks. The ongoing relevance of historical precedents underscores the continued importance of balancing competing interests in contemporary legal systems. Understanding this historical evolution enriches our understanding of the complexities surrounding searches incident to arrest and the protection of individual rights in the pursuit of effective law enforcement.

Cloutier is commonly known for the Supreme Court of Canada's recognition and refinement of the police's power to search lawfully arrested individuals.[11] This case is often placed in the same category with many of the other cases that we examine in this chapter, as it provides another example of the judiciary's approach in enunciating common law police powers. As a result, the Court in *Cloutier,* which decided the case in 1990, was certainly aware and influenced by the *Waterfield/Dedman* test – acknowledging that it was the Court's most recent approach for dealing with common law powers – but it did not directly apply the test. However, the historical antecedents of common law expansion calculi have undergirded search incident to arrest powers from the earliest jurisprudence of police powers.

In the following cases, we see how the Court has crafted incident-to-arrest searches as a common law police power, reconciling protected *Charter* rights alongside the police's law enforcement needs.[12] Over the course of three decades, the Court has refined and tweaked the scope and prerequisites demanded by the power to address various situations for searches: searches of the arrestee's body, ranging from frisk searches, to strip-searches, to rectal searches; and searches of the places and property of the arrestee, including one's car, one's home, or one's cell phone. This common law power, like the *Waterfield* test itself, is crafted in a manner that ensures flexibility like the other common law police powers. The Court in these cases is comparably trying to grant effective tools to the police, who find themselves facing unpredictable and potentially dangerous circumstances daily, while also trying to provide protections to individuals who have been arrested and deprived of their liberty, but still possess rights that must be respected by the state.

Search Incident to Arrest: *Cloutier v Langlois*

The critical legal question posed in *Cloutier* was whether the right to search a person who has been lawfully arrested arises automatically once the police arrest them or whether the police need to provide additional justification that they have reasonable grounds in conducting a search.[13] In this case, two officers of the Montreal Urban Community Police stopped a vehicle driven by Pierre Cloutier after he had made a right turn from the centre lane, breaching a municipal bylaw. When the officers were writing up a notice of the violation, they discovered that a warrant of committal had been issued against Cloutier for unpaid traffic fines. When the officers returned to Cloutier's car, they informed and requested that he accompany the officers back to the police station. Before asking Cloutier to enter their patrol car, the officers carried out a "frisk" search: "[T]he hands of the accused were placed on the hood of the car, his legs spread and the constables patted him down."[14] Throughout the duration of the exchange, the tone of the conversation became quite heated.

After the incident, Cloutier, a practising lawyer, filed an action against the officers for assault, arguing that the arrest was illegal and that the police officers had not been authorized to search him. The trial court found that the arrest was lawful, thus eliminating Cloutier's principal argument. However, the lower courts wavered on whether the police's common law power to search an individual arose automatically from the lawful arrest or whether the officers needed the existence of additional reasonable grounds as a prerequisite to conduct the search. Writing for the Supreme Court of Canada, Justice Claire L'Heureux-Dubé provided an excellent survey of the history of this power. She outlined the influential cases and scholarly commentary from Britain, the United States, and Canada, ultimately finding that "[w]hile at common law the British courts did not impose reasonable grounds as a prerequisite to the power to search a person lawfully arrested, neither have they gone so far as to recognize a power to search as a simple corollary of arrest. The Canadian courts on the other hand do not seem to have hesitated in adopting the latter approach."[15]

L'Heureux-Dubé J set the confusion straight, stating that the common law power of the police to search an individual arises automatically, or incidentally, to the lawful arrest of that person.[16] In trying to justify the necessity of the power, she commented that "[a] frisk search incidental to a lawful arrest reconciles the public's interest in effective and safe enforcement of the law on the one hand, and on the other its interest in ensuring the freedom and dignity of individuals. The minimal intrusion involved in the search is necessary to ensure that criminal justice is properly administered."[17] She explained that a frisk search is a relatively non-intrusive procedure where the "outside clothing is patted down to determine whether there is anything on the person of the arrested individual. Pockets may be examined but the clothing is not removed, and no physical force is applied. The duration of the search is only a few seconds." However, L'Heureux-Dubé J asserted that the "exercise of this power is not unlimited." She outlined three conditions that officers must abide by when using this common law power, otherwise their actions will be considered "unreasonable and unjustified at common law."[18]

First, this power does not impose a duty. Acknowledging that police have some discretion in conducting searches, she suggested that where the police are satisfied that the law can be "effectively and safely applied without a search," officers may see fit not to conduct a search. The officers must be able to fully assess the circumstances in each case in order to determine whether a search meets the underlying objectives.[19] Second, the search "must be for a valid objective in pursuit of the ends of criminal justice."[20] The justice offered three valid purposes for conducting a search: 1) seeking to discover and apprehend objects that may be used to threaten the safety of the police, the accused, or the public; 2) seeking to confiscate objects that may help facilitate the arrestee's escape; and 3) seeking to preserve objects that could be used as evidence against the accused in a criminal trial. The restriction that the search must be "truly incidental" to the arrest means that the police must be attempting to achieve some valid purpose connected to the arrest. This means that searches intended to "intimidate, ridicule or pressure the accused in order to obtain admissions" would not be considered as pursuing a valid objective.[21] This leads into the third requirement, that a search must not be conducted in an "abusive fashion." The police's use of physical or psychological constraint should be "proportionate to the objectives sought and the other circumstances of the situation."[22]

With the scope of this common law power more carefully articulated, L'Heureux-Dubé J moved to consider the frisk search performed on Cloutier. The evidence, she found, indicated that the police considered it necessary to search the respondent. His "unpleasant," "highly agitated and verbally abusive" conduct aroused a safety concern for the police officers as they conducted the arrest and escorted him to the police station in their patrol car.[23] To L'Heureux-Dubé J, performing a frisk to ascertain whether Cloutier possessed anything on his body that could be used as a weapon against the officers satisfied the second requirement of a proper objective. Further, she relied on the lower courts' rulings and found that the police did not use either excessive force or constraint in performing the search.[24] All considered, she found that as incident to the lawful arrest of Cloutier, the frisk search was justified.

Body Searches and Bodily Samples: *R v Golden*, *R v Stillman*, and *R v Saeed*

In 2001, the Supreme Court of Canada examined whether the common law authorized police to perform a strip-search incident to arrest in the case of *R v Golden*.[25] In this case, the police were conducting surveillance on Ian Golden, who they suspected of being a drug dealer. On the day in question, the police observed the accused sitting inside a Subway sandwich shop interacting with two individuals who entered the restaurant. Through the aid of a telescope, the officers witnessed Golden giving both of these individuals a "white substance."[26] Given the circumstances, the officers believed that the substance was cocaine and authorized a "take-down" group of officers to arrest the accused.[27] When the police entered the Subway, they arrested Golden and the other two individuals as well as locating cocaine at the table where Golden had been sitting. The officers patted down Golden but found no weapons or visible drugs. Intent on performing a more extensive search beneath the accused's clothing, the officers began escorting Golden to the public washrooms located in the basement, but they resorted to a visual inspection at the top of the stairway. In pulling down the accused's pants, the officers spotted plastic wrap protruding from between Golden's buttocks. Attempting to pull it out, the officer was hip checked by Golden, almost resulting in the officer falling down the stairwell. The officer relocated the accused back to the restaurant, where the officers bent the accused over one of the tables and made a second attempt to remove the baggie from the accused's buttocks. After an accidental defecation, the accused finally unclenched his muscles and the officer, wearing rubber dishwashing gloves, was able to remove the package, which contained ten grams of cocaine.

After hearing these rather explicit facts, the Court agreed that strip-searches could be included under the umbrella definition of incident-to-arrest searches, but, like many other common law powers, this particular invasive search needed to be subject to limitations and guidelines.[28] The Court reiterated that incident-to-arrest searches, including strip-searches, were only constitutionally valid at common law where they were conducted as an incident to lawful arrest and performed for a valid purpose, such as "discovering weapons in the detainee's possession, in order to ensure the safety of the police, the detainee and other persons, or for the purposes of discovering evidence related to the reason of the arrest, in order to preserve it and prevent its disposal by the detainee."[29]

Due to the "inherently humiliating and degrading" nature of strip-searches, the Court was uncomfortable with granting police the automatic authority to carry out a strip-search based on the reasonable and probable grounds for the lawful arrest. Thus, the Court held that the police must establish additional reasonable and probable grounds justifying the strip-search. The Court, borrowing guidelines set out by the UK legislature, set out several factors that should be considered by the police in deciding whether, and, if so, how, to conduct a strip-search:

1 Can the strip-search be conducted at the police station and, if not, why?
2 Will the strip-search be conducted in a manner that ensures the health and safety of all involved?
3 Will the strip search be authorized by a police officer acting in a supervisory capacity?
4 Has it been ensured that the police officer(s) carrying out the strip-search are of the same gender as the individual being searched?
5 Will the number of police officers involved in the search be no more than is reasonably necessary in the circumstances?

6 What is the minimum force necessary to conduct the strip-search?
7 Will the strip-search be carried out in a private area such that no one other than the individuals engaged in the search can observe the search?
8 Will the strip-search be conducted as quickly as possible and in a way that ensures that the person is not completely undressed at any one time?
9 Will the strip-search involve only a visual inspection of the arrestee's genital and anal area without any physical contact?
10 If the visual inspection reveals the presence of a weapon or evidence in a body cavity (not including the mouth), will the detainee be given the option of removing the object himself or having the object removed by a trained medical professional?
11 Will a proper record be kept of the reasons for and the manner in which the strip-search was conducted?[30]

While the police must satisfy these preconditions for conducting a strip-search incident to arrest, the Court reiterated that it is also necessary for the strip-search to be conducted in a manner that does not infringe section 8 of the *Charter*.[31] In the circumstances of this case, the majority found that while the arrest was lawful and the search was related to the purpose of the arrest, the police did not carry out the strip-search in a reasonable manner. The majority was particularly troubled by the police's decision to conduct the strip-search "in the field" (in the booth of a restaurant) as opposed to taking Golden to the police station.[32] It was highly unlikely that Golden could destroy or get rid of the evidence while being under police custody. However, his refusal to give up the evidence to the police did not justify the police's actions of stripping him down in the middle of a public place, performing a rectal examination, and dislodging the drug package from his body. These actions showed considerable disregard for Golden's dignity and his personal safety. The dissent, composed of Chief Justice Beverley McLachlin and Justices Charles Gonthier and Michel Bastarache, disagreed with the majority's stance and felt that the police did not need to provide additional justification that they had reasonable and probable grounds to conduct a strip-search.[33] They felt that as long as the officers had an objectively valid reason for the arrest and the search, and the search itself was not conducted in an abusive fashion, the strip-search should be allowed.

A few years earlier, the Supreme Court examined in *R v Stillman* whether the police could seize bodily samples in incident-to-arrest searches.[34] William Stillman, a seventeen-year-old boy, was the main suspect in a murder and sexual assault case. From the victim's body, the police found semen and evidence of a bite mark. During their investigation with the suspect, the police repeatedly asked Stillman for bodily samples, to which the young man refused. Once the accused's lawyers left, the police forcibly took these samples – plucking scalp and pubic hair, doing a buccal swab, and creating a plasticine teeth impression – all despite his protests. At a later point, the Royal Canadian Mounted Police (RCMP) were able to obtain another teeth impression and further buccal swabs with the help of a dentist. The Court found that the search performed by the officers in this case went beyond the typical "frisk" search usually accompanied by a lawful arrest. The accused had refused to provide the police with samples when asked. Instead of respecting his wishes or seeking a warrant, the police forcibly took the bodily samples.

The Court reiterated that the common law power of searches incident to arrest did not extend beyond the purpose of 1) protecting the police or public; 2) preventing the escape of the arrestee; or 3) preserving evidence that could be destroyed or lost.[35] However, here, the Court found that the search and seizure satisfied none of these purposes. The evidence seized – the hair, buccal swab, and dental impressions – was in no danger of disappearing. The common law power could not be so broad to empower police officers to seize bodily samples whenever they wish. The justices found that the police actions were an "abusive exercise of raw physical authority."[36] Justice Peter Cory stated that

> [n]o matter what the pressing temptations may be to obtain evidence from a person the police believe to be guilty of a terrible crime, and no matter what the past frustrations of their investigation, the police authority to search as an incident to arrest should not be exceeded. Any other conclusion could all too easily lead to police abuses in the name of the good of society as perceived by the officers. When they are carrying out their duties as highly respected and admired agents of the state they must respect the dignity and bodily integrity of all who are arrested. The treatment meted out by the agents of the state to even the least deserving individual will often indicate the treatment that all citizens of the state may ultimately expect. Appropriate limits to the power of search incidental to arrest must be accepted and respected.[37]

The Court found that Stillman's right to be free from unreasonable search and seizure, under section 8 of the *Charter*, was seriously violated since neither the search nor the seizure were authorized by statute or common law.

However, *R v Saeed* in 2016 considered some of the similar elements raised in both *Golden* and *Stillman* but struck a different chord.[38] Here, the Court was considering whether the police were authorized under their power of search incident to arrest to conduct penile swabs. The police arrested Saeed after they suspected him of attacking and sexually assaulting a young woman. Due to the allegations, the police believed that the victim's DNA would still be found on the accused's penis and that a penile swab should be taken. The accused was handcuffed to the wall of a "dry-cell" at the station in order to preserve the evidence.[39] Without seeking a warrant, the supervising officer ordered that a penile swab be performed as a "search incident to arrest." The officers permitted Saeed to conduct the swab, whereby he pulled down his pants and wiped the cotton-tipped swab along the length and around the head of his penis. The officer tested the swab and discovered that it contained the victim's DNA.

The majority, consisting of McLachlin CJ and Justices Thomas Cromwell, Michael Moldaver, Richard Wagner, Clément Gascon, Suzanne Côté, and Russell Brown, held that Saeed's section 8 rights were not breached and that the evidence found from the penile swab was properly admitted. The majority's main argument was that the penile swab did not seek to seize the accused's bodily samples but, rather, the DNA of the victim. As a result, the Court maintained that the accused does not have a privacy interest in the complainant's DNA.[40] The penile swab, especially when conducted by the accused, was less invasive in the majority's eyes than the police's actions in *Stillman*, where they forcibly took dental impressions and bodily samples. Perhaps more importantly, however, the majority found that the search satisfied one of the valid purposes of an incident-to-arrest search – namely, that of preserving evidence that was likely to be destroyed or lost. Unlike the accused's own bodily materials or impressions, which could be collected at a later date with a warrant, there was urgency in uncovering possible evidence of the victim's DNA on the accused before that evidence was degraded or washed away.[41]

The majority noted that just as the Court had in the past, the guidelines and conditions for common law searches incident to arrest could be properly tweaked to accommodate valid law enforcement objectives while also providing *Charter* protections to the accused. Here, the Court provided two requirements for conducting a valid penile swab incident to arrest, which was in fact very similar to how it dealt with strip-searches in *Golden*. First, before the police could request a penile swab, they must have separate reasonable grounds to believe that a penile swab will "afford evidence of the offence for which the accused was arrested."[42] This justification is in addition to the reasonable grounds for arrest. In determining whether reasonable grounds have been established specifically for a penile swab, the majority recommended that the police consider the "timing of the arrest in relation to the alleged offence, the nature of the allegation, and whether there is evidence that the substance being sought has already been destroyed."[43]

Comparable to strip-searches, the majority acknowledged that a penile swab had the potential to be a "humiliating, degrading and traumatic experience."[44] Thus, it set out a list of guidelines, similar to what the Court provided in *Golden*, for how police should determine whether a penile swab was necessary and, if so, how such a search should be conducted:

1 The penile swab should, as a general rule, be conducted at the police station.
2 The swab should be conducted in a manner that ensures the health and safety of all involved.
3 The swab should be authorized by a police officer acting in a supervisory capacity.
4 The accused should be informed shortly before the swab of the nature of the procedure for taking the swab, the purpose of taking the swab, and the authority of the police to require the swab.
5 The accused should be given the option of removing his clothing and taking the swab himself, and, if he does not choose this option, the swab should be taken or directed by a trained officer or medical professional, with the minimum of force necessary.
6 The police officer(s) carrying out the penile swab should be of the same gender as the individual being swabbed unless the circumstances compel otherwise.
7 There should be no more police officers involved in the swab than are reasonably necessary in the circumstances.
8 The swab should be carried out in a private area such that no one other than the individuals engaged in the swab can observe it.
9 The swab should be conducted as quickly as possible and in a way that ensures that the person is not completely undressed at any one time.
10 A proper record should be kept of the reasons for and the manner in which the swabbing was conducted.[45]

With this list of factors in mind, the majority found that the penile swab in Saeed's case did not violate his rights. While the accused was validly arrested, the police possessed reasonable grounds to believe that the "complainant's DNA had been transferred to the accused's penis during the assault and that it would still be found on his penis."[46] As mentioned, the majority was also satisfied with the purpose of the search – namely, to discover and preserve evidence on Saeed before it was washed away. Moving to the manner in which the swab was performed, the Court found that the police officers were "sensitive to the need to preserve the accused's privacy and dignity."[47] According to the facts, Saeed was informed in advance of the procedure, he was allowed to conduct the swab himself, the procedure occurred in private, and it was conducted in a quick, smooth fashion. There was no physical contact between the officer and the accused, and the officers took detailed notes regarding the reasons for, and the process of, taking the swab. The Court ultimately held that the swab did not fundamentally violate the accused's human dignity.

Searching Property Incident to Arrest: *R v Caslake, R v Fearon,* and *R v Stairs*

R v Caslake

Search incident to arrest is a common law power that has no readily ascertainable limits on its scope. We have seen the Supreme Court of Canada's efforts to set boundaries that allow the state to pursue its legitimate interests while vigorously protecting individuals' right to privacy in the context of body searches and seizures. However, in *Cloutier*, L'Heureux-Dubé J referred to the possible expansion of this common law power to search the premises and property of the arrested individual but refrained from commenting on the existence or scope of that power. The Supreme Court endeavoured to address this question more directly in *R v Caslake*, where it considered whether the police could conduct a search of the car when they lawfully arrested the driver.[48]

In *Caslake*, a police officer arrested the appellant, Terence Caslake, for possession of narcotics. The arrest took place on the highway after the officer discovered that the appellant had dropped off nine pounds of marijuana in a field alongside the road, presumably for someone else to pick up. The officer took Caslake into police custody and had his vehicle towed to a garage across the street from the police station. Six hours after the arrest, another officer went to the garage and searched Caslake's impounded vehicle without a warrant or the appellant's permission. The officer found cash and two packages of cocaine. However, the officer who conducted the search testified that he had only been acting according to the RCMP's policy, which required officers to take inventory of the contents and condition of vehicles when impounded by the police. At trial, the officer explained that this standard practice was to "safeguard the valuable belongings of the owner of the vehicle and to note the general condition of the vehicle."[49] Facing charges for possession of marijuana and possession of cocaine, Caslake challenged the latter conviction, arguing that the search of his impounded vehicle was unreasonable under section 8 of the *Charter*.

If the police sought to rely on the common law doctrine of search incident to arrest to authorize their actions, the Supreme Court was adamant that they had to respect the limits of the doctrine.[50] To the Court, the most important of these limits, articulated in *Cloutier*, is that the search must be truly incidental to arrest: "[T]he police must be able to explain, within the purposes recognized in the jurisprudence (protecting the police, protecting the evidence, discovering evidence) or by reference to some other valid purpose, *why* they conducted the search."[51] True to the requirements set out in *Cloutier*, the police did not need to possess additional reasonable and probable grounds for the search, independent of those required for the arrest. There was also general agreement that the scope of a search incident to arrest could extend beyond the body of the arrestee to one's vehicle. The reason for this action – the "need for the law enforcement authorities to gain control of things or information" – outweighed an individual's privacy rights.[52] As mentioned, however, the clincher was that an officer's subjective reasons for carrying out a search at the time of the arrest must be objectively reasonable, falling into the valid objectives outlined by the Court in *Cloutier*.

In examining the facts of this case, the majority noted that if the police had searched the car for the purposes of collecting evidence for trial, the search would have been motivated by a valid objective.[53] However, the officer admitted in his testimony that his sole reason for searching the car was to inventory its contents and condition. To the majority, including Chief Justice Antonio Lamer and Justices Cory, McLachlin, and John Major, this motive for conducting the search was unrelated to the purpose of the arrest of Caslake. Thus, the search was not authorized by the common law because it did not comply with the conditions that accompanied the power. L'Heureux-Dubé, Gonthier, and Bastarache JJ disagreed with the majority's strict finding, noting that there was little reason why an inventory search could not be considered a type of incident-to-arrest search or that regardless of the officer's subjective belief for conducting the search, he still had the right to search the car under the common law power of search incident to arrest.[54]

R v Fearon

In *R v Fearon*, the Court examined whether electronic devices, found on the accused, could be searched by police under the common law doctrine of search incident to arrest.[55] While investigating an armed jewellery robbery, the police were able to track down the getaway vehicle and arrested two individuals – Kevin Fearon and Junior Chapman. When the police conducted a pat-down search of Fearon, incident to his arrest, they discovered a cell phone in his pocket. Without a warrant or consent of the appellant, the officers searched the phone and uncovered an inculpatory text message draft and a picture of the handgun wielded in the robbery. The police used the evidence they found on the phone to get a warrant to search the suspected getaway vehicle, where they discovered the handgun. Fearon argued that the police's search of his cell phone had been unreasonable and had violated his section 8 *Charter* rights.

The Supreme Court of Canada held that the common law permitted the search of cell phones and similar devices discovered on the suspect incident to their arrest.[56] However, the Court acknowledged that a search of a cell phone had the potential to significantly invade the privacy interests of the accused, more so than a typical search incident to arrest.[57] Cell phones could "generate information about intimate details of the user's interests, habits, and identity without the knowledge or intent of the user, [and] may retain information even after the user thinks that it has been destroyed."[58] While the majority acknowledged that searches of cell phones could vary in scope, the majority found that "the law needs to provide the suspect with further protection against the risk of wholesale invasion of privacy."[59] As a result, the majority reapplied the Court's chosen approach in *Golden* and *Stillman* for dealing with invasive searches. They modified the existing common law framework, placing additional requirements on police when they perform searches of cell phones. By placing these types of limits, the Court aimed to better balance the competing interests at stake and bring cell phone searches into compliance with section 8 of the *Charter*.

The majority held that a "police officer will not be justified in searching a cell phone or similar device incidental to *every* arrest"; rather, a search will comply with the common law doctrine and section 8 of the *Charter*, where

1 The arrest is lawful.
2 The search is truly incidental to the arrest in that the police have a reason based on a valid law enforcement purpose to conduct the search, and

that reason is objectively reasonable. The valid law enforcement purposes in this context are:

a protecting the police, the accused, or the public
b preserving evidence; or
c discovering evidence, including locating additional suspects, in situations in which the investigation will be stymied or significantly hampered absent the ability to promptly search the cell phone incident to arrest.

3 The nature and extent of the search are tailored to the purpose of the search.
4 The police take detailed notes of what they have examined on the device and how it was searched.[60]

With these considerations in mind, the majority found that the facts satisfied the first two requirements listed above. Fearon was lawfully arrested for robbery, and the search fulfilled a number of valid law enforcement objectives: "The search of the phone was directed at public safety (locating the handgun), avoiding the loss of evidence (the stolen jewellery) and obtaining evidence of the crime (information linking Mr. Fearon to the robbery and locating potential accomplices)."[61] The trial judge also found that it was "reasonable for Sergeant Hicks to believe that the arrestee, Mr. Fearon, may have communicated through the cell phone before, during or after the robbery with other perpetrators or with third parties," providing the officer with a reasonable prospect that the phone might contain evidence of the offence.[62] These facts suggested that the search of the cell phone was truly incidental to Fearon's arrest for robbery.

However, the officers who inspected the phone and its contents failed to provide to the Court any details outlining precisely what they searched, how they had searched the phone, and why they had conducted the search. The majority was troubled by the officers' lack of evidence concerning the nature and extent of their search of Fearon's phone. Finding that the officers failed to satisfy the third and fourth requirements, the majority concluded that the search was not reasonable and that it breached Fearon's section 8 *Charter* rights.[63] Regardless, the majority refused to exclude the evidence found on Fearon's phone under section 24(2), citing that the invasion of Fearon's privacy was "not particularly grave" and that excluding "cogent and reliable" information would undermine the truth-seeking function of the justice system.

Justices Andromache Karakatsanis, Louis LeBel, and Rosalie Abella comprised the Court's dissenting reasons and opined that the majority's tactic and proposed modifications generated problems of "impracticality, police uncertainty, and increased after-the-fact litigation."[64] While they thought that the suggestions for detailed note-taking and limits on what officers could discover were desirable, those requirements in themselves did not do enough to moderate these extraordinary police search powers. Writing for the three justices, Karakatsanis J spoke to how the digital revolution had created a new intensely private and personal sphere for Canadians, one that the police should not be allowed to enter haphazardly:

> In short, the cell phone acts like a key or portal which can allow the user to access the full treasure trove of records and files that the owner has generated or used on any number of devices. It is not just the device itself and the information it has generated, but the gamut of (often intensely) personal data accessible via the device that gives rise to the significant and unique privacy interests in digital devices. The fact that a suspect may be carrying their house key at the time they are arrested does not justify the police using that key to enter the suspect's home. In the same way, seizing the key to the user's digital life should not justify a wholesale intrusion into that realm. Indeed, personal digital devices are becoming as ubiquitous as the house key. Increasingly large numbers of people carry such devices with them everywhere they go (be they cell phones, mobile computers, smart watches, smart glasses, or tablets).[65]

Karakatsanis J argued that the "weighty privacy interest that an arrested person has in a personal digital device will outweigh the state interest in performing a warrantless search incident to arrest," except for in exigent circumstances.[66] She acknowledged that in situations where the police were unable to obtain a warrant because the officers had 1) a reasonable basis to suspect that a search may prevent an imminent threat to safety or 2) reasonable grounds to believe that the imminent destruction of evidence could be prevented by a warrantless search, the police may be allowed to conduct a search of a cell phone without a warrant. However, the dissent advocated for judicial preauthorization (such as a tele-warrant) to properly consider the significant interference of the privacy interest that cell phone searches pose.[67]

Search Incident to Arrest in the Home: *R v Stairs*

In a 2022 Supreme Court of Canada decision, *R v Stairs,* the apex Court had another opportunity to decide on a common law police powers case.[68] The divided Court in *Stairs,* however, took very different positions on issues arising from a search incident to arrest. The Court held that where safety is concerned, officers may justifiably search an individual who has been arrested or the place controlled by the arrestee. However, the majority and the dissenting opinions disagreed on whether officers transgressed beyond reasonable limits, as prescribed in prior decisions, while conducting the search of Stairs's home. What is most observable about this case is that the Supreme Court, at a high level, restricted and limited police searches of an arrestee's home. Notwithstanding this, the majority and dissent came to differing conclusions as to whether the search was justified within the circumstances of the case.

In *Stairs,* the police received a 911 call from a civilian who had witnessed a male driver, who was swerving on the road, repeatedly hit his female passenger. Based on the caller's description, three officers were able to quickly locate the car parked in the driveway of an unknown house. The officers knocked on the front door and loudly announced their presence, but no one answered. Fearing for the woman's safety, the police entered the house through a side door. Upon the police's entry and further announcements, a woman with fresh injuries to her face came up the flight of stairs leading from the basement. Stairs did not follow. Instead, he ran past the bottom of the stairwell and barricaded himself in the basement laundry room. The police went downstairs with their firearms drawn and demanded that the accused emerge from the room with his hands up. Eventually, he complied with their orders, and the officers arrested and led Stairs to the main floor. However, after the arrest, the police conducted a visual "clearing search" of the basement living area. The police claimed that the purpose of the search was to ensure that nobody else was present and that there were no hazards or weapons sitting out in the open. During the search, the police found an open Tupperware container containing meth lying in plain view on the floor behind the couch. This resulted in Stairs being charged with possession of drugs for the purposes of trafficking under section 5(2) of the *Controlled Drugs and Substances Act,* in addition to charges of assault and breach of probation.[69]

At trial, Stairs was convicted of all charges, and the trial judge concluded that the search of the basement and the subsequent seizure of the drugs did not breach his section 8 *Charter* rights. Stairs appealed the conviction for the drug offence. However, in a split decision, the Ontario Court of Appeal upheld the conviction. In appealing his conviction to the Supreme Court, Stairs argued that the common law standard of search incident to arrest must be modified for searches conducted in a home, given the very high privacy interests that Canadians hold within their homes.[70] He argued that when the police conduct searches of the home for safety purposes, they should only be able to do so if they have reasonable grounds to believe (or at least suspect) that there is an imminent threat to public or police safety. Stairs claimed that in his case, this standard was not met. There was no immediate threat to the officers' or the public's safety since the police had already arrested and handcuffed Stairs. He asserted that the search of the basement living room by the police was therefore unconstitutional and that the drug evidence found should be excluded.

The majority of the Supreme Court – composed of Wagner CJ and Justices Moldaver, Malcolm Rowe, Nicholas Kasirer, and Mahmud Jamal – agreed that the common law standard for these types of searches should be made stricter. However, the majority disagreed with the test that the appellant recommended and took their own steps to modify the standard.[71] The majority reiterated the baseline common law standard of search incident to arrest, which allows the police, when they lawfully arrest an individual, to conduct a pat-down search and examine the area within the physical control of the person arrested. As a reminder, this search power arises automatically from the fact that the police have arrested the person and allows the police to seize anything in the arrestee's possession or in the immediate surrounding area that could harm the safety of the police or the arrested individual, facilitate the person's escape, or be used as evidence against the individual charges upon arrest. But when the police go outside the zone of physical control within the context of an arrestee's home, the majority acknowledged that the standard should be raised to recognize that the police have entered the house without a warrant. In these circumstances, the Court found that it was not enough to satisfy the existing common law standard; rather, the police must meet a higher standard: 1) they must have reason to suspect that the search will address a valid safety purpose; and 2) they must conduct the search in a reasonable manner, tailored to the heightened privacy interests in the home.

The majority explained that these conditions aimed to temper the police's search powers within the home:

Simply because the police have entered the home for a valid reason does not give them *carte blanche* to wander through the home at large where the circumstances do not call for it. As we have explained, the more extensive the warrantless search, the greater the potential for violating privacy. Thus, when the police search a home incident to arrest in areas outside the physical control of the arrested person at the time of arrest, they require reasonable suspicion ... The police are highly constrained when they go beyond the area within the physical control of the arrested person. As a general rule, the police cannot use the search-incident-to-arrest power to justify searching every nook and cranny of the house. This common law power remains an exception to the general rule that a warrant is required to justify an intrusion into the home. The search should be no more intrusive than is necessary to resolve the police's reasonable suspicion.[72]

With this modification of the standard, the Court asked whether in this instance the police had reason to suspect that there were safety risks that could be addressed with a search of the basement living room. In other words, did the officers satisfy the threshold of reasonable suspicion in this instance? The majority found that there was a constellation of both subjective and objective factors that led to the officer's reasonable suspicion. Officer Vandervelde, who conducted the clearing search, testified that the search was performed to ensure that "no one else was there" – whether that was an individual (unknown to police) who potentially posed a risk or required assistance.[73] The other reason was to ensure that there were "no other hazards," such as weapons or firearms sitting out in the open that could be used against the officers or occupants. From an objective point of view, the Court agreed that it was reasonable for the police to clear the area of hazards and other occupants while dealing with an emotionally charged situation where things could get out of hand.

The majority also found that the search was conducted in a reasonable manner. The search took place right after the arrest, and the police merely conducted a visual scan of the living area to ensure that no one else was present and that there were no weapons around. They did not move any items or open doors or cupboards. The police also appropriately limited their search to the basement living area adjacent to the laundry room where Stairs had been arrested. The Court commented that if the police had searched the upper floors or other rooms of the home, the search would have been deemed unreasonable. Given the police's objective – ensuring the safety of both the police and the occupants in the house – the majority found that the search was the least invasive possible. As such, the majority ruled that Stairs's section 8 *Charter* rights were not violated and that the evidence should be included.

However, the dissenting Justices Karakatsanis, Brown, and Sheilah Martin agreed with the appellant. They would have found that the common law power authorized police to conduct a search incident to arrest inside a home only where the police had reasonable suspicion of an imminent threat to the officers or the individuals involved. In penning the dissenting opinion, Karakatsanis J was steadfast on the use of warrants for searches within the home: "The warrant requirement is a foundation check on police powers. Any exception should be exceedingly rare. Still, some exceptions exist – including the common law power of search incident to arrest."[74] Karakatsanis J pointed out that most safety risks that arise from an arrest in a home – for which a warrant cannot be feasibly procured – will generally be recognized as "imminent." If the safety concern is not imminent and the police have already arrested the individual in question, the officers should be in the position to request a warrant before conducting any further searches of the home.

The dissent also commented that, while reasonable suspicion is a relatively low threshold, it still requires "the officer to articulate some basis to suspect safety may be at risk."[75] Here, the dissenting justices found that there were no particularized facts to justify a safety search, only generalized feelings of uncertainty about the presence of weapons or other people. The police only searched the basement once the accused had been handcuffed and the victim had gone upstairs. Thus, both known parties were under police control. The police also had no tip off that there would be weapons – the 911 caller had not seen any weapons, nor had the police found any weapons on Stairs when they arrested him in the laundry room. The dissent found that the searching officer gave no basis to ground a reasonable suspicion that anybody's safety was at risk following the accused's arrest. Thus, Karakatsanis, Brown, and Martin JJ would have found that the search and seizure was unlawful and violated the accused's section 8 rights. Given that the home attracts a high privacy interest and generally cannot be searched without a warrant, the dissenting justices believed that the search of the basement and the seizure of the drugs was a major incursion on Stairs's *Charter*-protected interests, and they would have been inclined to have excluded the evidence from admission.

Though the Supreme Court of Canada did not address the ancillary powers doctrine in *Stairs*, the Court's division on the extent of search powers under section 8 of the *Charter* is palpable. In the common law, one's home generally demands the utmost protection from state incursion as it has a high privacy interest that is protected under section 8. Notably, *Stairs* does not cite or refer to the Court's decision in *Fleming*.[76] This may simply be a consequence of the entrenched nature of the police power that was under review in *Stairs*.

Conclusion

In the *Charter* era, search incident to arrest, which had deep roots in common law, has been transformed into a new source of expanding police powers, and this development has been a matter of concern. The Supreme Court of Canada, from *Golden* to *Stairs*, has employed various and distinct methods to broaden the scope of search incident to arrest, marking a departure from the earlier *Charter*-era cases of *Cloutier* and *Caslake*. In those previous cases, one could reasonably argue that the Court defined the boundaries of search incident to arrest as limitable and rooted in the protection of privacy rights and as apprised of the notion of the home as a sanctuary. With the help of the common law, the line of the sanctuary has become increasingly liminal. As Richard Jochelson and David Ireland have noted in other works,

> in the ambiguous language of possibility, tremendous slippage has occurred. Ancillary powers and the evolution of search incident to arrest have provided for multiple contexts where warrant requirements are excused. In turn, this development has compelled the court to essentially draft limitations and criteria for each newly emerging power. As a result, privacy interests have been moderated, and the court has in turn countenanced lower standards than reasonable and probable grounds.[77]

An Empirical Analysis of Ancillary Power Generation and Deployment

4

with Lauren Gowler

While the *Canadian Charter of Rights and Freedoms* has been framed as a check on the unfettered expansion of government power, it can also be used to facilitate such expansion.[1] In this chapter, we present and explore empirical evidence demonstrating a vast expansion of police powers over time. This expansion has not only occurred in spite of the protection against state intrusion that the *Charter* was intended to represent; it has also relied on *Charter* analysis in coming to pass. In other words, the *Charter* has been used to facilitate state intrusion through police powers rather than to prevent it. Equally concerning is that this apparent co-opting of the *Charter* has been facilitated by the courts themselves. This raises serious questions about the role of Canadian courts, both as the guardians of the Constitution and as the arbiter between the rights of the individual and the enactments of a duly elected Parliament.[2]

A central feature of the *Charter* is that it assigns to the judiciary the responsibility of interpreting individual rights and determining whether encroachments on these rights are permissible. This is achieved through section 1, which permits the curtailment of the rights set out in the *Charter* only where such "can be demonstrably justified in a free and democratic society."[3] Judicial interpretation in this context occurs against the backdrop of the *Charter*'s legal supremacy: the *Charter* holds primacy over all non-constitutional legal documents in Canada. The result, perhaps unintended, has been the accrual of power in the courts running parallel to, and independent of, that of Parliament. Central to the interpretive function of judges is the crafting of legal tests that give content to the meaning of disputed principles in Canadian law. In doing so, judges draw on several sources to develop this content, such as previous court decisions, legal principles, and societal changes or norms.

One such principle that has emerged in the *Charter* era is constitutional stewardship, which is grounded in a view of the court system as a bulwark against the tyranny of the state in constitutional cases.[4] On this construction, the interpretive function of courts can be viewed as administering law as much as articulating it. Applied in the police powers context, where courts are interpreting the law regarding police actions, this construction of constitutional guardianship amounts to the judiciary's policing of policing.[5] In such cases, it falls to the Court to delineate the rightful scope of police powers and define the boundaries between the rights of the individual and the power of the state. At times, the Court will be met with novel issues for which there is no common law precedent, and it is in these circumstances where the Court is tasked with deciding whether to underscore individual rights or reassemble the language of rights and freedoms in order to generate new police powers. Notwithstanding the Supreme Court of Canada's repeated efforts to incrementally adopt and apply the ancillary powers doctrine to novel circumstances, what has been left in the wake of these decisions is a vast array of police practices that have been constitutionally protected by the courts.

One glaring issue with this result is that these practices have not been tested against legislative and democratic scrutiny, which, in turn, has had costly and dire consequences for vulnerable populations in society. Consider, for instance, the misuse of police powers in contexts of low visibility stops where there is little-to-zero accountability and scrutiny of the actions by the police. Importantly, the common law position on ancillary police powers is inherently confined to conduct that has led to charges being laid. The data that we have collected that, cumulatively, makes up decades-long police power jurisprudence does not expressly represent the countless police encounters that have not resulted in charges being brought forth by the federal or provincial Crown. What can be implied from the quantitative data is the street-level impact of the ancillary powers doctrine on policing in Canada. In other words, the generation and deployment of judge-made powers has given the police vast powers that have limited the fundamental rights and freedoms protected under the *Charter*. The quantitative data highlights the growth of these powers within the courtroom and indirectly reflects how novel or unregulated police conduct has been given a green light by the courts. Consequently, these judge-made laws have shaped policing policies and practices across the country.

This chapter endeavours to present and analyze the empirical data that has been collected from 2018 to 2021. The generation and deployment of police powers by courts today continues to be a pressing issue in the current jurisprudence; being conferred on police by the judiciary, these powers are not only established outside of the normal democratic process, but they are also virtually *Charter* proof.[6] The generation of such powers should be the subject of the highest scrutiny as the coercive power of the state is expanded by the very institution meant to keep it in check. To provide some context, this chapter first reflects on how the gap-filling rationale behind the ancillary powers doctrine changed the trajectory of policing across Canada by galvanizing investigative detention powers in *R v Mann*.[7] We present *Mann* as a through line that ties together turn-of-the-century case law with more recent decisions.

The Spectre of *Mann*

Narrativizing the development of case law is key to understanding what, if any, practical implications may arise in decisions that are released by courts. The growth of investigative detention in the jurisprudence is a helpful reminder of how the data we present below is representative of a tapestry of judge-made law that has had a profound impact on the review of police conduct. *Mann*, much like *Dedman v The Queen*, stands as a seminal case that has delineated the boundaries of investigative detention.[8] *Mann* is vital for our discussion because, through its narrativization, we can see the symbiotic relationship between the theoretical viewpoints of academics, the empirical data that has been derived from the case law, and the practical aspects of street-level policing. It is situated in a period of great expansion of common law police powers by the courts. Courts have shown a willingness to expand police powers in a wide variety of circumstances where novel or unregulated police conduct is judicially reviewed. The lineage of cases that began with *Dedman* grew to include powers of detention in various encounters between citizens and police. Consequently, these powers have contracted the fundamental rights protected under the *Charter*.

The facts in *Mann* were straightforward. Officers were investigating a reported break and enter in downtown Winnipeg. The report described the suspect as a "21-year-old aboriginal male, approximately five feet eight inches tall, weighing about 165 pounds, clad in a black jacket with white sleeves."[9] As the officers approached the crime scene, they observed Mann walking casually on the sidewalk. The officers questioned Mann about his name and age. Mann complied with a pat-down. During the pat-down search, one officer felt a soft object in Mann's pocket. The officer reached inside Mann's pocket and found drugs and baggies. They subsequently charged him pursuant to the *Controlled Drugs and Substances Act*.[10] The Supreme Court was thus tasked with determining whether the police were in violation of the *Charter* in their investigative detention and search incident to Mann's detainment. Surprisingly, the Court paid little attention to the racial dynamics of the case as Mann was of Indigenous descent.

In *Mann*, the majority of the Supreme Court acknowledged that judicial intervention was necessary with respect to investigative detentions as they were an unregulated aspect of policing in 2004. The majority in *Mann* maintained that courts must "exercise [their] custodial role" in creating the power of investigative detention and search incident to detention (for officer safety) to fill in the legislative gaps.[11] However, the impact of *Mann* on policing went well beyond the articulation of the necessary standard to establish a lawful detention; it widened the scope of investigation, detention, and search powers at the street level and substantially narrowed rights under sections 8 and 9 of the *Charter*. The now decades-old ruling in *Mann* was ill-received in academic circles for its assertion of broad discretionary powers of investigation on the street level. It was noted that the recognition of investigative detention and search incident to detention powers would have a stark impact on racialized minorities and Indigenous people in Canada. With respect to *Mann*, former professor of law and current Ontario judge, James Stribopoulos, stated that

> the reality that abuses of this new power will have a disproportionate impact on visible minorities went unmentioned. The legacy of *Terry v Ohio*, which gave birth to the "stop-and-frisk" power in the United States, was similarly ignored. More troubling, however, is that even with the issues it did choose to address, the court raised more questions than it answered. The resulting uncertainty is rather incompatible with the stated goal of regulating these low-visibility encounters.[12]

To critics, *Mann* appeared to give police reason to evade section 9 protections if the reasonable grounds standard and the *Waterfield* test could be met before a reviewing judge.[13] Therefore, policing strategies that were already problematic for many communities had now been declared lawful under the ancillary powers doctrine in *Mann*. *Mann*'s place in the body of law was problematic back in 2004, considering that by 2003, the issue of racial profiling in policing was working its way through the Ontario Court of Appeal in *R v Brown*.[14] Yet, surprisingly, the Court in *Mann* remained largely silent on issues surrounding race-based policing and suspect selection, as highlighted by Professor David Tanovich:

> *Mann* was a case about reactive policing. The police had a description of a known suspect that made reference to race and stopped Mann based on the fact that he matched that description. Generally speaking, racial profiling or policing based on racialized stereotypes does not occur when the police are relying on race because it forms part of the suspect's description. The problem, however, is that given our history of overt and systemic racism, race often unconsciously becomes the dominant part of the description used by the police. This is likely to occur where the non-racial aspects of the description of the suspect and location where the crime occurred are not sufficiently specific to safeguard against false positives. In other cases, the race component of the description will be used as a pretext to stop persons of colour who the police wish to investigate. When either of these situations arise, racial profiling is implicated and section 9 of the *Charter* is violated.[15]

In the wake of *Mann*, the power of investigative detention has been relied upon extensively by courts. The data we present below tells a story of how the role of the police has progressed into one that is quasi-judicial and discretionary. The recognition of investigative detention is evidence of the discretionary power of the police. This decades-long development in the common law has had a profound impact on race-based policing. The growth of police powers has protracted the reform of serious issues with policing and has indirectly invigorated systemically racist policing policies that treat "certain members of our society as a perpetual suspect class."[16] Two high-profile 2019 Supreme Court of Canada cases – *R v Le* and *Fleming v Ontario* – are positive signs that the judiciary may be pulling the reins on the expansion of police powers.[17] While *Le* directly rebukes race-based policing practices and is not part of the lineage of cases that arose after *Dedman*, the *Le* majority's effort to highlight the impact of carding may speak to a broader trend of delimiting police powers in recent years:

The impact of the over-policing of racial minorities and the carding of individuals within those communities without any reasonable suspicion of criminal activity is more than an inconvenience. Carding takes a toll on a person's physical and mental health. It impacts their ability to pursue employment and education opportunities (Tulloch Report, at p. 42). Such a practice contributes to the continuing social exclusion of racial minorities, encourages a loss of trust in the fairness of our criminal justice system, and perpetuates criminalization.[18]

The majority's efforts to push back against the over-policing of racialized communities indirectly engages with the oft-problematized decision in *Mann*, which re-enforced policing practices that are inherently racist, such that, in the years post-*Mann*, carding racialized individuals more often than their white counterparts became the status quo.[19] Alongside *Le*, the Supreme Court of Canada released *Fleming* in 2019, which gave the Court the opportunity to, once again, comment directly on the police's ancillary powers doctrine.[20] The decision by the Supreme Court stood in significant contrast to the prior trend of granting and expanding police powers. In its decision, the Court declined to grant the police the power to arrest an individual who is otherwise acting lawfully with the purpose of preventing a breach of the peace. The police claimed that this power falls within the scope of police duties that include preserving the peace, preventing crime, and protecting life and liberty. However, the Court rejected this argument on the grounds that this power is not reasonably necessary in order to fulfill those duties. The Court further held that the preservation of the peace is not a reasonable justification for interfering with the liberty of an individual who is acting lawfully and is not subject to investigation for committing a crime.

With the growth of pre-crime technology, it is imperative that the judiciary return to its guardianship role in the relationship between the individual and the state. The power considered in *Fleming* should be viewed with the knowledge that algorithmic policing, hot-zone policing, and facial recognition technology are being used by police departments. New policing practices, brought on by emerging technology, have the potential to seriously interfere with civil liberties. Thus, it is imperative for the courts to recognize that the ancillary powers doctrine cannot become a vehicle for pre-crime technology. In the following section of this chapter, we will discuss the importance of empirical data in our research and then pivot to detailing the methodology we used in procuring the data that has been analyzed. We will then engage with the data and present our most recent findings. Following a survey of the data, we will return to a discussion of how *Fleming* can be considered a positive step toward a new chapter of police powers jurisprudence. Of course, a cautious approach must be taken if we turn to recent appellate-level cases that have come after *Fleming*. We will engage with three appellate cases that have grappled with common law police powers to emphasize the need for stronger language from the Supreme Court with respect to the ancillary powers doctrine to better serve the constitutional obligations of the judiciary.

Methodology

The study that was conducted on the deployment and generation of police powers is rooted in empiricism. Felicity Bell has stated that empiricism includes quantitative analysis that usually involves statistics.[21] Empirical methods may be archival, such as analyzing court files or records.[22] In this study, data was collected pertaining to court decisions addressing the use of police powers and whether the use of those powers was justified. The data was analyzed into statistics to determine trends in the decision-making patterns of the courts over various periods of time. This section of the chapter is intended to contextualize the importance of the contribution of a study that is of a quantitative nature to the discussion of police powers. In this study, the facts take the form of statistics relating to the Supreme Court of Canada's willingness to justify the use of ancillary police powers. Discussions on the powers of police are often framed through normative theoretical explanations and social science perspectives that seek to unwrap the social context through which police powers emerge. The data that empirical legal studies provides allows us to place the theoretical and abstract explanations into a systematic, somewhat scientific, framework.

Bell highlights research that has investigated the value of quantitative studies by focusing on the possibility of uncovering objective truths through forms of empiricism.[23] The law's effects must include a critical focus on social consequences and policy implications. Empiricism reveals these consequences and implications in a way that goes beyond the face value of the law. Changes in policy with respect to ancillary powers necessarily implicate the need for empirical legal studies. As observed by Nard, "policy choices must stand or fall based on empirical evidence. Empirical scholarship is a window on the pathologies of the law and allows us to gauge the effect and efficiency, or lack thereof, of legal mechanisms as they presently operate within our society."[24] Moreover, empirical legal studies act as a bridge between the academic and legal profession. Data reveals the discrepancy between the actual decision-making of the courts as opposed to claims of what they are doing and what we may think they should be doing. The data and statistics analyzed in this study provide a grounded, scientific basis for conclusions to be made. The law cannot rely solely on theoretical hunches in making changes; rather, empirical legal research is required for institutions to evolve in a meaningful way. The importance of empirical facts in legal proceedings and judicial decision-making within social science research training has also been emphasized.[25] The quantitative study that was undertaken here reveals trends that may have otherwise remained as theories or anecdotes rather than solidified proof of actual trends.

This chapter incorporates and expands upon the data collected in the previously published article "Generation and Deployment of Common Law Police Powers by Canadian Courts and the Double-Edged *Charter*," which was based on an empirical investigation of common law police powers between 1985 and 2017.[26] Here, we have imported the methodology used in that study and applied it to the intervening time in order to create a more complete and up-to-date data set. We examined reported cases across Canada from 1 January 2018 to 31 May 2021. Cases were gathered from three legal databases: WestLawNext, QuickLaw, and CanLII. Search terms, including keywords such as "police powers" and "*Waterfield*," were used to identify relevant cases. The "citing cases" function in WestLaw was also used on the *Dedman* case to reveal all reported cases that have cited *Dedman* as precedent in Canada on that database.

The collected cases were reviewed by law students trained in legal methods in order to determine their relevancy. The first step was to ascertain whether a case directly addressed common law police powers. French-language cases were evaluated after being run through Google Translate. Cases that directly addressed common law police powers were then divided into "generation" and "deployment" categories. Generation cases were those that referred to the novel ad hoc creation of new common law police powers or a significant alteration to an established power using the *Waterfield/Dedman* test. Cases that were categorized under deployment were those in which a court decided whether a police power established in a previous court decision applied in the case at hand. In other words, deployment refers to any common law police power applied after its initial creation by another case in Canada. The cases were then further subdivided within these categories based upon their outcomes. Thus, collected cases were ultimately assigned to one of the four categories: "Generate," "Decline to Generate," "Deploy," and "Decline to Deploy." Cases were also grouped within these four categories by court level and type of power considered in order to identify further potential trends.

A total of 780 cases from within the time frame were reviewed. Of these, 355 were identified as being relevant to the generation or deployment of common law police powers. This number includes all reported cases at all court levels and jurisdictions that matched the search criteria, including both criminal and civil matters. Many of the cases dealt with more than one common law police power. Where a case dealt with more than one type of police power, it was counted once under each of the police powers that it dealt with. For example, if a case dealt with both the power of investigative detention and search incident to detention, then it was counted once under each of those categories. In some of the cases that dealt with multiple powers, a court deployed one power but declined to deploy another. Thus, a single case might be counted multiple times in the Deploy/Decline or Generate/Decline tables, depending on the number of powers and outcomes within that case. The total number of instances that addressed the deployment of police powers was 395, accounting for cases that dealt with multiple powers.

Both appellate and trial cases were considered. Cases that were decided at the trial level were categorized under "trial level." These first instance cases included decisions that may have been made either at the provincial court level or the superior court level. The cases that were appeals were put under the "appeal" category. These included decisions made by the Court of Appeal of the relevant province as well as appeals made to the Superior Court of that jurisdiction. All of the cases that were decided by the Supreme Court of Canada were put under the category "SCC." Each instance at each level was counted as a separate case. For example, if a case was heard initially by a superior court and, subsequently, there was an appeal, this would count as two separate cases. This method allowed us to accurately measure how many courts would generate or deploy these powers.

Ancillary Powers by Numbers: Data and Analysis

A significant majority of the cases identified within the time frame involved the deployment of established police powers rather than the generation of new powers. There were 22 instances between the years of 2018 and 2021 where a court dealt with a generation of police powers, while there were 355 cases that addressed the deployment of police powers. This aligns with the

FIGURE 3 Relative Proportions of Generated and Declined Powers by Year

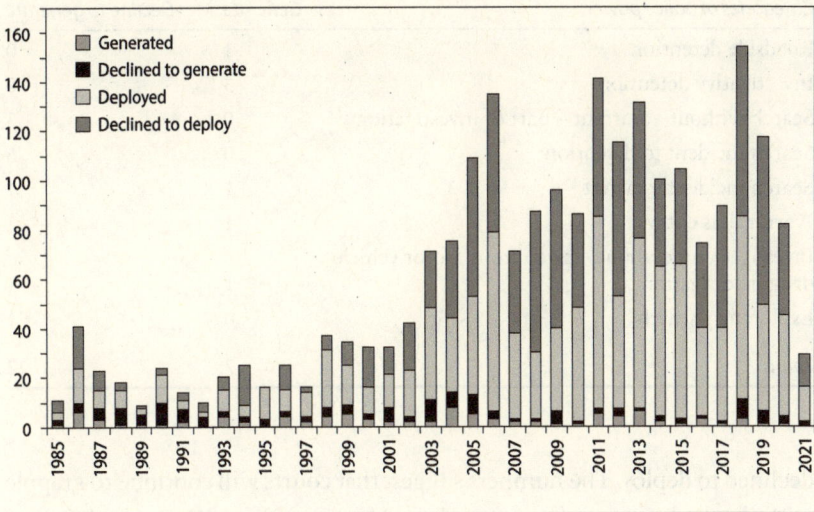

general pattern established by our prior research, which recorded 205 cases addressing generation and 1,699 cases addressing deployment between 1985 and 2017. The total number and relative proportions of the full dataset from 1985 to 2021 are included in Figure 3.

Since a court may deal with multiple powers in a single case, the number of powers recorded exceeds the number of cases. Thus, though there were only twenty-two generation-of-powers cases from 2018 to 2021, there were twenty-five powers considered for generation. Of these, seven were accepted by the courts, while eighteen were declined. The most active category of power within this time frame was investigative detention. In our previous research, powers related to roadside detention had been the dominant category of generation/decline to generate cases for over two decades (see Table 1).

Similarly, the period from 2018 to 2021 saw 417 power deployments considered by courts, with 195 of these being deployed and 220 declined. The preceding data, from 1985 to 2017, logged 1,349 power deployments considered, with 676 deployed and 673 declined. Deployment cases maintained a similar trend in terms of raw numbers compared to the numbers at the turn of the century. In Figure 3, it can be seen that 2018 had the highest occurrence of deployed/declined to deploy cases to date, with the courts favouring the deployment of powers in slightly more cases than they

TABLE 1 Generated/Declined Powers by Category, 2018–21

Categories of police power	Generate	Decline to generate
Roadside detention	1	0
Investigative detention	3	8
Search without a warrant – part of investigation	0	3
Search incident to detention	0	6
Search incident to arrest	1	1
Warrantless entry	1	3
Investigative technique – swab from motor vehicle drug investigation	1	
Exploratory search	0	1
Total	7	22

declined to deploy. The numbers suggest that courts will continue to grapple with the deployment of common law police powers as defence and Crown counsel are likely to rely on past ancillary powers jurisprudence to present their case with respect to the police conduct being reviewed. It is also a sign that the exponential effect that the generation of a new power has on how many deployment cases arise has not changed in the most recent data (see Table 2).

In total, courts have slightly favoured declining to deploy common law police powers over their deployment. Unsurprisingly, Table 2 shows that courts appear to be deploying search incident to investigative detention at a lower rate than search incident to arrest (35 percent versus 56 percent). Courts are less likely to take issue with a search when the police officer has

TABLE 2 Deployed/Declined Powers by Category, 1985–2021

Police power	Deployed	Declined	Total	% of deploy/decline
Investigative detention	273	300	573	48/52
Search incident to arrest	220	171	391	56/44
Search incident to detention	118	219	337	35/65
Emergency/forcible entry	145	97	242	60/40
Roadside detention	105	94	199	53/47
Total until 2017	676	673	1,349	50/50
Total 2018–21	185	210	395	47/53
Total	861	881	1,742	49/51

met the higher reasonable and probable grounds standard to justify an arrest. Table 1 is notable because of the stark difference in the percentage of cases where a power has been generated versus declined to generate cases. Courts have generated powers in only 28 percent of cases that were gleaned by the researchers, whereas courts have declined to generate a novel power in 72 percent of cases. In comparison, the years between 2002 and 2017 led to the percentage of cases generated rising to 49.5 percent from 37 percent in the years from 1985 to 2001. We acknowledge that the number of cases from 2018 to 2021 that were procured from the databases are not high. We also appreciate that the COVID-19 pandemic has influenced how courts have operated in the past two years. However, the reduction of generated cases is an overall positive sign when considering the Supreme Court of Canada's decision in *Fleming*, and it will warrant further analysis as more decisions are released in the coming years.

Table 1 also indicates that courts in recent years have been reluctant to recognize new police powers around investigative detention and search incident to arrest. Again, this finding requires further analysis of the data produced by courts in the coming months and years to confirm whether this is a notable change in how the courts delineate these powers or whether it is a mere deviation from the existing trends. In addition, cases that reviewed questionable incidences of investigative detention have led to the generation of three new powers that could lead to an uptick in deployed numbers. When charted over time, the data shows a general increase in power deployment cases. Notably, Figure 4 shows a sharp decline in deploy/refuse to deploy numbers during the COVID-19 pandemic. Thus, the lockdown period may have had a residual effect on the steep decline in cases and may be an outlier in the data. This increase is not steady, however, as the annual case volume rises sharply between 2001 and 2007. Though case volumes begin to fluctuate significantly after this period, they do so within a markedly higher range than volumes from the pre-2001 period (Figure 2).

The deployment percentages across the same time frames show a declining trend, with a 60 percent deployment rate from 1985 to 2000, 50 percent from 2001 to 2017, and 47 percent from 2018 to 2021 (Generation Springer; see Table 2).[27] Despite the lower rate of deployment, the years following the 1985–2000 period still account for a greater total volume of deployments since the total incidence of deployment post-2001 is 937 cases, while the total incidence of deployment between 1985 and 2000 is 147 cases. It is worth noting that the total incidence of deployment for the data collected since the previous article was published, which spans a three-year period from 2018

FIGURE 4   Power Deployment Cases over Time

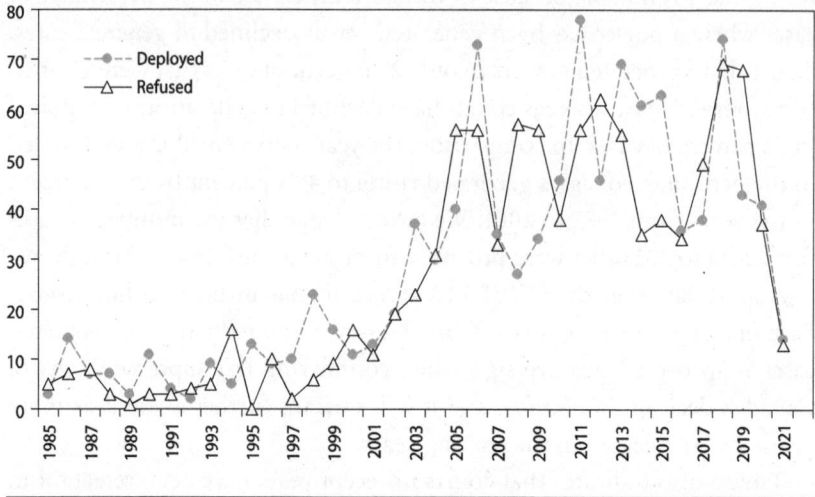

to 2021, with the 2021 dataset being incomplete, amounts to 151 cases – more cases than occurred in the entire fifteen-year period from 1985 to 2000. Thus, while the rate of power deployment has decreased over time, the post-2001 period has still seen 770 more power deployments than the period from 1985 to 2000. As was discussed in the earlier article, there may still be structural issues at play in the Canadian legal system that facilitate the high deployment numbers that have been observed over the last three decades. Canadian police receive their powers from myriad statutes that are criminal and quasi-criminal in nature. As such, gaps naturally exist in the patchwork of legislation enacted by both levels of government (see Figure 4).

The generation data, on the other hand, has not produced such clear trends, in part due to the low volume of generation cases relative to deployment cases (see Figure 5). The effects of a novel power generation by a court are much wider reaching than the effects of a deployment case since each new generation case creates another possible power for future deployment, in addition to existing ones. In Figure 6, the number of generation cases by year is charted cumulatively, alongside the number of cases where power deployment occurred each year, as seen in Figure 4. Doing so reveals a general correlation between the number of powers available to police and the rate of power deployment, though this correlation appears to weaken after 2006.

The result is intuitively consistent; the more police powers that are established, the more often deployment cases will come before courts and, as a

FIGURE 5   Cases Generating/Declining to Generate Powers over Time, 1985–2020

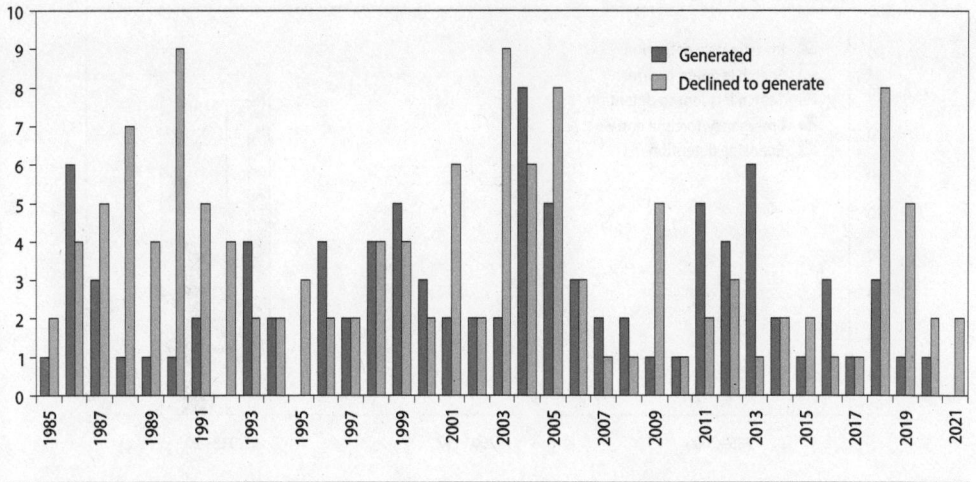

FIGURE 6   Cumulative Generation Cases versus Deployment Cases by Year, 1985–2020

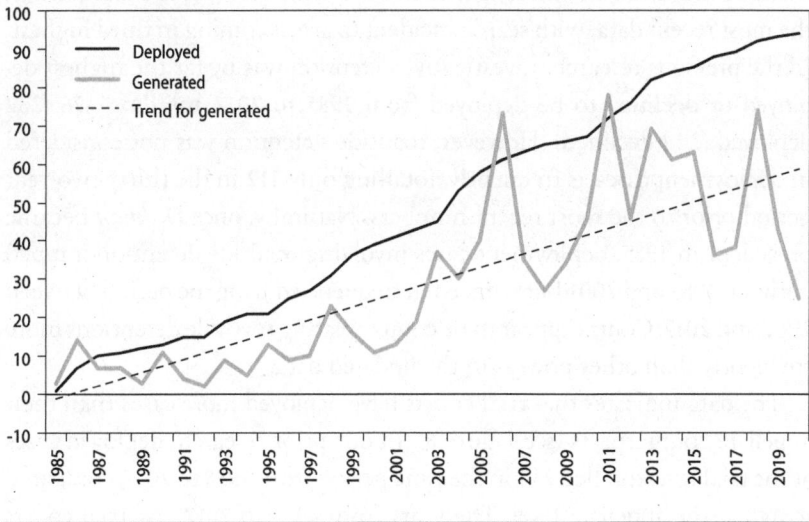

result, the more often powers will be deployed. However, this also raises a few questions. The most obvious of these is why the correlation appears to break down after 2006. We also wanted to know whether all types of police powers have proliferated equally or whether certain types of powers

FIGURE 7   Total Number of Powers Considered by Time Period

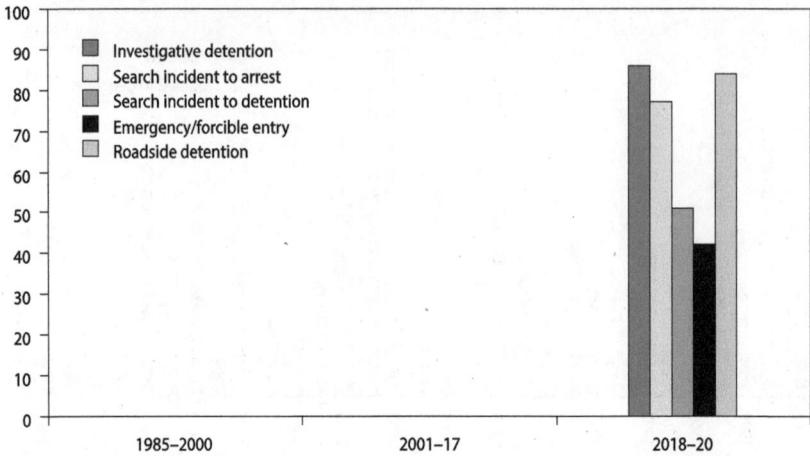

have waxed or waned outside of this general trend. Figure 7 shows that roadside detention and investigative detention are considered most often in the most recent data, with search incident to arrest coming in third highest. In the previous research, investigative detention was by far the highest deployed or declined to be deployed from 1985 to 2017, totalling 476 (232 deployed; 244 declined). However, roadside detention was not considered in deployment cases as frequently, totalling only 112 in the thirty-two-year period prior to the most recent numbers. Naturally, once *Dedman* became precedent in 1985, deployment cases involving roadside detention jumped between 1985 and 2001 but reduced in frequency during the period between 2002 and 2017. Courts appear to be contemplating roadside detentions more frequently than other powers in the updated data.

The data indicates that trial courts have deployed more cases than their appellate counterparts (see Figure 8). In our prior research, deployed cases at the trial level totalled 744 in the time period from 1985 to 2017, compared to 148 at the appellate level. The years from 1985 to 2017 saw trial courts declining to deploy powers 733 times compared to 74 at the appellate level. A perusal of the data from 2018 to 2021 is suggestive of a similar trend with respect to levels of courts. As noted in prior research, these numbers are unsurprising considering that "most fact-finding work occurs at trial and, in most cases, the propriety of police conduct is assessed at trial – predictably

FIGURE 8   Cases Deploying Powers by Court over Time

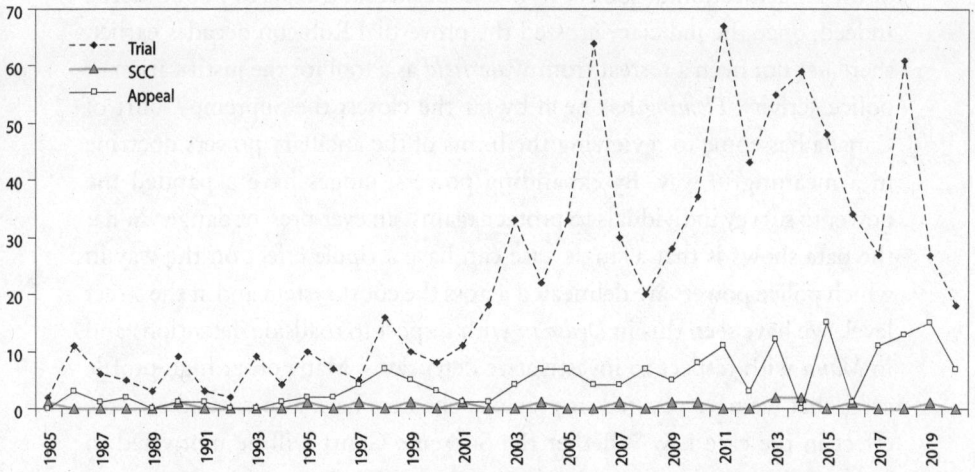

at greater numbers than appeal because fewer cases proceed to appeal relative to the trial process."[28] The data that is provided in Figure 6 tracks quite closely with our previous findings. These findings are also representative of the declined to deploy cases that would be before trial court judges at a higher rate than at the appellate level (including the Supreme Court of Canada).

As described in prior research, the "double-edged" nature of the *Charter* continues to play a role in each generation of a power by the courts.[29] The judiciary's role in the protection of constitutional rights and values has continued to be an exercise of law-making in the context of *Waterfield*. The judiciary's response to novel issues in policing has left citizens with less recourse under the auspices of the *Charter*. Judicial review of police conduct, when approached on an ad hoc basis, leaves citizens without a clear picture of the law. In other words, an encounter with police may be fraught with legal uncertainty if reviewing judges retroactively generate new powers when a novel situation is before them. Novel issues in policing will continue to arise in lockstep with advancements in technology and socio-economic factors that often underpin criminal activity. Thus, some form of judicial intervention will be necessary. We argue that more precision is necessary in the language used by the courts to find the proper balance between state and individual interests.

The proliferation of common law police powers is yet another symptom of the securitization of society in lieu of perpetual threats to public safety. Indeed, once the judiciary crossed the proverbial Rubicon decades earlier, there has not been a retreat from *Waterfield* as a tool for the justification of police activity. *Fleming* has been by far the closest the Supreme Court of Canada has come to reviewing the limits of the ancillary powers doctrine in a meaningful way. By expanding powers, judges have expanded the power to survey individuals to protect against an ever-present danger. What the data shows is that a single case can have a ripple effect on the way in which police powers are delineated across the court system and at the street level. We have seen this in *Dedman* with respect to roadside detentions and in *Mann* with respect to investigative detentions. Many other high-profile cases that we have covered in previous chapters have also created a ripple effect in the case law. Whether the Supreme Court will be motivated to overturn *Waterfield* and explicitly urge lawmakers to consider how novel police conduct should be handled by the judiciary is yet to be seen.

The data that we have endeavoured to present is key to understanding the way in which powers proliferate in the courts. In the next section, we will discuss the impact of *Fleming,* with a focus on how it stands as an echo of past dissenting opinions that voiced discomfort in the utilization and application of *Waterfield* as a legal test for novel and unregulated police conduct. The generation of powers impacts the way in which police conduct is reviewed and powers are applied. Nonetheless, courts are often reluctant to generate new powers, as the data has indicated. Numerous reasons exist for this reluctance; however, when the Supreme Court of Canada comments on *Waterfield,* the change that takes effect has the potential to be seismic.

A Turning Point: *Fleming v Ontario*?

The Supreme Court of Canada's decision not to expand on police powers in *Fleming* possibly echoed the underlying anxieties about ancillary powers that had, until now, largely been left in the shadows. The fears behind granting the police overly broad and permissive powers began early on and remained in the background in dissenting opinions. *Fleming* referred to the dissent in *Dedman* by Justices Brian Dickson, Jean Beetz, and Julien Chouinard, which held against granting police the power to engage in random vehicle stops:

> It has always been a fundamental tenet of the rule of law that the police, in carrying out their general duties as law enforcement officers have

limited powers and are only entitled to interfere with the liberty or property of the citizen to the extent authorized by law. It is necessary to distinguish the duties of police officers from the power, or lawful authority, they possess to execute those duties. The fact that a police officer has a general duty to prevent crime and protect life and property does not mean that he or she can use any or all means for achieving these ends.[30]

The opinion of these judges reinforced the line between the role of the courts and Parliament: "[I]t is the function of the legislature, not of the courts, to authorize arbitrary police action that would otherwise be unlawful as a violation of rights traditionally protected at common law." Some members of the Court continued to echo the concerns behind creating *ex post facto* ancillary powers to meet the ad hoc needs of the police. These opinions took issue with granting the police *Charter*-proof powers that went against the fundamental values of our constitutional democracy. In *R v Kang-Brown* in 2008, the Court placed limits on search-and-seizure powers with the use of sniffer dogs.[31] In doing so, Justices Louis LeBel, Morris Fish, Rosalie Abella, and Louise Charron critiqued the use of ancillary powers being used to create police powers, a duty that they believed belonged to Parliament:

> Any perceived gap in the present state of the law on police investigative powers arising from the use of sniffer dogs is a matter better left for Parliament. Jurisprudence based solutions which would openly or implicitly advocate the creation of new common law rules reducing the standard of scrutiny of state intrusion into privacy do not represent an appropriate exercise of judicial power in the circumstances of this case. When rights and interests as fundamental as personal privacy and autonomy are at stake, the constitutional role of the Court suggests that the creation of a new and more intrusive power of search and seizure should be left to Parliament to set up and justify under a proper statutory framework.[32]

Additional advice from the Supreme Court continued, albeit in the margins of dissenting opinions. These underlying concerns were rooted in an approach that aimed to defer to Parliament to create statutory frameworks to address the use of police powers that infringe on fundamental rights and interests. The need for a "more prudent approach to the interplay between concept and *Charter* values and rules" was recognized by LeBel and Fish JJ in *R v Orbanski*.[33] They wrote that the "adoption of a rule enabling the courts to limit *Charter* rights through the development of common law police powers on the basis of the needs of police investigations would "pre-empt any serious *Charter* review of the limits, as the limits would arise out of initiatives of the courts themselves."[34] The judges acknowledged that the use of common law ancillary powers that focused on the needs of the police would lead to the deprivation of individual liberty and freedom. Further, they recognized that it is not for the courts to provide solutions for these issues through jurisprudence; rather, it is the role of the executive branch that has statutory powers to delineate the boundaries of lawful police conduct. These dissenting opinions anticipated much of the data presented in this chapter.

Fleming attempted to reassert the need to balance the judiciary's position as guardians of the Constitution. In *Fleming*, Justice Suzanne Côté, for the Supreme Court, asserted that the "ancillary powers doctrine is designed to balance intrusions on an individual's liberty with the ability of the police to do what is reasonably necessary to perform their duties."[35] The very fact that the police were targeting someone who was acting lawfully failed the reasonably necessary branch of the *Waterfield* test. The *Fleming* Court also established that if this power were to be recognized, the type of arrest that was conducted by the police would not be reviewable due to the lack of charges being laid. Thus, the Court determined that the "impact on law-abiding individuals, its preventative nature and the fact that it would be evasive of review" militated in favour of not recognizing this new power in the common law.[36]

The way in which the Court described the type of arrest that was central to *Fleming*, especially its ability to evade judicial review, is similar to an investigative detention that does not lead to charges being laid. Thus, we must praise the Court in *Fleming* for rejecting the manner of arrest that was conducted in the case while also remembering the impact of *Mann* on low-visibility detentions. While the decision in *Mann* recognized the power of investigative detention and search incident to detention, it did so to the detriment of individuals who fit a particular description and who are wrongly suspected of committing a crime. Consequently, *Fleming* highlights the impracticability of low-visibility arrests, whereas *Mann*, decades earlier, failed to consider the impracticability of low-visibility detentions. Instead, it ostensibly broadened the discretionary powers of police to conduct low visibility stops on citizens.

Despite the overarching concerns expressed, common law ancillary police powers continued to increase steadily in deployment at all levels until 2018.[37] As we have endeavoured to show, each generation of a power had far-reaching consequences. Each deployment that we have on record does not reflect the number of low-visibility police encounters that were not reviewed by courts. Simply put, the true number of individuals affected by the generation of a power may remain elusive. Despite these concerns, *Fleming* marks a victory for the dissenting opinions and concerns over the use of ancillary police powers that we have seen over the years. The decision marks a re-emergence of values that support the protection of individual rights against the might and weight of state power. In some respects, *Fleming* has recalibrated the judiciary's relationship with the ancillary powers doctrine. Yet powers such as investigative detention and roadside detention are still deployed with some frequency in the data. Additionally, the data suggests that courts have remained consistent in their willingness to grant search powers to police when the search is conducted truly incidental to a lawful *de facto* arrest that arises from reasonable and probable grounds. Thus, in the following section, we will consider how three appellate-level cases treat investigative detention, search incident to arrest, and roadside detention respectively. What we suggest is that though the language in *Fleming* signals a shift in the Supreme Court's application of the ancillary powers doctrine, the shift may not be as pronounced in later rulings.

Cases Post–*Fleming v Ontario*

Since its release in 2019, scholars have debated whether *Fleming* offers an indication of where the Supreme Court of Canada is heading in the future with respect to police powers. Will the justices aim to "pump the brakes" on the expansion and deployment of common law ancillary police powers, or were the facts of *Fleming* so situationally based that the Supreme Court's decision to decline the requested power was more of a one-off exception? Post-*Fleming*, the provincial and appellate courts have acknowledged the Supreme Court's general concerns regarding this doctrine. However, these lower courts have continued to approve the deployment of common law police powers – particularly when it comes to search-and-seizure powers – and, in several cases, have shown a willingness to generate new powers over the past several years.

We will focus on two cases, *R v McKenzie*[38] and *R v McColman*,[39] to provide a brief snapshot of the nascent trends and tendencies in several courts since

Fleming. These three cases provide different treatments of the body of case law that has become part of the discourse around common law police powers. In *McKenzie,* the Manitoba Court of Appeal's interpretation of *Mann* arguably accentuated the standard required to validly establish an investigative detention under the common law. In *R v Stairs,* the majority of the Supreme Court of Canada relied on decades of search incident to arrest jurisprudence that was developed in the common law to determine that the accused's home was justifiably searched incident to arrest.[40] Further, in *McColman,* the majority of the Ontario Court of Appeal relied on *Fleming* to refuse to expand powers of roadside detention to include detention on one's own property; the majority of the Court of Appeal was very clearly influenced by the tone in *Fleming* when they rejected the expansion of detention powers in the context of an impaired driving investigation.

R v McKenzie

One wintery January evening, two police officers were dealing with a motorist in the back lane of a residential neighbourhood in Winnipeg. During this interaction with the motorist, one of the officers spotted a man running through the yard of a nearby property. The man was clenching the left side of his body with his elbow, leading the officer to suspect that he might be injured. Officer Beattie called out to see if the man was okay. When the man and the officer made eye contact, Officer Beattie immediately recognized the man as Clinton McKenzie, a long-standing member of a Winnipeg street gang who was known by police to carry weapons. Appearing startled at encountering the officers, McKenzie immediately changed his direction and quickened his pace to a full-out sprint. Observing this change, Officer Beattie then suspected that McKenzie might be carrying a concealed weapon. The officers called after McKenzie to "stop," but the accused continued running – leading Officer Beattie to pursue. Eventually, the officer caught up after the accused had fallen from a snowbank, and he pinned McKenzie against the wall of a house. In the pursuit, a fanny pack, which McKenzie was wearing around his waist, had become three-quarters unzipped. When Officer Beattie was inspecting McKenzie's body for weapons, he lifted the flap of the fanny pack fully open and shone his flashlight inside, discovering the metal hilt of a handgun. Officer Beattie immediately handcuffed McKenzie and arrested him for possession of a handgun. Before placing the accused into the police cruiser, the officers confiscated the firearm, which was fully loaded, and searched McKenzie's jacket finding drugs and items indicative of drug trafficking.

At trial, McKenzie applied to have the drug and the firearm evidence excluded on the basis that the officers had violated his sections 8 and 9 *Charter* rights. However, the trial judge found that McKenzie had not been arbitrarily detained and that the warrantless search of his fanny pack was reasonable. Justice Suche was satisfied that the police had acted in good faith in a fast-moving and potentially dangerous situation, and she refused to exclude the evidence under section 24(2). McKenzie appealed to the Manitoba Court of Appeal, arguing that the trial judge had misconstrued the facts and erred in her evaluation of section 24(2). Thus, the question before the Court was whether the police had lawfully and reasonably exercised their common law powers in their detention of McKenzie and the search of his fanny pack. Justice Christopher Mainella, for the Court of Appeal, first examined the detention using the *Waterfield* framework.[41] Under the first stage of the test, he found that the officer's actions of detaining McKenzie for a weapons offence investigation fell under the police's common law duties to prevent crime and protect life. Turning to the second stage, the Court of Appeal reviewed the case law surrounding investigative detentions, referencing the Supreme Court's decisions of *Mann* and *R v MacKenzie:* "A police officer may detain an individual for investigative purposes where they have reasonable grounds to suspect that the individual is connected to particular criminal activity and that such a detention is reasonably necessary in the circumstances."[42]

In *McKenzie,* the Manitoba Court of Appeal agreed with the trial judge that there was a constellation of objective facts that led Officer Beattie to reasonably suspect that McKenzie was possibly concealing a weapon. Specifically, the Court of Appeal highlighted factors such as "the accused's mannerisms were consistent with that of a person carrying a weapon while running; upon seeing the police, the accused attempted to flee; and he had a criminal reputation and a propensity to carry weapons."[43] The appellate justices also agreed with the trial judge's view that the detention was conducted in a reasonable manner. The duration of the investigative detention was brief, and the police's limited use of force was appropriate given that the inquiry possibly involved a weapon. The Court of Appeal found that it was important that Officer Beattie take immediate action to eliminate a possible serious threat to peace and public safety, even if the officers were briefly interfering with the accused's liberty. Ultimately, the Court of Appeal found that it was reasonably necessary for the police to detain McKenzie to ascertain if there was a weapons threat. Thus, the investigative detention in the Court's eyes was a justifiable exercise of police powers under the *Waterfield* framework.

Next, Mainella JA moved to evaluate the officer's search of McKenzie's fanny pack. He started with a recap of the police's search powers incident to investigative detention, citing *Mann:* "A police officer may conduct a protective pat-down search for weapons incident to an investigative detention where the officer has reasonable grounds to believe that his or her safety or that of others is at risk."[44] The justices highlighted the debate post-*Mann* on what legal threshold must be satisfied before police could conduct a protective search for a weapon incident to a lawful investigative detention. The justices agreed that the standard should be that of "reasonable suspicion" of a safety risk posed by the detainee. Here, however, the accused raised an interesting submission. McKenzie argued that *Mann* stood for the proposition that a search incident to a detention must follow a "rigid sequence of a pat-down search first, before a bag or pocket may be opened or otherwise searched."[45] He asserted that since the police went straight to searching his fanny pack before conducting a pat-down search, the search of the fanny pack was unreasonable.

However, the Manitoba Court of Appeal disagreed with this interpretation, finding that *Mann* did not lay down such a bright line rule and that McKenzie's argument was not convincing considering *R v MacDonald:*

> It strikes us as incorrect and entirely artificial to say that legally Beattie was limited in his split-second decision, where there was a real threat to his safety, to use his sense of touch on the outside of the fanny pack as opposed to completely opening the already partially open zipper and using his eyesight when he was careful to conduct a minimally intrusive search that was limited in its scope to locate weapons. We agree with the trial judge's observation that "Beattie's second-by-second actions" should not be "parse[d] too finely" (at para 58). What is ultimately controlling is how intrusive the character of the search conducted was in light of what was reasonably necessary to alleviate the risk to the officer or third party ... We accept as accurate (particularly in light of *MacDonald* at para 39) Steel JA's comment in *Willis* that "it is undesirable to measure with extreme nicety whether [police officers'] safety or that of the public in any particular search requires more or less than a quick pat-down" (at para 36).[46]

The accused argued that allowing a search in circumstances like this would "leave former gang members who 'chose to jog' to be forever ... at the mercy of police search," especially when officers could opt to do a more intrusive search through pockets and forgo a protective pat-down.[47] The Court was unconvinced by this claim, calling it an "unfortunate hyperbole," and it reasserted that it found that Officer Beattie's search was both in conformity with his common law police powers and conducted reasonably.[48]

Ultimately, the Manitoba Court of Appeal had chosen to adopt a loose application of *Mann*'s searches incident to investigative detention. While it had not explicitly created a new power, the Court had shown its willingness to expand the scope of legal searches incident to investigative detentions. Unlike in *Mann*, the reasonable suspicion standard that was applied by the Court in *McKenzie* was not tied to a recent or ongoing crime in the factual matrix. If we recall, in *Mann*, the investigative detention was conducted based on Mann's likeness to the perpetrator and his proximity to the scene of the crime. The crux of the investigative detention was the investigation of a break and enter that had been reported. However, in *McKenzie*, the accused was not being investigated for a crime that was recent or ongoing. The officer's suspicion was based on a prior reputation and observable behaviour. This distinction is key to understanding how powers such as investigative detention may still expand in the wake of *Fleming*. It speaks to the need for stronger language from the Supreme Court as to how gaps in policing legislation should be addressed by the judicial branch. In *Stairs*, the Supreme Court had the opportunity to comment on search incident to arrest powers in one's home.[49]

R v McColman

Should a police officer be authorized to stop and question a person on their own private property to determine if the person may have been driving while impaired when the police officer has no reason to suspect that the person has been drinking? This was the question before the Ontario Court of Appeal and the Supreme Court of Canada in the *McColman* case. The Ontario Court of Appeal provided some analysis with regard to common law police powers; however, the Supreme Court did not grant leave "on the issue of whether the police had the common law authority to conduct the stop."[50]

In *McColman*, two police officers, while on patrol, decided to conduct a sobriety check on a vehicle that was leaving a restaurant and gas station. The officers followed the vehicle down the highway but did not activate their lights or signal for the driver to stop right away. Instead, Officers Lobsinger and Hicks followed the vehicle until the driver, McColman, arrived at his destination – his parent's home – and turned into the private driveway. Up until that point, there was nothing out of the ordinary about McColman's driving. He was not swerving on the road or rolling stop signs. His car was in functioning order, and he did not appear to be breaking any of the Ontario *Highway Traffic Act* rules.[51] Nevertheless, the officers followed McColman onto his private driveway, activated their lights, and exited their police cruiser.

When the police approached McColman, who was now standing outside of his car, they immediately noticed that he was unsteady on his feet and that his eyes were bloodshot. As the officers started talking with him, they could smell a strong odour of alcohol on his breath. When one of the officers asked if he had consumed any alcohol that evening, he admitted that he may have had ten beers. At that point, the officers arrested him for impaired driving and transported him to the police station. There, the accused provided two breathalyzer samples, both of which registered over the legal limit. At the trial, McColman sought to exclude the breathalyzer evidence obtained from the stop, arguing that he was arbitrarily detained contrary to section 9 of the *Charter*. The trial judge dismissed his application and convicted him of impaired driving. The Ontario Superior Court of Justice allowed his appeal and found that the police had no authority to conduct a sobriety or highway safety stop on private property under the common law or under section 48.1 of the *Highway Traffic Act*. The Superior Court of Justice excluded the evidence under section 24(2) and entered an acquittal. The Crown appealed to the Ontario Court of Appeal, seeking an expansion of the common law police power.

However, the Ontario Court of Appeal was reluctant to expand this power. In his judgment, Justice Tulloch (as he then was) recalled the Supreme Court of Canada's warnings from *Fleming* to "tread lightly" in expanding common law police powers and that "complex legal developments," especially those that establish police powers and restrict the individual's activities and interests, should best "be left to the expertise of the legislature."[52] Yet, as we have seen, the Supreme Court has also been very clear that the courts "cannot abdicate their role of incrementally adapting common law rules where legislative gaps exist."[53] In this case, the Court of Appeal refused to expand the police power as requested by the Crown. Tulloch JA, for the majority, walked through the *Waterfield* framework. Under scrutiny was the power to pursue a vehicle off the highway and detain the driver to conduct a random sobriety check on a private driveway, where there are no grounds to suspect an offence has been or is about to be committed.

In this case, the Court recognized that this proposed power interfered with an individual's ability to move around freely on their own driveway and private property. Driving on a highway is a highly regulated activity, and drivers often expect the rules of the road will be enforced and anticipate being pulled over by police. However, at home, individuals have greater liberty to do as they wish and have no expectations that the police, without any suspicion of wrongdoing or any particular safety concerns, may enter onto their driveway to arbitrarily detain them. Passing the threshold consideration, the Court moved to the first stage of the test finding that the proposed police power fell within the general scope of the police's common law duties to prevent crime and protect life and property. The majority stated that "pursuing drivers off the highway and onto private property to conduct random sobriety checks is related to these duties. The carnage of impaired driving knows no bounds when it comes to the difference between public and private property."[54]

However, the serious considerations arose at the second stage of the test: Does the action involve a justifiable exercise of police powers associated with that duty? In the majority's view, the Crown failed to demonstrate that pursuing and detaining an individual on their own private property without any suspicion of wrongdoing was reasonable or necessary to combat impaired driving. Considering the powers that police already possess to combat impaired driving and the greater intrusion on liberty posed by stops on private property, Tulloch JA found it difficult to see the need for the courts to fill a legislative gap:

> I cannot conclude that the power to conduct a groundless stop on private property is reasonably necessary ... The police can conduct a random stop under section 48(1) as soon as the vehicle enters the highway. They also have the option to observe the driver without detaining them, and based on those observations, develop a reasonable suspicion that would give them a basis to detain.[55]

The Court of Appeal laid out the options available to the police:

> A police officer may choose to follow a driver along a highway to see if the manner of driving gives rise to a reasonable suspicion that the driver is intoxicated. Alternatively, the police officer may immediately stop the driver to see if there is evidence to support making a demand. However, where there is no indication from the manner of driving that the driver is intoxicated, police officers should not be entitled to follow a driver,

after forming a crystallized intention to effect a stop, and wait to do so until after the driver has entered onto private property. This would allow the police to enter private property and detain people based on a claimed prior intention to stop the car, formed in the absence of any actual suspicion of impairment.[56]

The majority of justices were also concerned about the potential for abuse that such a power would leave open. Tulloch JA explained that the random nature of the stops means that the power to detain "would generally not result in the laying of charges, [and] the affected individuals would often have no forum to challenge the legality" of the detention.[57] Further, he argued that "since the valid exercise of the proposed police power depends entirely on whether, in the officer's own mind, the officer intended to stop the vehicle before it pulled off the highway, judicial oversight of this power could prove challenging."[58] These low visibility encounters with police would leave some marginalized individuals at greater risk. However, the Crown argued that declining to authorize this police power would lead to "an absurd consequence" – drivers would be able to flee to private property to escape the enforcement of highways laws.[59] To the majority, this concern was misplaced:

> This is not a case of escape: there is no suggestion that Mr. McColman's actions were an artifice designed to evade police. In a true case of escape, the police may well have the authority to continue pursuing that person. It is important to bear in mind that the question is whether the police are entitled to stop someone on private property without any cause for suspicion. Certainly, drivers should not be entitled to escape onto private property to avoid culpability. However, police officers should not be allowed to follow drivers onto private property to investigate their driving where there are no grounds to suspect any wrongdoing.[60]

Ultimately, the majority found that the police did not have the authority to randomly check the sobriety of the accused on his property under the common law, and, thus, the police in this instance arbitrarily detained him contrary to his section 9 *Charter* rights.

In 2022, *McColman* was taken to the Supreme Court of Canada, which heard arguments from counsel on the issue of whether police have lawful authority to perform a sobriety stop on private property. Justice Michelle O'Bonsawin, for a unanimous Court, found that the *Highway Traffic Act* did not support the Crown's argument that the impugned police conduct was lawful. Yet this conclusion was reached without the need to analyze the circumstances through the lens of the ancillary powers doctrine. In fact, the Supreme Court chose not to hear arguments on whether the police officers were justified under the common law. Instead, the Supreme Court implicitly endorsed the majority of the Ontario Court of Appeal in its refusal to hear arguments on the issue when the majority had clearly found no justification for the police conduct under the common law.[61]

Even though the Supreme Court did not add to the law with respect to the ancillary powers doctrine, it still provided some commentary in *obiter* at paragraph 63 of the decision. Under the section 24(2) analysis, the Court invoked *Dedman* to comment on police conduct that fell outside the legal ambit of the law. Specifically, O'Bonsawin J cited Dickson CJ's admonishment of any police conduct that interferes with one's liberty or property and that falls outside the scope of police conduct authorized by law, both common and statutory.[62] Importantly, the Supreme Court stated that "[i]n situations marked by legal uncertainty, police officers should not rely on that uncertainty but instead should err on the side of caution."[63] This statement suggests that the Supreme Court had signalled, yet again, for a need to militate away from endorsing police conduct that interferes with one's rights when the law is uncertain. The Supreme Court ultimately allowed the appeal on the basis that the evidence should not have been excluded under section 24(2) and restored the original conviction imposed by the trial judge.[64] In its section 24(2) analysis, the Court found that the seriousness of the offence outweighed the first two factors in *R v Grant*.[65] Regardless of whether the police unlawfully infringed on the accused's property rights, the Court identified impaired driving as a serious offence and that "society has a vital interest in combatting drinking and driving."[66]

In each of the three cases that we have reviewed, a novel circumstance came before the justices. The outcomes of all three cases were nuanced yet, arguably, dissonant in their tenor. In Ontario, a majority led by Tulloch JA (as he then was) rejected a very intrusive power to detain a person without suspicion of wrongdoing on their own property, whereas a unanimous Manitoba Court of Appeal chose to interpret *Mann* to include instances of detention where no crime was being investigated prior to the investigative detention of the suspect. In the latter case, McKenzie, the accused, was not suspected of wrongdoing. Should courts draw a line as to what must be addressed by legislators? It appears that Tulloch JA's decision invites democratic intervention, whereas Mainella JA's decision maintains the status quo with respect to ancillary police powers. While the judiciary acknowledged the need to protect police when they make split-second decisions, it arguably comes at the cost of limiting, not preserving, rights under the *Charter*. It is imperative that an air of predictability be preserved in the way in which policing is conducted so that citizens can recognize and assert their rights during a police encounter. Otherwise, the fundamental rights that are enshrined in the *Charter* may simply be trammelled by the state, and the judiciary's guardianship role will be less effective and pronounced. Thus, it is incumbent on the judiciary to vocalize the need for legislators to proactively fill legislative gaps in policing.

Conclusion

Gathering empirical evidence and categorizing common law police powers into quantifiable data is one important facet of common law police powers. Indeed, the rule of law can be measured to determine and predict trends and futurities. Notwithstanding the corpus of law that we have analyzed, there still lies the very real problem of policing and the impact of the rule of law on marginalized communities in Canada. Thus, practical, real-world solutions to policing cannot be found in case law. Instead, considering the exercise of police powers rather than the generation of such powers can provide a different perspective on the issues of expansion and proliferation in the common law. Professor Michael Plaxton, in his review of police powers after Dicey, states that

> [d]iscussions of the rule of law will carry us only so far, certainly not as far as many critics of the Supreme Court's police powers jurisprudence have supposed.[67] To effectively argue that police discretion poses a problem to be solved, we must focus on how it is exercised, not how it is created. Critiques must not be supported by sweeping appeals to the rule of law, but by hard evidence about the limits of police expertise that goes beyond the merely anecdotal.[68]

The articulation of police powers in this context reveals the ambiguities between the practical real-world application of common law court decisions and their intended implementations. Though judges should not be looked upon to lay the foundation for police reform, the judiciary must not abdicate its role of limiting police conduct in the face of growing state securitization. The nub of our argument is that the delineation of police powers requires clarity and precision to see through its proper implementation. We further argue that guidance and rules with respect to police duties must spring out of the legislative process. Reviewable police conduct is merely the tip of the iceberg with respect to common law police powers; the real quantum of police intervention on the margins of common law powers would amount to a shadowy figure of police powers, akin to the hidden instances of crime that criminologists contend remain immune from statistical scrutiny. Discretionary decisions by police that impact individuals often go unnoticed by courts in low-visibility encounters. Many of the cases before a judge focus on split-second decisions by officers that are necessarily incidental to policing and are generally seen as such in the judicial review of police conduct.

Another less apparent use of powers, and one that was central to *Fleming*, occurs in cases where police conduct is in favour of preventing crime. Perhaps there is something to be said about the benefit of at least having police conduct within the legal ambit of the law to be regulated and governed by the Court. One may question whether courts should be conferring powers onto police as frequently as the data above has shown. Even though the judiciary cannot remain completely silent when a gap in legislation inevitably reaches the courts, precision and clarity will ultimately help to address and problematize low-visibility encounters that are unreviewable. Much of what has been discussed with respect to police powers has been based on judicial discretion and activism. There are myriad ways that the generation of powers has perpetuated race-based policing practices around the country. When we look at the data, we see the growth of detention powers throughout the decades. Empirical statements that are retrieved from data are essential to the conversation around police powers. However, we must not shy away from making normative statements in order to propose a novel vision of policing that is transformative yet practicable.

The decision-making process in meeting the standard of reasonable suspicion is a low standard of belief that is highly susceptible to unconscious biases. The jurisprudence on police powers has recognized and developed this standard over the course of decades, which has been articulated, quite notably, in cases such as *R v Simpson* and *Mann*.[69] Naturally, the application of *Waterfield* in *Mann* expanded the state's power of investigative detention under the common law and minimized the *Charter*'s protective force under section 9. This likely had sweeping effects on racialized communities. The data that we have shown in this chapter indicates that such powers proliferated in the lower courts once the generation or accentuation of a power took legal effect in the common law. Yet the impact of decisions like *Mann* cannot truly be ascertained. Once powers expand under the common law, it gives police the green light to conduct activity that can structurally reinforce race-based policing.

The phenomenon of racial profiling within policing is well known in Canadian society. Numerous studies across Canada, the United States, and Great Britain have revealed that Black people are more likely to experience multiple police stops and searches.[70] In 2020, the Ontario Human Rights Commission released a report as part of its inquiry into racial profiling and racial discrimination of Black persons by the Toronto Police Service.[71] The data that was obtained from the Toronto Police Service confirms that Black communities are subjected to a disproportionate burden of law enforcement in a way that is consistent with systemic racism and anti-Black racial bias. For instance, Black people are more likely to be arrested, charged, and subjected to excessive uses of force by the Toronto Police.[72] Furthermore, a Canadian study revealed that there is a direct relationship between how closely people are monitored by the police and how likely they are to get caught for breaking the law.[73] What this means is that if Black residents are systematically stopped and searched more frequently than others, they are more likely to be detected and arrested for illegal activity than their white counterparts who engage in the same behaviours. The tendency to over-police Black communities, subjecting them to systematic stop-and-search practices disproportionately, consequently leads to an over-representation of Black people in the Canadian criminal justice system.[74]

Comprehensive studies of the effects of these powers have not been fully investigated in the literature on encounters between Indigenous persons and the police, and such studies should be undertaken in the near future. It has been noted in the literature that "the police's relationship with Indigenous communities has been tumultuous since the beginning of colonialism, and Indigenous communities have often dealt with being under-protected as well as over-policed."[75] In turn, studies have shown that Indigenous accused persons believe that the justice system affects them deleteriously when it comes to how seriously they are charged.[76] The over-representation of Indigenous persons in corrections systems and in state-involved deaths is also well documented.[77] Despite these observations, race-based data for Indigenous-involved police encounters remains under-counted and not fully studied from an empirical perspective.[78] Significant progress has been made in attempting to redress Indigenous involvement with the criminal justice system by interrogating Indigenous constructions of moral responsibility, intergenerational trauma, the limits of Indigenous-specific sentencing, Indigenous justice systems, restorative justice programs, and the corrections and parole systems.[79] Little thorough research has been undertaken exploring similar themes in the context of ancillary powers and how they affect Indigenous accused persons, though examples of such unjust police encounters have made impressions in notorious events and ensuing media responses.[80]

As legal professionals, justice system workers, and law students struggle to implement the recommendations of the Truth and Reconciliation Commission of Canada,[81] a comprehensive study of empirical work employing quantitative and qualitative approaches to exploring the role of ancillary powers in the policing of Indigenous persons is vitally needed. A book-length treatment would be needed to begin to understand the complexities and lived experiences of the communities and individuals affected. This approach would hold significant relevance for Indigenous people, interweaving issues of constitutional rights, historical relationships, and contemporary law enforcement challenges. Some work has been undertaken with respect to the relationship of the criminal justice system to affected communities, but further work on the role of ancillary powers in these contexts is warranted.[82]

PART 3
Critiquing Police Powers

The Doctrine's Proportionality Problem   **5**

The ancillary powers doctrine – and its accompanying *Waterfield* test –
incorporates certain proportionality constraints.[1] Courts only authorize
ancillary police powers that are reasonably necessary to fulfill law enforcement duties.[2] These common law powers must respect proportionality requirements to satisfy the condition of reasonable necessity.[3] As part of the
proportionality analysis, courts evaluate the importance of an ancillary
police power, its impact on liberty, and whether it is necessary for officers
to restrict liberty to fulfill a police duty.[4] The ancillary powers doctrine's
proportionality analysis appears to resemble constitutional proportionality
analysis under section 1 of the *Canadian Charter of Rights and Freedoms*.[5]
However, the ancillary powers doctrine's proportionality test is flawed in
many respects and employs a weaker proportionality framework compared
to section 1 of the *Charter*. When applying the ancillary powers doctrine,
judges may not consider how common law police powers can result in selective enforcement and racial profiling.[6] And judges may not incorporate
adequate transparency and oversight mechanisms that foster a police power's
reasonableness.[7] However, the ancillary powers doctrine's proportionality
framework has other defects that tend to be overlooked.

This chapter argues that the ancillary powers doctrine's proportionality
framework has fundamental problems that undermine the legitimacy of
common law police powers. It advances the following three arguments.
First, the ancillary police powers doctrine's proportionality analysis fails to

consider three types of harms: collective, non-egalitarian, and repetitive.[8] Yet these types of harms can justify stronger transparency and oversight mechanisms for a particular common law police power or militate against the creation of a new ancillary police power altogether. Second, the ancillary powers doctrine's proportionality analysis is inaccurate due to information failures.[9] When applying the *Waterfield* test, courts authorize common law police powers that apply for the future.[10] For this reason, judges tend to lack information about how police officers have exercised, and will exercise, this power.[11] Years later, empirical studies may reveal that officers have enforced a particular police power disparately or selectively.[12] Yet this evidence is crucial for proportionality analysis because it highlights the deleterious effects of police powers on individual rights.[13] The ancillary powers doctrine's proportionality analysis is flawed because judges lack vital information about whether enforcement patterns are discriminatory and whether remedies can redress such abuses adequately.[14] Third and interrelatedly, the judiciary's inability to conduct accurate proportionality analysis undermines the ancillary police powers doctrine's justifiability. Proportionality doctrine fulfills a justificatory function; the state must justify its laws and decisions that restrict liberty.[15] Yet inaccurate proportionality assessments erode the validity of such justifications and, ultimately, corrode the ancillary powers doctrine's legitimacy.

Proportionality and Justification

The concept of proportionality is central to the ancillary powers doctrine.[16] The common law authorizes judges to create new police powers to fill legislative gaps.[17] However, judges only create novel police powers that respect necessity and reasonableness constraints – requirements that aim to ensure proportionality between state objectives and individual rights.[18] These constraints can be summarized as follows. First, the proposed police power must be necessary to fulfill a police duty – for instance, to prevent crime, maintain public order, or protect people and property from harm.[19] Second, the proposed police power must be a reasonable exercise of police authority, such that "less intrusive measures not be valid options in the circumstances."[20] The ancillary powers doctrine's proportionality requirement fulfills an important justificatory role.[21] The proportionality doctrine obliges the state to justify restrictions of individual liberty and demonstrate that they are rational, legitimate, and impose acceptable trade-offs.[22] Its use aims to prevent needless, irrational, and excessive governmental coercion.[23] In doing so, the proportionality doctrine promotes principles of limited government.[24]

The state is called to account, and must publicly justify governmental action that violates constitutional rights.[25]

Proportionality analysis also legitimizes the judiciary's counter-majoritarian role within a democracy.[26] In democracies with strong-form judicial review, unelected judges have the power to strike down democratically enacted laws.[27] For this reason, the judiciary must justify its authority to overrule democratic will and to legitimize its counter-majoritarian function.[28] Proportionality analysis helps achieve this aim.[29] Through this analysis, courts must provide public reasons, and respect a justificatory framework, that legitimize their decisions.[30] This process allows the other branches of government, members of the legal profession, and the public to understand and accept judicial decision-making.[31] Typically, within constitutional law, proportionality analysis incorporates the following elements.[32] First, as a threshold requirement, the state must pursue a legitimate and sufficiently important objective to restrict individual rights.[33] Second, the state must restrict rights through suitable – or logical – means to achieve its aim.[34] Third, the state must impair constitutional rights minimally.[35] Fourth, the advantages of restricting individual rights must outweigh their disadvantages.[36]

Proportionality analysis fulfills other functions. Judges can more justifiably strike down laws, or invalidate governmental action, that breach proportionality constraints and result in needless or excessive coercion. Each aspect of proportionality analysis guards against different forms of governmental wrongdoing. The government may enact laws that violate fundamental rights for trivial or illegitimate reasons, which treat individual rights as unimportant. The state acts arbitrarily when it limits individuals' rights through means that are not suitable to achieve governmental objectives. The state may inflict needless or excessive coercion and narrow the strength of constitutional protection because it impairs rights too harshly to achieve its aim. Or, in restricting individual rights, the negative effects of such restrictions outweigh their benefits, which accords primacy to governmental interests over individual rights. The proportionality analysis seeks to ensure that the state does not needlessly, irrationally, or excessively trample rights and interests to achieve its ends.

The Ancillary Powers Doctrine: Overlooking Three Types of Harm

The ancillary powers doctrine incorporates some proportionality constraints.[37] The doctrine employs a necessity threshold: ancillary police powers must fulfill a law enforcement duty.[38] Courts also analyze whether the police duty is sufficiently important to justifiably restrict liberty, considering whether officers must necessarily limit liberty to fulfill the relevant duty and the degree to which the police power limits freedom.[39] The ancillary powers doctrine also evaluates how state action impacts individual interests and whether governmental conduct was minimally intrusive.[40] However, the ancillary powers doctrine differs from section 1 of the *Charter*'s proportionality analysis in certain important respects. Notably, the ancillary powers doctrine does not rigorously evaluate the benefits and burdens of a police power.[41] Without robust proportionality analysis, courts discount how ancillary police powers can produce three types of harms, each of which are examined in turn: collective, non-egalitarian, and recurrent.

First, the ancillary powers doctrine's proportionality analysis does not consider how a common law police power can result in collective harms, meaning diffuse harms against community members.[42] As discussed more below, Indigenous and racialized communities are disproportionately subject to these collective harms. The ancillary powers doctrine overseas collective harms for the following reason. In applying the *Waterfield* test, courts focus primarily on how a particular police power can restrict freedom in a particular case.[43] However, judges may not consider how the widespread exercise of these powers can result in racial profiling, decrease the community's trust in the police, contribute to social exclusion, or make individuals feel targeted rather than protected.[44] Ancillary police powers may produce collective harm in various ways. Individuals may lose confidence in the police vicariously through others' negative experiences with law enforcement.[45] Those who are subject to racial profiling may share their stories with friends and family members who become more distrustful of law enforcement.[46] Similarly, the unlawful exercise of certain police powers can be filmed and shared widely through traditional news and social media, which can further lower trust in the police.[47] The asymmetric impact of law enforcement encounters aggravates these realities. Research indicates that negative police powers are roughly six times more impactful than positive ones.[48] The upshot: one unlawful police encounter may generate wide-ranging negative effects within the community. And the ancillary powers doctrine generally discounts these effects.

Second, police powers produce non-egalitarian harms that disproportionately impact Indigenous and racialized persons.[49] Racial profiling produces salient non-egalitarian harms.[50] Individuals who are racially profiled can suffer negative physical and mental health outcomes and may feel socially excluded from the community.[51] Non-egalitarian harms also carry significant expressive (or symbolic) value. Individuals who are racially profiled and are subject to non-egalitarian harms are treated as second-class citizens.[52] Studies indicate that certain ancillary police powers are exercised disproportionately against racialized persons.[53] Compared to white drivers, Black drivers are more likely to be pulled over by police officers.[54] Similarly, research demonstrates that Black high school students are more likely to be searched by the police compared to white high school students.[55]

Third, some police powers subject the same individual to recurrent harms. Certain studies show that Black adolescents are more likely to be frisk searched on multiple occasions by the police than white adolescents.[56] Empirical research demonstrates that compared to white drivers, Black drivers are more likely to be stopped multiple times by the police.[57] Similarly, judicial decisions and media reports highlight how certain individuals are pulled over repeatedly by the police.[58] Repetitive harms are both different and worse than one-off harms for various reasons. Police encounters, such as traffic stops and frisk searches, can be intimidating, humiliating, and demeaning.[59] Recurring police encounters can compound these harms, and repetitive harm causes other consequences. Individuals who are repeatedly stopped by law enforcement are more likely to believe that they were treated unfairly and that the police acted abusively.[60] Individuals, in turn, may change their conduct to avoid unwanted police encounters.[61] They may drive down different roads or leave earlier for work in case they are pulled over by law enforcement.[62] They may become hypervigilant and may fear being pulled over when they drive past a police car.[63] Repetitive harms can produce physical and psychological effects that one-off harms do not.

Ancillary Police Powers, Information Failures, and Legitimacy

Beyond overlooking these three types of harms – collective, non-egalitarian, and repetitive – the ancillary powers doctrine's proportionality analysis generates two other concerns. First, when assessing whether a police power is reasonably necessary, courts cannot conduct accurate proportionality assessments due to information failures. Courts must decide whether to create common law police powers based on imperfect information. Judges do not know whether officers will exercise a police power discriminatorily. Courts cannot assess whether judicially created oversight mechanisms ensure adequate transparency and accountability in policing.[64] Nor do they know whether certain legal remedies will redress police misconduct effectively. The low-visibility nature of police encounters exacerbates these problems.[65] Relatively few police encounters end up in court.[66] And defendants tend to plead guilty to criminal charges, such that courts do not typically scrutinize whether police officers' conduct was lawful.[67] For this reason, existing legal protections – the exclusionary rule, *Charter* damages, stays of proceedings, and civil suits – may not deter and remedy police misconduct optimally.[68] But judges cannot forecast the effectiveness, or ineffectiveness, of legal protections and remedies. As Cass Sunstein notes, judges "do not know what they do not know."[69]

Courts, for their part, cannot acquire this type of information proactively.[70] Judges cannot gather data like other branches of government.[71] They are largely bound by the information that parties present to courts.[72] Furthermore, judges cannot order other branches of government to undertake empirical studies. Nor can they conduct their own studies that would provide information about how police powers are exercised. These information failures produce major error costs.[73] Common law police powers can misfire. Police officers may abuse their powers in ways that judges did not expect.[74] Due to access-to-justice barriers, individuals whose rights are violated may not seek private or public law remedies.[75] Various factors limit the judiciary's capacity to improve access to justice. Judges lack the power of the purse and cannot spend money to improve access to justice.[76] Furthermore, given their limited institutional competence, judges are reticent to engage with legal issues that require the other branches of government to redistribute resources.[77]

But these information failures also undermine the accuracy of the ancillary powers doctrine's proportionality analysis. Rather than assess the constitutionality of past legislative action under section 1 of the *Charter*, courts that apply the ancillary powers doctrine authorize common law police powers that apply prospectively.[78] Given the prospective nature of these powers, courts that apply the *Waterfield* test lack empirical data about a police power's enforcement. Instead, years after a police power is judicially authorized, scholars and human rights commissions conduct empirical studies that evaluate how police officers have exercised it.[79] Only then do researchers discover that a police power produces collective, non-egalitarian, and recurring harms. And only then can courts properly evaluate a police power's benefits and burdens and, ultimately, its proportionality. Courts thus assess an ancillary police power's proportionality, and justifiability, based on incomplete and possibly erroneous information.

In contrast, courts tend to have more access to such information when individuals contest the constitutionality of statutory police powers. It may take years for such a challenge to go to trial and for the case to wind its way through the appellate process. During that time, scholars may conduct empirical studies that demonstrate a police power's disparate enforcement patterns, harms, and deleterious effects. Courts, for their part, can evaluate a statutory police power's proportionality more accurately in such contexts because they have access to greater and more complete information.

Traffic Stops, Information Failures, and Disproportionality

The decisions *R v Ladouceur* and *Luamba v Procureur général du Québec* illustrate how the availability of information shapes the accuracy of the proportionality analysis and the legitimacy of police powers.[80] The Supreme Court of Canada authorized random traffic stops in *Ladouceur*, which took place in 1990.[81] The majority of the Court decided that police officers can lawfully conduct random traffic stops to maximize motor vehicle safety and to prevent injuries and deaths on public ways.[82] The Court noted that random traffic stops result in arbitrary detentions that violate section 9 of the *Charter*.[83] Yet the Court determined that these stops were reasonably justified in a free and democratic society based on the ancillary powers doctrine and section 1 of the *Charter*.[84]

The Court considered the following elements as part of its proportionality analysis. The majority of the justices noted that random traffic stops pursue a sufficiently important legislative objective: preventing injuries and deaths on public roadways.[85] They observed that random traffic stops were a suitable means to achieve that objective.[86] The justices concluded that random traffic stops result in a minor inconvenience that minimally impacts individual rights.[87] They concluded that the police power's benefits – preventing fatalities on public roadways – outweighed its deleterious effects – restricting drivers' freedom for brief periods.[88] The majority of the justices also concluded that various legal safeguards would prevent abusive random traffic stops and selective enforcement.[89] The Court observed that officers could not conduct a criminal investigation and could only ask questions related to motor vehicle safety.[90] Furthermore, the Court noted that judges could exclude unconstitutionally obtained evidence where officers acted unlawfully.[91]

The *Ladouceur* decision exemplifies how information failures result in inaccurate proportionality analysis. When weighing the benefits and burdens of random traffic stops, the majority of the Court did not properly consider how this police power could result in racial profiling that produces collective, non-egalitarian, and repetitive harms.[92] Although the Court characterized the harms of random traffic stops as "minor inconveniences," research indicates that proactive police encounters can result in physical and mental suffering, feelings of social exclusion, decreased trust in the police, and more.[93] And the Court overestimated how legal safeguards would prevent and remedy unlawful traffic stops.[94] These deleterious effects were largely ignored, or underestimated, in the Court's proportionality analysis in *Ladouceur.*

In *Luamba*, which took place in 2022, the Superior Court of Quebec overturned the *Ladouceur* decision within the province.[95] The Court decided that random traffic stops resulted in arbitrary detentions, violated the constitutional right to equality, and limited the right to liberty in a manner that was inconsistent with the principles of fundamental justice.[96] The Court concluded that these violations were not reasonably justified in a free and democratic society and, ultimately, did not restrict rights proportionally to achieve the state's objective.[97] In *Luamba*, the decision's reasoning was based primarily on empirical data, qualitative information, and expert evidence that elucidated flaws in the majority of the Supreme Court of Canada's proportionality analysis in *Ladouceur.*[98] The evidence adduced at trial demonstrated that police officers disproportionately pull over Black drivers.[99] Several witnesses testified about the harms that they experienced from traffic stops and suggested that police officers racially profiled them.[100] Moreover, the state failed to provide evidence that demonstrated how random traffic stops improve highway safety and decrease motor vehicle–related mortalities.[101] For these reasons, the Superior Court of Quebec decided that random traffic stops were unconstitutional. The *Luamba* decision highlights how the availability of information influences the accuracy of proportionality analysis and the legitimacy of police powers.

Inaccurate Proportionality and the Legitimacy of Ancillary Police Powers

Inaccurate proportionality analysis also undermines the ancillary powers doctrine's legitimacy.[102] Previous sections have highlighted how proportionality analysis is associated with the concept of justification in public law.[103] As discussed above, the proportionality doctrine serves to justify state action that impinges on rights and interests and aims to legitimize the judiciary's role within a democracy.[104] Yet a flawed proportionality analysis undercuts both justificatory enterprises. Consider first how an inaccurate proportionality analysis undermines the justifiability of governmental coercion. In criminal law contexts, the notion of "justification" implies that conduct that is normally morally wrong is morally acceptable in the circumstances.[105] For instance, although use of force is normally wrong, police officers may justifiably use force against others to prevent harm, investigate crimes, and apply the law.[106] Similarly, state coercion is presumptively wrong because it limits freedom.[107] But state coercion is justifiable where it is necessary and reasonable to protect fundamental interests and, ultimately, respects proportionality constraints.[108] Needless or excessive coercion are morally objectionable because they violate proportionality requirements and lead to unnecessary harm or suffering.[109]

Proportionality analysis also aims to ensure that the state does not commit its own moral wrong when it limits rights to protect core interests.[110] Like in use-of-force contexts, governmental coercion is justifiable when the state restricts freedom in a necessary, reasonable, and proportionate fashion.[111] Proportionality ensures that the state balances individual and societal interests and achieves equilibrium between fundamental rights and governmental objectives.[112] As guardians of the Constitution, courts conduct proportionality analysis to ensure that rights are restricted based on sufficiently compelling moral reasons.[113] This justificatory enterprise acknowledges that it is normally wrong for the state to restrict individuals' fundamental rights but that the state can justifiably do so when it respects proportionality requirements.[114] These considerations highlight how the state commits a moral wrong when it limits rights in a manner that violates proportionality constraints; the state inflicts needless harm, coercion, or suffering in such contexts.[115] Proportionality analysis evaluates whether the state imposes coercion that is necessary and reasonable – and, thus, justifiable – such that the state does not commit its own wrong when it limits rights.[116]

Yet due to inaccurate proportionality analysis, courts authorize police powers that coerce individuals unjustifiably and result in various forms of governmental wrongdoing. For instance, officers may exercise ancillary police powers, such as random traffic stops or frisk searches, against factually innocent persons.[117] In doing so, officers commit a moral transgression; they limit the fundamental interests of individuals who have done nothing wrong and are not suspected of wrongdoing.[118] In other contexts, officers may selectively enforce certain powers against racialized persons, which exemplifies the distinct moral wrong of discrimination.[119] The exercise of certain police powers can degrade, humiliate, and intimidate individuals, which demeans human dignity.[120] Inaccurate proportionality analysis can result in these forms of unjustifiable coercion that typify governmental wrongdoing.

Consider next how the ancillary powers doctrine's inaccurate proportionality analysis can undermine the judiciary's role within a democracy. Recall how proportionality analysis aims to legitimize the judiciary's counter-majoritarian function.[121] As discussed above, courts can invalidate state action more justifiably in contexts where the state needlessly or disproportionately violates individual rights to achieve governmental objectives.[122] The judiciary's role is counter-majoritarian in that it helps prevent a tyranny of the majority and protects individuals against majoritarian governmental power.[123] Furthermore, constitutional review is justified because it redresses governmental coercion that violates proportionality constraints and constitutes a moral wrong. But the ancillary powers doctrine is inconsistent with the judiciary's counter-majoritarian role. Rather than safeguard individuals' rights against governmental coercion, unelected judges authorize police powers that expand state authority and limit these rights. Furthermore, courts do so in a manner that circumvents traditional democratic guardrails, such as debate between lawmakers, notice-and-comment procedures, legislative committees and subcommittees, and multiple readings of a bill.[124] Judges do so based on flawed proportionality analysis that is plagued by information failures and that ignores collective, non-egalitarian, and repetitive harms.[125]

Conclusion

This chapter has argued that the ancillary powers doctrine's proportionality framework is objectionable for several reasons. When judges apply the *Waterfield* test, they generally do not consider how police powers can result in various types of harm. Yet these harms constitute meaningful deleterious effects that militate against a police power's proportionality. Furthermore, judges face information failures when they apply the ancillary powers doctrine, which can result in an inaccurate or erroneous proportionality analysis. This chapter also drew on the *Ladouceur* decision to show how courts that face information failures – and conduct flawed proportionality analysis – can authorize police powers that result in needless and excessive coercion. As the *Luamba* decision illustrates, courts may obtain information that highlights how a police power violates proportionality constraints because it results in collective, non-egalitarian, and repeated harms. Judges may invalidate a police power when they obtain more complete information and can conduct a more accurate proportionality analysis that fully captures a police power's deleterious effects.

But the ancillary powers doctrine's proportionality analysis also undermines the legitimacy of judicially created police powers. Proportionality analysis partly aims to justify the judiciary's counter-majoritarian role within a democracy. Yet the ancillary powers doctrine is inconsistent with the judiciary's counter-majoritarian function and with the obligation to justify restrictions of individual rights. Courts that conduct inaccurate proportionality analysis can authorize police powers that inflict needless harm and are not justifiable. The inaccuracy of proportionality analysis undermines the judiciary's justification for creating police powers that restrict individual liberty and, ultimately, the legitimacy of the judicial branch as a creator of police powers.

Ancillary Police Powers and the Black Experience in Canada

The tenuous relationship between Black communities and the police is well documented in Canada as it is in many other Western nations.[1] Black people are disproportionately more likely to be stopped and searched by the police;[2] to experience police disrespect and harassment;[3] and to be on the receiving end of police use of force.[4] While it is police use of force involving Black and other racialized people that typically garners the greatest levels of public attention and, at times, serves as a catalyst for social unrest, police stop-and-search powers are of course much more common and, given their far-reaching impact, should also be of great public concern. This chapter examines the Black experience with police stop and search in Canada. The chapter begins by situating the tenuous relationship that Black communities have with the police in Canada in a historical context. The chapter then provides further contextualization by examining public perceptions of police bias before examining racial differences in police stop and search as gleaned from both "official" and "unofficial" sources of police data. The chapter concludes by considering the impact that police stop-and-search practices have on the populations most subject to them.

Historical Context: Black People and Policing in Canada

Canada's Black population has long been subject to police suspicion, surveillance, and the target of police action, including stop and search, arrest, and use of force, and much attention to the relationship between Black Canadians and the police has been centred in Toronto and Ontario, the region with the greatest number of Black people. In his historical analysis of systemic racism in Ontario's criminal justice system, for example, Clayton Mosher documents how the police used public order offences discriminately as a means of controlling Toronto's Black population in the early twentieth century.[5] As the immigration reforms of the 1960s opened Canada's doors to immigrants from non-European countries, an influx of Black immigrants arrived in the country, many of whom settled in the Greater Toronto Area (GTA).[6] It was not long after this time that tensions between Toronto's growing Black communities and the police began to escalate and then peaked following a series of police shootings involving Black males in the late 1970s.[7]

On 9 August 1978, a white police officer shot and killed twenty-four-year-old Buddy Evans in a Toronto nightclub.[8] The officer's acquittal, following an eleven-week inquest, prompted a rally organized by the Sikh-led Action Committee against Racism. A year later, thirty-five-year-old Albert Johnson was shot to death in his own home by two white officers.[9] This shooting again sparked community mobilization. Dudley Laws, who would become an important figure in the fight against police discrimination, formed the Albert Johnson Defense Committee against Police Brutality. In October 1979, members and supporters of this committee gathered outside of city hall to protest the death of Johnson.[10] The two officers involved in the Johnson shooting were ultimately acquitted of manslaughter charges, and the Ontario government responded to the demonstrations with institutional reform. In 1981, the province enacted a three-year pilot project under the *Metropolitan Police Force Complaints Project Act* called the Office of the Public Complaints Commissioner.[11] The office, which intended to provide an improved civilian complaint system to deal with incidents of police brutality, faced much criticism from members of Toronto's Black communities because it was seen to be biased in favour of the police.[12]

A second series of police shootings involving Black men in the late 1980s prompted further community mobilization and contestation toward the police. Days after the 1988 police shooting of forty-four-year-old Lester Donaldson in his Toronto rooming house apartment, the Black Action Defense Committee organized a demonstration in front of the police division where the suspected officer worked. A second police shooting that year further angered members of Toronto's Black communities, increasing racial tensions in the region. On 8 December 1988, seventeen-year-old Michael

Wade Lawson was shot in the back of the head by a Peel Regional police officer using an illegal hollow-point bullet, a type of enhanced ammunition banned under Ontario's *Police Services Act*.[13] Public demonstrations continued after the acquittals of the officers involved in these cases.

In response to this social unrest, the provincial government formed the Task Force on Race Relations and Policing, with a mandate "to address promptly the very serious concerns of visible minority communities respecting the interaction of the police community with their own."[14] The task force concluded that racialized Ontarians felt that they were policed unfairly, and it noted that the lack of public confidence posed a major challenge to effective policing.[15] The task force also made a number of recommendations on hiring, training, and accountability measures related to the policing of an increasingly diverse province and called for the creation of a civilian oversight body to investigate police shootings.[16] In 1990, in response to this recommendation, the provincial government created the Special Investigations Unit to increase police accountability in the investigation of cases involving the serious injury or death of a civilian.[17]

Throughout the 1990s and into the 2000s, public concern about police relations with Black communities persisted and began to centre on the frequency and nature of police contacts with Black people. In 2002, this attention increased drastically following the publication of the *Toronto Star*'s first series on race and justice, which drew upon almost half a million police-civilian encounters documented by the Toronto police.[18] A lead article in the series, entitled "Police Target Black Drivers," presented the *Toronto Star*'s analysis of 7,500 "out-of-sight" traffic offences – offences that only come to light after a driver has been stopped by the police.[19] The *Star*'s analysis showed that Black drivers accounted for almost 34 percent of all drivers charged with out-of-sight violations, even though Black people accounted for just 8.1 percent of Toronto's population. Police Chief Julian Fantino questioned the *Star*'s analysis and findings, proclaiming: "We don't do profiling at this service."[20] Many Black Torontonians disagreed. The *Toronto Star* ran the following passage summing up the thoughts and experiences of Grace Edward Galabuzi, a well-known Black community activist, who is now an eminent professor:

> "It's sadly inevitable for young Black men," lamented the 40-year-old community activist and researcher at the Centre for Social Justice. One stop was particularly ironic. He was pulled over driving from Pearson

International Airport, in an upscale Audi 4000, having just flown home from an Ottawa conference on police harassment. The officer refused to give Galabuzi a reason for the stop, arguing that "security reasons" prevented him from explaining his actions. Galabuzi, then 29, complained to the officer about this "humiliating" scrutiny but was warned not to cause trouble. Heeding that caution, he stopped protesting and was allowed to go on his way.[21]

The stories recounted by other Black Torontonians painted a similar picture: "'I've had so many experiences with police,' said a twenty-five-year-old professional, 'that I just immediately become aware when they're around and make sure I'm driving carefully and going the limit.'" Likewise, a seventeen-year-old boy provided an account of how different people around him felt when in the presence of the police: "When I'm driving with my brother, and he sees a cop in the rearview mirror, he's shook." He continued: "But when I'm with a white friend, and he sees a cop in the rearview mirror, he's still chillin."[22] With its novel data and gripping stories, the original *Toronto Star* series received praise from many in Toronto's Black communities and from civil liberties and human rights organizations.[23] However, in addition to Chief Fantino's denials of racial bias, the Toronto Police Association filed a $2.7 billion class action libel suit, claiming damages against the *Star* on behalf of all sworn officers.[24] The suit was later dropped, and the allegations of racial bias were supported by a group of Black officers who said that they had themselves been the victims of racial profiling.[25]

The *Star*'s work was pivotal in terms of propelling issues of race and police contact into the public consciousness in Canada. Several years later, the *Toronto Star* struck again in a series entitled "Race Matters," this time releasing its analysis of over 1.7 million "contact cards" filled out by the Toronto Police Service (TPS) between 2003 and 2008.[26] This data on police stop-and-question activities, which will be discussed in more detail below, again showed a high level of racial disproportionality in police activity, with Black and Brown people being greatly over-represented in the police records.[27] In the years following the release of "Race Matters," the phenomenon of police "carding," especially as it relates to police activity targeting Indigenous and Black people, garnered attention across Canada, prompting public demonstrations, government reviews, and legislative reform. Before taking a closer look at the data on police stop and search, we first examine how Black Canadians view the police.

Public Perceptions of Police Bias

Perhaps unsurprisingly, given the history of police-race relations detailed above, research conducted over the past three decades has consistently documented racial differences with respect to citizens' perceptions of the police, with perceptions of police bias quite prevalent in, but not limited to, the Black population. The first major study into citizens' views of the police was carried out as part of the Commission on Systemic Racism in the Ontario Criminal Justice System in the early 1990s. This commission surveyed over 1,500 members of the general public in the GTA and found that over half of Black, white, and Chinese respondents believed that the police treat Black people differently than white people.[28] This study was replicated in 2007, fifteen years later, to examine whether there were changes in citizens' perceptions of the police. What may be of surprise, in light of the myriad race relations initiatives that were implemented in the intervening period, is that the 2007 study found that perceptions of police bias had actually increased among both Black and white respondents. For example, in 1994, 76 percent of Black respondents felt that the police treated Black people worse or much worse than they treated white people. By 2007, this figure had risen to 81 percent.[29] Similarly, in 1994, 51 percent of white respondents felt that the police treated Black people worse or much worse than they treated white people. By 2007, this figure had risen to 59 percent.[30] A subsequent replication of this survey conducted in 2019 shows that perceptions of police bias against Black people had increased marginally among both Black and white respondents, with 82 percent of the former and 62 percent of the latter reporting that the police treat Black people worse than white people.[31] Similar findings have emerged from other studies.

In 2017, for example, the Toronto Police Service Board (TPSB) commissioned a survey to investigate citizens' perceptions of, and experiences with, the TPS following the implementation of measures to regulate police "carding" in Ontario. This large-scale study also involved approximately 1,500 respondents who were surveyed in areas across the city of Toronto. Overall, the results indicate that a majority of respondents considered the TPS to be honest and fair. For instance, some 68 percent of respondents felt that the TPS's officers are honest, and 65 percent believed that the TPS could be trusted to treat members of their racial group fairly.[32] However, as in other work, racial differences emerged. Whereas 78 percent of East Asians and 76 percent of white respondents believed that the Toronto police treated members of their racial group fairly, only 26 percent of Black respondents felt this way.[33] Black respondents were also the least likely of all groups to believe that Toronto police officers are honest and that they live up to their motto.[34] Conversely, Black respondents were most likely to believe that the TPS's officers with whom they have interacted are biased against members of their own racial group.[35]

In addition to documenting racial differences with respect to perceptions of the police, this line of research has also demonstrated that racial differences in perceptions of police bias emerge, at least in part, from racial differences in levels of contact and perceived treatment at the hands of the police. Indeed, researchers found a strong positive relationship between personal and vicarious contact with the police and perceptions of police bias – respondents who reported that they or someone they knew had recently been stopped by the police were more likely to perceive the police as biased.[36] As Black people are much more likely to experience police stops, and to perceive these encounters negatively, it makes sense that they hold such strong perceptions of police bias.

The Black Experience with Police Stop, Question, and Search in Canada: What the Data Tells Us

Although concerns about the police targeting of Black and other racialized populations in Canada have existed for decades, there has been a lack of access to official sources of data documenting such practices. Unlike in England and many regions of the United States, Canadian police agencies have not been mandated to collect information on the race of individuals they stop and/or search.[37] As a result, the Canadian public has historically had little access to official police data that would support the long-standing claims by Black people that they are subject to disproportionate police stop-and-search practices. While legislation has begun to mandate the public release of racially disaggregated police data in certain contexts (around the use of force in Ontario, for example), Canadian police agencies are still not required to collect race-based data on stops and searches, hampering efforts to accurately assess the extent to which racial disparities in such police activities exist and to uncover the reasons for any observed differences. To date, only two Canadian police agencies have systematically collected data on police stops that included information on the race of the individuals stopped for the purpose of making that information public. Other available data has typically been made public when media or other parties have gained access through freedom-of-information laws, and this data has been rather limited in scope.

Official Police Data

Shortly after the publication of the *Toronto Star*'s 2002 series and following repeated allegations of racial bias in police stops in the city, Bill Closs, the chief of the Kingston Police Service, entered into an agreement with Scot Wortley, a University of Toronto professor, to initiate a pilot project to collect and publicly release race-based data on police stops for the first time in Canada. The announcement of this project came on the heels of intense criticism following the arrest of two innocent Black teenagers, Mark Wallen and Adrian Parkes, who were handcuffed and searched after having a gun pulled on them by a Kingston police officer while walking home from basketball practice.[38] For twelve months, beginning in the fall of 2003, Kingston police officers were required to document the race, age, gender, and home address of all the people that they stopped and questioned as well as information about the time, location, reason for, and outcome of the stop. Over the study period, information on over 16,500 stops was recorded.[39] Wortley's analysis of the data shows that Black residents of Kingston were three times more likely to be stopped by the police at least once than were white people and that these racial differences in stops were most pronounced for young people.[40] Importantly, the analysis showed that these racial differences in police contact could not be explained by racial differences in criminal activity or violation of traffic laws, leading the researchers to suggest that their findings supported the allegations of racial profiling.[41] As was the case with the release of the *Toronto Star*'s findings, the Kingston study led to a great deal of criticism from within police circles and a high level of antipathy directed at Chief Closs for embarking on the project.[42]

With the Kingston study complete, a great deal of public, political, and academic attention turned to the issue of racial profiling in Canada. As in other jurisdictions, debate raged over the causes of the racial disparities, and polarized camps formed, alleging police bias, on the one hand, and defending police actions, on the other.[43] While activists, civil liberties organizations, and human rights groups used this data to support further examination and reform of police action, many parties that were aligned with the police continued to deny the possibility that racial bias existed in police stop-and-search practices.[44] The politically charged nature of these discussions and the criticisms levelled against Chief Closs likely dissuaded other police services from engaging in similar research projects. The only other police agency to have done so since is in Ottawa.

As part of a settlement in a racial-profiling case, the Ottawa Police Service agreed to collect information on traffic stops conducted by its officers for a two-year period beginning in 2013.[45] The decision to focus solely on traffic stops is questionable, given that pedestrian stops account for a high number of police stops and the fact that civilian race is initially much more obvious in the latter than in the former. Notwithstanding this limitation, the outcome of the Ottawa study was very similar to that of the Kingston study; the researchers found that Black drivers and Middle Eastern drivers were much more likely than white drivers to be stopped by the police. Indeed, Middle Eastern drivers were 3.3 times more likely and Black drivers 2.3 times more likely to be stopped by the police than their representation in the driving population would predict.[46] Again, these differences were most pronounced for young people and for young males in particular.[47] As was the case in Kingston, offence seriousness did not account for the racial differences observed in the study.

The Ontario Human Rights Commission (OHRC), which initially fought for the study to be undertaken, had the following to say about the results:

> From the OHRC's perspective, the York University researchers' findings are highly consistent with the phenomenon of racial profiling. Over-representation of various racialized groups and sub-groups (broken down by sex and age) exists when looking at traffic stops generally, the reason for the stop, the outcome of the stop, and the police district where the stop took place. In stating their conclusions about the disproportionately high incidence of traffic stops of various race sub-groups in the six police districts, the researchers note that anomalies are extensive in number and severe in disproportionality. These disproportionalities exist despite some officers acknowledging that they failed to correctly enter the race data due to concerns about how it would affect their employment.[48]

In both the Kingston and Ottawa data collection projects, the police officers in each service knew that their police agencies were under scrutiny for alleged racial bias, potentially influencing who they decided to stop as well as the accuracy of their reporting practices when they did interact with members of the public. The initial data on police carding, discussed above, does not suffer from this weakness because the information collected was intended only for internal police purposes. Police "carding," or "street checks," emerged as a public issue following the release of the *Toronto Star*'s "Race Matters" series.

This phenomenon is called "carding" in reference to the "contact cards" (often also referred to by other names) used by police agencies to collect information about members of the public. Unlike the data from Kingston and Ottawa, carding data is not collected after every stop (pedestrian and/or traffic) nor, typically, when criminal charges are laid but, rather, when individual officers want to record the details of a civilian encounter and personal information about the civilian for the purposes of intelligence gathering. In 2012, "Race Matters" was followed up by "Known to Police," a series of articles by the *Toronto Star* that also focused on contact card data, this time collected between 2008 and mid-2011. The *Toronto Star*'s analysis found that while Black people comprised 8.3 percent of Toronto's population, they accounted for 25 percent of the contact cards filled out over this period.[49] The data also showed that Black people were more likely to be stopped in each of the city's seventy-two police patrol zones and that, again, Black people were more likely to be stopped in areas that were predominantly white.[50] This *Star* series once again drew public attention, and the chair of the TPSB announced that steps would be taken to address carding disparities.[51] Unfortunately, this pronouncement led to little action on the part of the TPS itself to reform the practice.

Since the publication of the *Toronto Star*'s investigative work into carding, data on this type of police activity has been made public from police agencies across the country, demonstrating with relative consistency the over-representation of Black (and Indigenous) people in police-carding databases. Wortley provided the following summary in his report on street checks in Halifax, Nova Scotia:

- Between 2011 and 2014 the Ottawa police recorded 23,403 street checks. Results indicate that Black civilians were more than three times more likely to be subject to a street check than their representation in the general population. Middle Eastern civilians were two times more likely to be subjected to a street check, while Whites were under-represented.
- Between 2010 and 2015 the Hamilton police conducted over 18,500 street checks. Black people were four times more likely to be subject to a street check than their representation in the general population would predict.
- In 2014, the London Police conducted 8,400 street checks. Black and Indigenous people were over three times more likely to be entered into the street check dataset than their representation in the London population.
- The Peel Regional Police conducted 159,303 street checks between 2009 and 2014. Analysis of the street check data reveals that Black residents are three times more likely to be entered into the street check dataset than White residents.

• Between 2006 and 2015, the Halifax Regional Police conducted 68,483 street checks. Analysis reveals that Black Haligonians are three times more likely to be entered into the HRP street check dataset than their representation in the general population would predict.[52]

Furthermore, data made public from Edmonton demonstrates that between 2012 and 2016, Black people in the city were almost four times more likely than white people to be street checked. Similarly, data from Vancouver shows an over-representation of Black people in police-carding activities in the city, and although a new policy has reduced the overall number of street checks conducted, racial disparities persist.[53] Irrespective of jurisdiction, official police data demonstrates that Black people have historically been stopped and documented (carded) by the police at rates several times higher than their representation.

The practice of police carding has been viewed as particularly controversial given the rather opaque and unregulated nature of the practice. Prior to the introduction of regulations in Ontario in 2017, there were almost no checks and balances on the practice in the province or in any other jurisdiction in Canada. As such, serious concerns were raised about with whom the data was being shared and the data being used as a performance measure for police officers. The former was of great concern to civil liberties organizations and privacy groups who correctly pointed out that non-criminal information was being shared with potential employers and other agencies that were conducting background checks on individuals and that this was having a negative impact on the opportunities afforded to the disproportionately racialized people whose data was being shared for the purposes of making employment and other important decisions. In terms of the latter, community organizations rightly pointed out that using contact cards as a performance measure led officers to target Black, racialized, and otherwise marginalized people for unnecessary police stops in order to boost their carding numbers and thus improve their performance scores. In essence, police officers were benefiting professionally at the expense of Black and other racialized Canadians.

Findings from Survey and Interview Research

The findings drawn from the analysis of official police data support the conclusions drawn from nearly three decades of survey and interview research conducted with members of Canada's Black communities. Among earlier studies carried out with Black youth in and around the GTA, Robynne

Neugebauer-Visano conducted interviews with Black and white youth from across Toronto. While her findings demonstrated that teenagers from all racial backgrounds often complained about being hassled by the police, both white and Black youth in her study agreed that Black males were much more likely to be stopped, questioned, and searched by the police than teens from other racial backgrounds.[54] Similarly, Carl James conducted interviews with over fifty Black youth from six different cities in Ontario. James found that many of these youth reported that being stopped by the police was a common occurrence for them and that there was an almost universal belief that skin colour, not style of dress, was the primary determinant of attracting police attention.[55] As one of the Black male respondents noted,

> they drive by. They don't glimpse your clothes; they glimpse your colour. That's the first thing they look at. If they judge the clothes so much, why don't they go and stop those White boys that are wearing the same things like us. I think that if you are Black and wearing a suit, they would think that you did something illegal to get the suit.[56]

Over a decade later, Professor Akwasi Owusu-Bempah drew upon data collected from interviews with 328 young Black men from four of Toronto's most disadvantaged neighbourhoods to assess their perceptions of, and experiences with, the police. As in the research conducted by Neugebauer-Visano and James, Owusu-Bempah found that these young men reported frequent often fraught encounters with the police. For some of these young men, the sheer frequency of their contacts with police was perceived negatively, as Willie, a seventeen-year-old boy, explained: "I get stopped a lot – one night I was stopped four times in one night and questioned. It is annoying because they don't look at anyone else."[57] In addition to the frequency of stops, Owusu-Bempah found that many of the young men in his sample reported being stopped by the police under questionable grounds, often because they "fit the description." The following quotations from these young men are illustrative:

> Every time I get stopped it's bad. They always say that I fit a description even if I'm not even in the same area.
>
> I was at my house and the police busted in my back yard and said I matched the description.

> They said I looked like I stole something. They said if I matched their description they would have to restrain me.
>
> They said they were looking for someone. I fit [the] description.[58]

Black youth reporting that they are stopped by the police because they "fit the description" is not a new phenomenon.[59] Nor is a sentiment that police stops often signal a level of disrespect for the Black people who experience them. As Owusu-Bempah found in his research, this feeling of disrespect was a common experience for Black youth in Toronto: "If you live in my 'hood they always stop you, pat you down, ask you to empty your pockets and ask you where you are going. It is disrespectful."[60]

In recognizing the increasing presence of Black Canadians outside of urban areas, James's research has also examined the police experiences of Black youth residing in suburban areas in the GTA. Although many people move to the suburbs as a result of upward mobility and to shield their children from the "social ills" and violence associated with the inner city, James's findings suggest that stereotypical assumptions about Black people and Black youth continue to negatively influence their experience with the police in these environments.[61] Indeed, one young man interviewed as part of his research commented:

> Law enforcement also stereotypes us and assumes because we are Black we all partake in drugs etc. They also assume that all Black youth live in poverty and are struggling which is not true. People in the stores assume I am going to steal which is not true. I go out of my way to try not to look [like a] suspect. People are always staring at me thinking I am a thief.[62]

This sentiment is apparent in the interviews conducted with young Black men across the suburban neighbourhoods included in the study. As a result, James suggests that for Black youth, life in the suburbs is understandably no different from that in urban areas when it comes to the treatment they receive from law enforcement officials; the high levels of surveillance they experience and the treatment they receive from the police continue to reinforce notions of otherness and a lack of belonging.[63]

The results of these studies by academics are complemented by qualitative research undertaken on behalf of organizations such as the OHRC and the TPSB. In the early 2000s, the OHRC conducted a study to examine Ontario residents' experiences with racial profiling. Over eight hundred people, many of whom were Black, participated in the research and reported that they had been the victims of racial profiling. Respondents provided detailed descriptions of their experiences with racial profiling and conveyed detailed information about the negative impact of these experiences at both the individual and the community levels.[64] Similar stories were shared with researchers as part of public consultations conducted by the Ontario government's Roots of Youth Violence Inquiry. Black and Indigenous young people told the inquiry that they felt targeted by the police and that this unfair police treatment eroded their trust in the police and the justice system as a whole.[65]

Following the implementation of measures to regulate carding in Ontario, which came into force in 2017, the TPSB commissioned a broader qualitative study on the impact of the regulation on Torontonians' perceptions of, and experiences with, the TPS.[66] It was found that 11.3 percent of the respondents to their survey (which comprised 1,503 participants) had been carded by the police in Toronto, and, of these respondents, 41.8 percent were Black, 11.5 percent were white, 10.9 percent were Arab, and 10.9 percent were South Asian.[67] Finally, as part of an inquiry into police carding in Halifax, Nova Scotia, a series of consultations were held with members of the general public to gain insight into their experiences with this police practice. In total, over 250 community members, both youth and adult, shared their perspectives. A major theme that emerged from these consultations was anger and frustration over the high frequency of unwanted police stops and a belief that Black people were more likely to be targeted by the police than white people. The following quotations capture the sentiment of Black Haligonians and their experiences with police street checks:

> I have a son. He's twenty years old. He gets stopped by the police all the time. At least three or four times a month. He gets stopped because of his window tint, to check to see if the car is stolen, for his vehicle registration and for no reason at all. Interesting thing is, he has never been asked to change the tint because it ain't illegal. Once, when he questioned why the cop stopped him, he became a victim of police brutality. He's scared now. Now when the cops stop him, he immediately calls me, and I will stay on the phone and drive to where he is so I can protect him.
>
> Listen, when you're a Black man in Halifax, you're gunna get stopped by the police. I've been stopped all over. I've been stopped in Black communities and in White communities. In poor areas, in nice areas. In the city and out in the country. When I'm walking, when I'm driving. It don't

matter. If you're Black, you're automatically suspicious and you're gunna get stopped, you're gunna get questioned.

My son is twenty-nine years old. He was stopped while driving my new car after he left the library downtown. He has dreads. He was stopped in the middle of the day and he didn't do anything. He was not given a ticket or a warning. The cops didn't tell him why he was stopped. They just asked him a bunch of questions and checked his documents. This was all based on the colour of his skin.[68]

As Wortley notes, many participants reported feeling "powerless, angry, frustrated, embarrassed or humiliated" by their street check encounters, causing a great deal of stress and undermining the legitimacy of the police for those targeted and those around them.[69]

A final and important source of information on racial profiling and police stop-and-search practices comes from research with Black police officers, who occupy a unique position as both law enforcers and members of a group who experience a disproportionate amount of police attention. Following the publication of the initial *Toronto Star* series "Race Matters," then Toronto police chief Julian Fantino asked several senior Black officers to investigate how allegations of racial profiling were being perceived by Black members of the service. In response to this request, thirty-six Black officers met to discuss the issue of racial profiling. All of the participating officers agreed that racial profiling was a problem and that the criminal stereotyping of Black citizens was widespread within the TPS. The majority of respondents also reported that they themselves had been the victim of racial profiling. Three officers, in fact, reported that they had been stopped and questioned by the police on more than one occasion in the same week, and six officers reported that they had been stopped on more than twelve occasions in the same year. In a subsequent presentation of these findings to their fellow officers, the senior Black officers tasked with the investigation began with the statement: "We know that racial profiling exists."[70]

Similar research on the perceptions and experiences of Black police has recently been conducted with officers across the GTA. Owusu-Bempah conducted in-depth interviews with a non-random sample of fifty-one Black male police officers from five different Toronto-area police services.[71] He has argued that this sample can provide unique insights into the reality of racism within law enforcement because of the respondents' dual identities and experiences as both Black males within Canadian society and their experiences as police officers. Almost all the Black male police officers involved in this study reported that they had observed racial profiling and other forms of racially biased policing on the job and had worked with fellow officers who engaged in racial profiling and openly condoned the practice.[72] Indeed, the majority indicated that they themselves had been subjected to racial profiling on multiple occasions, even after becoming a police officer.[73] One of these officers recounted the following experience:

> I have been stopped as a result of racial profiling. I was driving a Mercedes at the time and I saw a cop. I was dropping off my daughter at a community centre in Jane and Finch. He saw me and drove into the parking lot of a community centre, I could see he was on his computer so he was probably running my plates. Then he went and parked across the street. I was anticipating that he was going to stop me and I was getting angry. As I pulled out of the community centre he pulled me over. I told him that I was a police officer and that I was unhappy. When I told him, he went red and walked away.[74]

In line with the experiences of members of the general public, the Black officers who said they had experienced unjustified police stops also reported feelings of anger and frustration. Furthermore, all agreed that such racial bias has had a negative impact on Canada's Black communities and fosters distrust between the police and Black people. Many of the officers argued that racially biased policing is a result of racial stereotypes that associate the Black population with both criminality and dangerousness.[75]

The Consequences of Unjust Stops and Perceived Mistreatment

Unnecessary and unwarranted police stops are not just a nuisance for the people who experience them. Indeed, there are a variety of social and psychological consequences that result from racial profiling and unjust police stop-and-search activities. As illustrated in the quotations provided earlier, individuals who believe they have been the victims of discriminatory policing often feel angry, frightened, and frustrated by their encounters. A growing body of research suggests that the residents of heavily policed neighbourhoods exhibit high levels of worry and anticipation caused by the possibility of being stopped by the police at any moment and the potential for criminalization and from the anger and resentment stemming from the perception of unfair treatment at the hands of the police.[76] Research has recently begun to systematically document the association between the experience of procedurally unjust policing and mental health. For example, Alyasah Ali Sewell and colleagues, examined the impact of aggressive policing at the neighbourhood level. They combined individual-level health data collected by the New York City Department of Health and Mental Hygiene with neighbourhood-level stop-and-frisk data from the New York Police Department.

The results of this study show that living in a neighbourhood with a higher occurrence of frisking was associated with experiencing a higher level of psychological distress for neighbourhood residents, while living in a neighbourhood with a higher density of force was associated with experiencing fewer feelings on measures such as sadness and effort.[77] However, further analysis indicates that these findings are gendered. Women were not affected by living in a neighbourhood where pedestrians are more likely to be frisked and where use of force is more concentrated.[78] Indeed, the use of force acted as a protective factor for women's mental health, perhaps by reducing fear of crime.[79] Conversely, their results show that men who live in neighbourhoods where pedestrians are more likely to be frisked were more likely to report feelings of nervousness and worthlessness as well as more psychological distress.[80] Likewise, in neighbourhoods where pedestrians were more likely to have force used against them, men were more likely to report feelings of nervousness, effort, and worthlessness and more severe psychological distress.[81]

The impact of aggressive policing on men's mental health specifically was examined by Amanda Geller and colleagues, who drew on the results of a survey conducted with 1,261 young men living in New York City. Their respondents were asked about their experiences with the police, whether and how many times they had been stopped, where the encounter took place, about the conduct of the officer during the stop, if they were frisked or searched, and whether the officer used abusive language or some kind of physical force against them.[82] The participants also reported their perceptions of procedural justice (the level of fairness) and answered questions designed to measure levels of anxiety and trauma (post-traumatic stress disorder [PTSD]).[83] Their findings suggest that young men who report police contact, and intrusive contact in particular, displayed higher levels of anxiety and trauma associated with their experiences.[84] Furthermore, while procedurally just treatment was associated with fewer negative mental health symptoms, the level of stop intrusion was predictive of PTSD – individuals experiencing the most intrusive stops displayed more symptoms associated with trauma.[85]

Geller and colleagues concluded by suggesting that the young men living in high-crime, disadvantaged neighbourhoods who are stopped by the police face the parallel disadvantage of compromised mental health.[86]

In addition to contributing to physical and mental health problems, racial profiling can also compound social disadvantage by increasing the chances of criminalization for those most targeted by the police. In *Paying the Price: The Human Cost of Racial Profiling,* the OHRC drew specific attention to the detrimental impact that racial profiling has on the life chances of Indigenous youth, a problem also experienced by other over-surveilled groups, such as Black Canadians.[87] Because Black people are exposed to higher levels of police surveillance, they are also much more likely to be caught breaking the law than are white people who engage in the same forms of law-violating behaviour. A survey of Toronto high school students, for example, found that 65 percent of the Black youth who reported selling drugs[88] said that they had been arrested in their lifetime, compared with just 35 percent of the white youth who reported selling drugs.[89]

Similarly, data recently published by the *Toronto Star* shows that between 2003 and 2013, Black people accounted for 25.5 percent of people arrested for cannabis possession by the TPS while accounting for 8.4 percent of Toronto's population.[90] Key here is that cannabis arrests increased in tandem with the practice of police carding in Toronto over this period.[91] As rates of carding increased, so did the number of cannabis possession arrests laid by the Toronto police. Therefore, race-based targeting may help explain why Black people are over-represented in arrests for cannabis possession even though empirical evidence suggests that rates of cannabis use are similar across racial groups.[92] A plethora of American research has illustrated how the war on drugs has fuelled the mass incarceration of Black and Latino individuals in the United States.[93] In sum, discriminatory police stop-and-search practices may contribute directly to the over-representation of Black people in Canada's criminal justice system.[94]

Furthermore, unjust policing practices can have a negative impact on the functioning of the criminal justice system and can contribute to criminal offending. Citizens' perceptions of police legitimacy (the extent to which they believe the police are a legitimate authority) are formed, in part, by the way in which the police treat members of the public during police-citizen encounters. If citizens are treated unfairly by the police or are stopped unjustly, they are less likely to view the police as a legitimate authority.[95] Perceptions of illegitimacy can have two important implications for criminal justice and society at large. First, the police/criminal justice system and the public have an interdependent relationship. The public is reliant on the system to fight crime and punish offenders, but the system is dependent on the public to bolster its legitimacy and to properly administer justice. Without confidence in the system, citizens become alienated and reluctant to co-operate with the police and the courts as victims, witnesses, complainants, and the accused. Such a situation can thwart the efforts of the police to control crime and maintain social order.[96]

Finally, there is growing concern that perceived injustice itself causes criminal behaviour.[97] Katheryn Russell, for example, argues that perceptions of criminal injustice can set the stage for criminal offending.[98] Indeed, recent research has demonstrated that early unwarranted police contact is crim-inogenic for Black youth. Juan Del Toro and colleagues, for example, found that among Black and Latino adolescent males (ninth and tenth grade), those who were stopped by the police reported more frequent delinquent behaviour six, twelve, and eighteen months later, independent of prior delinquency.[99] Thus, by unnecessarily stopping, searching, and questioning young Black men, the police may be contributing to crime rather than reducing it. This is an assertion that we should all take seriously.

Conclusion

As far as street-level bureaucrats go, the police wield an immense amount of power. On the least extreme end of the spectrum, they have the power to interrupt people in public as they go about their business. On the most ex-treme end of the spectrum, they can take life. While the latter is thankfully quite rare in Canada, for many, the former is not. As this chapter has dem-onstrated, Black people in Canada experience disproportionately high levels of police stops, and these stops have a detrimental impact at the individual, community, and societal level, ranging from exacerbating mental health problems to contributing to legal cynicism and feelings of social alienation. Given the important role of the police in our society and the immense impact of the exercise of their stop-and-search powers, we must seriously consider what limits are placed on them. This point was aptly articulated by eminent Canadian criminologists Anthony Doob and Rosemary Gartner, following their review of the literature on the effectiveness of police stops as a crime prevention tool:

> The police have a number of important roles to play in public safety and in the operation of the criminal justice system. The findings that we cite here which suggest that certain approaches to crime and public protection

either do not work or have overall negative impacts should be placed in this larger context. Perhaps the conclusion that one could come to that might be the least controversial would be the need to monitor and evaluate police policies related to street stops to ensure that the benefits outweigh the possible harm that could come from such interventions. This is the same conclusion that one could apply just as easily to medical or educational interventions as police interventions. An important point to remember is that one cannot conclude something is effective, just because assertions are made that it is. Data are important. And sometimes, the findings are complex. Certain kinds of activities of the police can have quite positive effects if the community is engaged in an appropriate fashion. But looking at the issue that we started with – street stops by the police of people who have not apparently committed an offence – it is quite clear that to us that is easy to exaggerate the usefulness of these stops, and hard to find data that supports the usefulness of continuing to carry them out. This is not to say that the police should not be encouraged to continue to talk to people on the street. But evidence that it is useful to stop, question, and/or search people and to record and store this information simply because the police and citizens "are there" appears to us to be substantially outweighed by convincing evidence of the harm of such practices both to the person subject to them and to the long term and overall relationship of the police to the community.[100]

The Doctrine as a One-Way Ratchet   **7**

Much of street-level policing stems from the ancillary powers doctrine, whereby courts create new police powers that fill legislative gaps.[1] Various police powers, including roadblocks, investigative detentions, stop-and-frisk searches, safety searches, sniffer-dog searches, and searches incident to arrest, were created by the Supreme Court of Canada rather than by Parliament.[2] Ancillary powers tell half the story about the scope of what the police can and cannot do lawfully. Statutes tell the other half. Legislation and case law authorize the police to stop vehicles at random, and courts have upheld this power as constitutional.[3] The *Criminal Code* confers the power to arrest individuals without warrant, while other provincial acts provide additional powers of arrest.[4] Then there is everything else that federal, provincial, and municipal law prohibit and that the police have the power to enforce. Examples include traffic offences (e.g., driving with a defective headlight, changing lanes without signalling) and other low-level offences that apply to pedestrians (e.g., jaywalking).[5] Municipal ordinances and bylaws, for their part, prohibit many other things, some well-known and others not (such as idling one's car, spitting on the ground, and so on).[6]

Police officers' investigatory powers and law enforcement powers, though, are largely discretionary.[7] Officers have statutory and common law duties to maintain public peace, prevent crime, and protect people and property from harm – police powers are a means to those ends.[8] Yet police powers are just that: powers. And police powers are largely discretionary.[9] When it comes to street-level policing, officers enjoy enormous discretion to determine whether they exercise a given power, which laws they enforce, and who they investigate, arrest, and charge.[10]

This chapter argues that the ancillary powers doctrine has shifted greater discretionary power to the police, while progressively limiting liberty and political equality – a process that resembles a one-way ratchet in criminal procedure.[11] Although the Supreme Court of Canada has created a litany of new police powers, neither Parliament nor the Court have imposed adequate transparency and oversight measures to govern these powers.[12] Furthermore, lawmakers and courts have failed to develop adequate public law and private law remedies for when these powers are exercised unlawfully.[13] The judiciary's treatment of police powers, therefore, incrementally chips away at individual liberty and equality. This too is half the story. The Court has upheld certain arbitrary police powers as constitutional, which has restricted liberty and equality even further.[14] The explosion in regulatory offences – traffic offences, municipal bylaws, and so on – has produced the same effect.[15] Together, common law police powers, arbitrary statutory powers, and the growth of regulatory offences all increase police power while restricting freedom and equality.

This chapter's core argument is that, as a one-way ratchet, the growth of police powers has resulted in domination, meaning that individuals are vulnerable to the unilateral threat of interference by police officers.[16] It explains why this domination in turn has bred distrust toward the police, disincentivized cooperation with law enforcement, and, ultimately, undermined the very law enforcement objectives that justify common law police powers. Since the courts have created police powers that limit individual liberty, yet Parliament has failed to constrain these powers, neither branch of government adequately protects individuals against domination by the police. The chapter concludes by explaining why individuals increasingly resort to informal police oversight mechanisms to protect themselves against domination from law enforcement.

Traditional Critiques of the Ancillary Powers Doctrine

The ancillary powers doctrine remains controversial within Canadian criminal law. One may defend its use for various reasons. Some contend that the ancillary powers doctrine is necessary because legislators cannot anticipate every police power in advance.[17] For this reason, courts should have the authority to recognize new law enforcement powers in certain circumstances. Others observe that in certain law enforcement contexts, especially those that involve technology, courts may create police powers more quickly and efficiently than lawmakers.[18] Interrelatedly, in contrast to statutory police powers, judicially created police powers may respond more precisely to a particular court case's factual matrix.

Yet, since its inception, scholars have criticized the ancillary powers doctrine on the following grounds.[19] First, some contend that it violates the separation of powers because unelected judges create new police powers that should be enacted by Parliament.[20] According to this view, the rise of the ancillary powers doctrine has modified the Supreme Court of Canada's role within criminal procedure.[21] More specifically, the Court has shifted away from its traditional counter-majoritarian function. Rather than safeguard individual rights, the Court creates police powers that endanger those rights.[22] Some observe that the judiciary also lacks the institutional competence to develop police powers in a manner that safeguards rights and interests adequately.[23] Others remark that the ancillary powers doctrine is undemocratic.[24] Judges are fewer in number and far less representative than lawmakers.[25] Judicially created police powers avoid most of the democratic process inherent to law-making.[26] Common law police powers involve less input from stakeholders.[27] Neither legislative committees nor subcommittees scrutinize these powers.[28] There is no democratic debate prior to creating a new ancillary police power.[29] In short, the ancillary powers doctrine and common law police powers are both undemocratic.

Second, some argue that the ancillary powers doctrine is inconsistent with the rule of law because judges create these powers after the fact and on an ad hoc basis.[30] When the Supreme Court of Canada creates a new police power, neither the police nor individuals know that such a power exists at the time that it is exercised.[31] The upshot: when exercising an ancillary power, officers cannot confirm that they are acting lawfully, while individuals cannot know the scope of the police's authority. The ancillary powers doctrine generates other rule-of-law concerns related to fair notice.[32] Since Parliament does not codify judicially created powers, the *Criminal Code* fails to inform individuals about what the police can and cannot do lawfully.[33]

Third, scholars posit that the Supreme Court of Canada has failed to consider the prospect of discrimination and racial profiling when it creates new police powers.[34] As a result, the Court has failed to incorporate adequate transparency and oversight mechanisms that aim to prevent, address, and remedy racial profiling.[35] The state does not require police officers to document the exercise of judicially created police powers, such as frisk searches and investigative detentions.[36] Nor does the state require police forces to collect and publish data regarding the ethnicity of individuals against whom these powers are exercised.[37] To be clear, scholars and human rights commissions have conducted empirical research that highlights how judicially created police powers are exercised disproportionately against Indigenous and racialized persons.[38] Yet we lack accurate data about how these powers are exercised disparately within certain police forces, within certain local communities, and on the provincial and national level.[39]

Ancillary Powers as a One-Way Ratchet

The ancillary powers doctrine has heavily influenced the development of Canadian criminal procedure. Many routinely exercised police powers have been created by the courts rather than by Parliament.[40] The Supreme Court of Canada has stated that Parliament has the authority to abrogate or modify common law police powers.[41] Yet, since its inception, Parliament has generally not codified common law police powers or altered them.[42] Furthermore, despite Parliament's inaction, the Supreme Court of Canada has created more and more police powers over time.[43] Within the past several decades, in the vast majority of Supreme Court of Canada decisions where the state has invoked a new common law police power, the Court has created it.[44] Indeed, Richard Jochelson and colleagues have shown that between 2002 and 2017, the Court created a new common law police power in every single Supreme Court of Canada decision where one was invoked.[45]

There are various reasons why the ancillary powers doctrine disincentivizes Parliament from codifying, limiting, or abrogating common law police powers.[46] First, the judicial creation of police powers creates path dependency.[47] Namely, Parliament relies on the Supreme Court of Canada to create police powers because it has done so for the past forty years.[48] The Court, in turn, relies on itself to create police powers because of the force of precedent (and because the justices know that Parliament will not legislate in this area).[49] Second, since the Court only creates police powers that are presumably constitutional, there is no reason for Parliament to modify a common law police power that meets the Constitution's requirements.[50] Furthermore, insofar as a common law police power fulfills crime control objectives, there is no reason why Parliament would abrogate it. Third, compared to the traditional legislative process, the ancillary powers doctrine involves less constitutional friction. The doctrine circumvents many of the negative externalities inherent to both the legislative process and the process of constitutional dialogue. Instead of enacting laws through a democratic process, courts provide a more efficient pathway that avoids democratic debate, political disagreement, legislative drafting, and the risk that the law will be struck down as unconstitutional.[51] It is more efficient for judges to create police powers than for lawmakers to enact them. The undemocratic nature of these powers, though, is precisely what makes their creation more efficient. Fourth, the ancillary powers doctrine diminishes the prospect of political blowback associated with police reform.[52] Various stakeholders, including civil society groups, individuals and communities, lawyers, and opposition parties, may harshly criticize legislatively enacted police powers. Politicians may believe that this type of flak may harm the prospect of re-election. None of this looks good for politicians. Yet, unlike lawmakers, judges are less democratically accountable and cannot be elected out of office. In some respects, the ancillary powers doctrine insulates lawmakers from political attacks surrounding legislatively enacted police powers.

Notice the cumulative effect of the Supreme Court's creation of new police powers and Parliament's failure to constrain them. More specifically, the ancillary powers doctrine results in a one-way ratchet, whereby courts expand police powers in a manner that increasingly limits individual freedom.[53] When the Court decides that the police can exercise some new power, individuals are no longer protected against interference that stems from that power.[54] To illustrate this point, consider the Supreme Court of Canada's interpretation of what makes searches and detentions unlawful.[55] Searches and detentions are unlawful in three contexts: when they are not authorized by law; when they are authorized by an arbitrary law; or when they are conducted unreasonably.[56] When the Court creates a new police power, it authorizes some type of police action that was not previously authorized by law: it transforms previously unlawful searches and detentions into lawful ones.[57] Conversely, whereas individuals were previously protected against certain interferences, the Court removes that protection.[58] This explains why each new ancillary power chips away at an individual's sphere of liberty.

Ancillary Powers and Remedial Mechanisms

There is another reason why the ancillary powers doctrine functions as a one-way ratchet. While the Supreme Court of Canada has created new police powers, it has not increased the scope of public law and private law remedies for police misconduct.[59] As a result, the ancillary powers doctrine limits freedom without providing sufficient remedies when individuals' rights are violated.[60] Several examples illustrate this point. Consider damages under the *Canadian Charter of Rights and Freedoms* first.[61] The term "*Charter* damages" implies that courts award damages for constitutional rights violations in accordance with section 24(1) of the *Charter*.[62] This remedial mechanism was first recognized in the decision *Vancouver (City) v Ward*.[63] In that decision, the police mistakenly believed that the plaintiff, Ward, would throw a pie at the prime minister.[64] The Royal Canadian Mounted Police unlawfully strip-searched the plaintiff in violation of the section 8 *Charter* right to be free from unreasonable searches and seizures.[65] At issue was whether section 24(1) of the *Charter* – the provision that allows courts of competent jurisdiction to accord appropriate and just remedies – authorizes compensation for constitutional rights violations. The Supreme Court of Canada decided that section 24(1) of the *Charter* allows individuals to recover *Charter* damages and awarded Ward five thousand dollars.[66]

The *Ward* decision is notable for the two following reasons, both of which highlight some drawbacks to *Charter* damages for police misconduct. First, in *Ward*, the accused was subject to a particularly demeaning type of search – a strip-search – that the Court observed is often "humiliating, degrading, and traumatic."[67] Second, the Court established the monetary amount of five thousand dollars of *Charter* damages for unlawful strip-searches.[68] Notice how the Court set a relatively low quantum of *Charter* damages for a relatively invasive search that the Court characterized as a "serious injury" but not "at the high end of the spectrum."[69] One of the major drawbacks to the Court's approach in *Ward* is that it produced a powerful anchoring effect in constitutional adjudication.[70] The "anchoring effect" is one of the most pervasive and robust cognitive biases.[71] When a set numerical value – the anchor – is disclosed to an individual, they will rely heavily on that anchor when making a decision.[72] More specifically, they will subconsciously appeal to the anchor's value as their decision's starting point and then adjust that value above or below that anchor.[73] All other things being equal, when an anchor is disclosed to a decision-maker, they will select a value that falls closer to the anchor than if no such anchor was disclosed.[74] Scholars have shown that the anchoring effect influences how courts calculate damages.[75] For instance, judges award a higher value of punitive damages when the law imposes a higher ceiling on them.[76]

The same is true for how courts calculate *Charter* damages. Since *Ward*, courts tend to accord relatively low *Charter* damage awards, especially in contexts where the police misconduct was judged to be less serious than the strip-search in *Ward*.[77] In quantifying damages, judges appeal to the anchor disclosed in *Ward*. Police interventions that are deemed less invasive than *Ward* tend to fall below five thousand dollars, whereas those that are deemed more invasive fall above five thousand dollars.[78] Yet, in both contexts, damages are still calculated by reference to *Ward*. The anchor established in *Ward* – and the force of precedent – explains why the quantum of *Charter* damages remains low. To be clear, the quantum of *Charter* damages may well exceed the five-thousand-dollar amount established in *Ward*. In some contexts, courts may award a higher amount.[79] Yet the amount of *Charter* damages tends to approximate the five-thousand-dollar amount set out in *Ward*, especially if the police's intervention is less intrusive than a strip-search. The relatively low quantum of these damages, however, can disincentivize individuals from bringing section 24(1) Charter damage claims against the police.[80]

Second, tort liability has evolved little since the rise of ancillary police powers. Compared to the number of new police powers that courts create, judges have devised few new torts to control police misconduct. The Supreme Court of Canada expressly rejected a tort of discrimination that would apply to instances of discrimination.[81] The Court observed that human rights tribunals were a more appropriate forum for such claims.[82] There are other limitations to tort liability for police misconduct. The value of civil damages for police misconduct remains relatively low, including in contexts where courts award punitive damages.[83] Insofar as individuals conduct a cost-benefit analysis, the potential legal costs of hiring a lawyer and bringing a claim may exceed the potential award.[84] Similar to *Charter* damages, the low quantum of tort damages may dissuade individuals from bringing tort actions against the police.[85]

Third, the exclusionary rule – section 24(2) of the *Charter* – also tends to provide little recourse for some ancillary police powers that are exercised unlawfully.[86] Section 24(2) of the *Charter* authorizes courts to exclude unconstitutionally obtained evidence.[87] Yet when police misconduct yields no evidence, there is nothing for courts to exclude.[88] Many street-level police encounters fit this paradigm. When police officers frisk search someone and find no evidence, section 24(2) of the Charter does nothing. So too in contexts where officers conduct an illegal traffic stop that yields no evidence.

Lastly, despite the prevalence of racial profiling and discrimination in the criminal justice system, the section 15 *Charter* right to equality plays virtually no role within criminal law and procedure.[89] *Ontario (Attorney General) v G* is one of the few Supreme Court of Canada cases where an accused successfully brought a section 15 *Charter* application.[90] In this case, the accused was found to be not criminally responsible for a sexual offence.[91] The law required individuals who were convicted or found not criminally responsible of certain sexual offences to be registered in a sex-offender database.[92] The accused argued that the applicable law violated section 15 of the *Charter* because it discriminated against individuals with mental illness.[93] The Court agreed.[94] This is a positive development. But the factual matrix in *G.* is far-removed from the type of discrimination that occurs in the criminal law's daily administration.[95] Indeed, even in Supreme Court of Canada decisions that have dealt directly with the problem of discrimination or abusive policing practices – such as *R v Le* and *R v Ahmad* – section 15 of the *Charter* played no role whatsoever.[96]

Liberty, Equality, and Domination

The ancillary powers doctrine, therefore, functions as one-way ratchet for two interrelated reasons. First, police powers have expanded in a manner that increasingly limits liberty, and, second, courts have not developed remedial mechanisms to prevent and rectify police misconduct adequately.[97] For these reasons, the ancillary powers doctrine generates profound implications for liberty and equality. On its face, the ancillary powers doctrine appears objectionable because of its impact on negative freedom (or negative liberty – the terms are used interchangeably). The term "negative freedom" implies freedom from interference by others.[98] According to the negative conception of liberty, an individual is free so long as they experience no concrete interference by others.[99] Negative freedom has deep roots in the classical liberal tradition, and it is embedded deeply within Canadian constitutional law.[100] The Supreme Court of Canada has observed that the *Charter*'s legal rights are primarily negative in nature, meaning that they provide freedom from concrete interference by the state.[101]

The problem seems to be that the ancillary powers doctrine reduces one's sphere of negative freedom and that individuals may lack a remedy when the police unlawfully interfere with their rights. Furthermore, the disparate exercise of police powers against Indigenous and racialized persons undermines political equality. This account, however, understates the extent to which common law police powers limit liberty and equality, especially when considered against the backdrop of statutory police powers. The republican theory of liberty better captures why the judicial expansion of police power undermines both freedom and equality.[102] To be clear, the theory is conceptually distinct from the Republican political party in the United States.[103] Instead, the republican theory of freedom (or republicanism) refers to the era of the Roman republic when the theory first emerged.[104] Whereas negative freedom implies non-interference, republicanism construes freedom as non-domination.[105] The term "non-domination" is broader than non-interference and entails that an individual is protected against the threat of unilateral interference by others.[106] Individuals enjoy non-domination when others lack the unilateral power to interfere with them.[107] As some scholars suggest, non-domination implies a form of "secured negative liberty."[108]

There is a fundamental distinction between negative freedom and republican freedom – a distinction that illustrates why the judicial and statutory expansion of police powers is objectionable. Negative freedom theory posits that interference is necessary to undermine liberty.[109] In contrast, republicanism recognizes the prospect of domination without interference.[110] The notion of "domination without interference" means that an individual is not free when others have the unilateral power to interfere with them, even if no actual interference occurs.[111] Domination without interference undermines liberty because individuals will adopt various liberty-limiting coping mechanisms to avoid concrete interference.[112] As Philip Pettit notes, individuals may become deferential to others or kowtow to them in order to escape interference.[113] Or they may adapt their preferences to those of the dominating party so as to avoid interference.[114] As Pettit observes, the conception of freedom as non-interference leads to absurd results.[115] Namely, individuals who live under the complete control of others are portrayed as free, provided that they experience no concrete interference by the dominating party.[116]

Negative liberty and republican liberty are also different in how they conceptualize the extent to which one enjoys freedom. In assessing one's freedom to do something, negative liberty theory posits that interference is present or absent.[117] When an individual experiences interference, they lack freedom. When they do not experience interference, they are free.[118] This binary understanding of freedom is particularly attractive for constitutional law, which is tasked with deciding whether rights have been infringed or not and with determining the appropriate remedy. Republican freedom, on the other hand, provides a more nuanced account of liberty. It recognizes that domination can exist across a spectrum.[119] Republican scholars note that domination can exist in various levels of intensity, occur in some settings but not in others, and arise in certain relationships but not in others.[120] Domination is exemplified by relationships that involve asymmetrical power dynamics.[121] Employees who can be fired at will are subject to domination by their employers.[122] An abusive spouse also subjects their partner to domination.[123] And when police officers wield the power to interfere with individuals at will – for instance, by pulling them over when they have done nothing wrong – individuals experience domination too.[124]

Notice how, in all of these contexts, it is clear to both parties – and to any external observer – which party wields unilateral power and which party is unilaterally subject to it.[125] In the eyes of republican theorists, domination has a subjective, inter-subjective, and objective component.[126] Subjectively, the dominating party understands that they wield unilateral power over the dominated party.[127] Conversely, the latter knows that they are vulnerable to the threat of interference by the former.[128] Inter-subjectively, the dominated party and the dominating party are both aware of the asymmetrical power dynamic between them, which in turn shapes their interactions with one another.[129] Objectively, individuals within society understand which party wields a unilateral power of interference and which party is vulnerable to its exercise.[130] At their root, these types of asymmetrical power dynamics – and the subjective, inter-subjective, and objective elements of domination – elucidate how unfreedom undermines equality.[131] In the republican tradition, individuals who are unfree lack political equality, and individuals who lack political equality are unfree.[132]

Republican scholars are particularly concerned with two features that tend to characterize domination, both of which are relevant to understanding how the judicial expansion of police powers limits liberty and equality. First, they observe that threats of interference are particularly objectionable when they involve an element of arbitrariness, meaning that the dominating party can interfere at will with the dominated party.[133] Second, republican theorists highlight the evils associated with unchecked threats of interference, meaning that there are inadequate safeguards to protect individuals against domination and to provide remedies when they experience interference.[134] As republican scholars point out, the threat of arbitrary interference generates certain psychological harms that negative freedom theorists tend to overlook.[135] Namely, individuals may become hypervigilant as a result of domination since they generally do not know – and cannot anticipate – when interference will occur.[136] The prospect of interference produces anxiety, and individuals may alter their routines, plans, and habits to ward off interference.[137] The broader republican conception of freedom as non-domination, therefore, captures certain limitations to negative liberty theory.

Common Law Police Powers and Domination

The ancillary powers doctrine – and judicially authorized police powers – contributes to domination for several reasons. First, individuals frequently lack remedies when the police infringe their rights – realities that highlight the unchecked nature of many police encounters.[138] Many ancillary powers are exercised in low-visibility contexts.[139] In the vast majority of contexts where police officers pull over a vehicle, frisk search an individual, or detain someone for investigative questioning, the intervention's lawfulness will never be scrutinized by a court.[140] Even in contexts where individuals do bring civil claims, it may be very difficult to prove police misconduct, especially in contexts of racial profiling.[141] For this reason, many discriminatory or unlawful police interventions go unremedied. Furthermore, individuals may be discouraged from bringing civil claims against the police given the high costs and low rewards.[142] Together, the low-visibility nature of police encounters, their lack of concrete judicial oversight, and the economic forces that dissuade civil claims against the police all highlight how the exercise of certain police powers goes unchecked.

Second, the exercise of ancillary police powers exemplifies the core features of domination. Police encounters involve an asymmetric power dynamic between officers and individuals. Furthermore, this asymmetric power dynamic involves the subjective, inter-subjective, and objective elements that typify domination.[143] The power differential between officers and individuals is obvious to both parties and to outside observers.[144] The potential risks of disobeying the police are also clear. The threat of the use of force lies behind every police interaction.[145] Non-compliance – real or perceived – carries a real risk of escalation, humiliation, and use of force.[146] Like in other domains of life, individuals also adopt coping mechanisms to avoid more serious forms of coercion during police encounters.[147] When approached by the police, individuals may behave deferentially, answer questions when there is no duty to do so, and remain with the police when they have the right to leave.[148]

Third, the Supreme Court of Canada's more recent case law alludes to the problem of domination.[149] In *Le,* the Supreme Court of Canada revisited the applicable test for investigative detention – an ancillary police power first created in *R v Mann*.[150] The majority of the Court noted that racialized persons are over-policed and subject to a disproportionate number of unlawful proactive police encounters: traffic stops, investigative detentions, frisk searches, arrests, and criminal charges.[151] Given the experiences that racialized communities have with the police, the majority of the Court noted that some racialized persons may feel as if they have no choice but to comply with the police in certain contexts.[152] Similarly, in *R v Grant,* Justice Ian Binnie stated that certain racialized persons may feel unfree to leave police interactions as officers may interpret their choice to leave as evasive and detain them accordingly.[153] The republican concept of domination encapsulates how certain individuals experience police encounters and how they may engage in certain coping mechanisms to avoid graver interference.

Fourth, in addition to creating new police powers, the Supreme Court of Canada has also authorized police officers to exercise certain powers arbitrarily – powers that exemplify the problem of domination.[154] The police power to conduct random traffic stops is an example. Building on its prior jurisprudence in *Dedman v The Queen*, the Supreme Court of Canada upheld the statutory random traffic stop power as constitutional in *R v Ladouceur*.[155] The Court explained that random traffic stops are lawful provided that the officers can justify them by one of three grounds: verifying the driver's licence; assessing the vehicle's mechanical fitness; and evaluating the driver's sobriety.[156] Although random traffic stops subject individuals to arbitrary detentions, the Court noted that these stops are justified in a free and democratic society in order to reduce driving-related harms and fatalities.[157] Today, officers can pull over vehicles when the driver has broken no law whatsoever; officers can exercise that power at will. Since officers need only to invoke one of these three grounds to lawfully stop any driver, they may invoke these justifications after the fact, which also elucidates the arbitrary nature of these encounters.[158]

Fifth, the cumulative effect of common law police powers, arbitrary legislative powers, and statutory prohibitions make individuals particularly vulnerable to interference. Officers can conduct random traffic stops. However, they also have the power to pull over drivers for a litany of traffic-related offences, which even prudent drivers tend to violate when observed for long enough by the police.[159] Together, an officer's lawful authority to pull over drivers for both lawful and unlawful conduct increases the arbitrary nature of traffic stops. Suppose, though, that an individual attempts to challenge a traffic stop's lawfulness, even though there may be little evidence that gives rise to an inference of impropriety. Their claim will likely fail if the driver committed a traffic-related offence or if the officer can provide sufficient justifications for why they conducted the random traffic stop. Here, too, the concrete interference with one's liberty goes unchecked.

In response to these arguments, one might contend that the ancillary powers doctrine – and common law police powers – also mitigates domination. The argument goes something like this. Some republican scholars posit that the criminal law aims to reduce domination.[160] According to this view, criminalization aims to protect individuals against domination by others by prohibiting conduct that harms, threatens, or endangers individuals or their property.[161] Police powers are a means to that end by empowering officers to prevent, repress, and eventually solve crimes that exemplify domination. Police powers, however, may still generate significant domination in certain respects even if they reduce it in others. For instance, proactive police encounters are exercised frequently against innocent persons.[162] The discriminatory enforcement of police powers results in physical and psychological harm, estrangement, and social exclusion.[163] Proactive police powers also instrumentalize innocent persons by treating the violation of their interests as an acceptable sacrifice in the pursuit of public safety.[164] The disparate exercise of police powers treats individuals' shared interests in dignity, liberty, and equality as less important.

Domination and Distrust

Unsurprisingly, domination breeds distrust of the police. This distrust undermines certain law enforcement objectives that justify ancillary police powers. There are several reasons why the cumulative impact of statutory and common law police powers decrease trust in law enforcement. First, since individuals cannot ascertain whether the police have acted unlawfully in certain contexts, they may infer that the police have abused their authority. Random vehicle stops are an example. Officers do not overtly state that they pulled over a vehicle or detained a person based on discriminatory motives.[165] Individuals thus assess the legitimacy of police action based on various factors: the officer's demeanour; the police officer's justification for the encounter; whether the officer treated the individual fairly and respectfully; and so on.[166] Yet empirical research shows that in many contexts, individuals do not believe the officer's justifications for a traffic stop.[167] In Halifax, for instance, survey studies showed that 70 percent of Black survey respondents did not believe the reasons that officers provided for the stop.[168] The Ontario Human Rights Commission conducted a survey, held focus groups, and received written submissions regarding individuals' encounters with the police in that province.[169] The results showed that Indigenous and racialized persons who were stopped by the police reported that they felt as if they were racially profiled by officers who stopped them as part of a "random" or "routine check."[170] Distrust stems from being subject to domination in the form of arbitrary, unchecked, and discriminatory interference.[171]

Second, individuals may believe that officers have abused their authority even when they have acted lawfully.[172] Scholars have shown that police officers and individuals evaluate the legitimacy of police powers differently, especially in contexts when courts do not adjudicate a police intervention's lawfulness.[173] Police officers tend to evaluate the legitimacy of their interventions in terms of "legality," meaning whether they exercised their power lawfully.[174] Individuals, on the other hand, evaluate the legitimacy of police action in terms of bounded authority.[175] The notion of "bounded authority" implies that individuals assess the legitimacy of police action according to their beliefs about the appropriate scope of police authority and applicable social norms.[176] Though the law authorizes the police to conduct frisk searches in certain contexts (e.g., their legality), individuals may construe these interventions as illegitimate in light of their beliefs about the appropriate limits of police authority (e.g., their bounded authority).[177] Bounded authority explains why individuals may perceive police action as arbitrary, discriminatory, and illegitimate even when it is lawful.[178]

There are various reasons why individuals view police interventions through the lens of bounded authority rather than legality. For one, in certain contexts, individuals may lack sufficient legal knowledge about the lawfulness of police action.[179] Furthermore, in many cases, there is no legal adjudication of the lawfulness of police action (recall the low visibility of many police encounters).[180] Through bounded authority, individuals may rely on their own perception of legitimacy – or that of their friends, family, or other community members without in-depth legal knowledge – to gauge the legitimacy of police action.[181] This explains why even lawful police encounters generate distrust when individuals perceive that officers wield arbitrary power over them.

Third, bad experiences with the police produce a disproportionately negative impact on trust in law enforcement.[182] Wesley Skogan's empirical research shows that all other things being equal, the effects of negative police encounters can be roughly four to fourteen times more impactful than positive ones.[183] Certain types of negative police encounters are roughly six times more impactful than positive ones.[184] Even positive traffic stops, however, tend to generate few statistically positive effects.[185] It is a mistake, though, to conclude that negative police encounters only impact those who are directly subject to them. Research studies show that an individual's trust in the police is shaped through both their personal and vicarious experiences.[186] Since individuals share their negative police experiences broadly with others, even a single bad police encounter can generate wide-ranging effects within communities.[187] This is particularly true for highly mediatized and emotionally salient instances of police misconduct.[188] Individuals may feel that they are also vulnerable to discriminatory police conduct because of their family members, friends, or acquaintances' negative experiences with the police.[189] An individual may reason that they are vulnerable to the same threat of arbitrary interference – to the same domination – that others experience, and this recognition characteristically breeds cynicism toward law enforcement.[190]

The Supreme Court of Canada, however, largely overlooks how both common law and statutory police powers result in domination that corrodes trust in law enforcement.[191] This is surprising given how the notion of "public confidence" pervades many other areas of the law.[192] For instance, public confidence plays a central role in the exclusion of evidence,[193] the law of bail,[194] the right to a trial within a reasonable time,[195] and the principle of judicial independence.[196] Yet in most decisions where the Supreme Court of Canada has created a new police power (e.g., investigative detentions, stop-and-frisk searches, and even strip-searches) or upheld a statutory power's constitutionality (e.g., the random traffic stop power), the Court did not consider how these powers could damage confidence in the police.[197]

The relationship between domination and distrust matters. Even lawful police interventions can demean human dignity, invade privacy, and humiliate individuals.[198] Beyond these harms, though, common law police powers may undermine some of the objectives that justify their existence.[199] The ancillary powers doctrine is justified on the basis that the police are pursuing valid law enforcement objectives: preserving peace, preventing crime, and safeguarding people and property from harm.[200] Yet police require the public's cooperation in order to achieve these objectives and, ultimately, to prevent and solve crimes effectively.[201] Individuals who distrust the police are less willing to call 911, report crimes, accept police authority as legitimate, and cooperate with police investigations.[202] The judiciary's expansion of discretionary police powers – and the domination they produce – can undercut the cooperation that is necessary to prevent and solve crimes optimally.[203]

Public Institutions, Self-Help, and Non-Domination

The evolution of police powers results in an undesirable constitutional dynamic – one that has led to a rise of informal police oversight mechanisms. In the realm of criminal procedure, Parliament and courts have largely failed to protect individuals against police-related domination. This failure has given rise to self-help measures that strive to prevent, expose, and remedy police misconduct. In order to better understand the rise of informal police oversight measures, consider how criminal law and procedure are typically portrayed.[204] Parliament enacts laws through a democratic process that reflects majoritarian preferences.[205] In many cases, legislatures and the police overlook the rights and interests of the political minority who lack sufficient political clout.[206] Courts exert a counter-majoritarian role that protects the political minority against the tyranny of the majority.[207] When an individual's rights are violated, courts provide redress. They strike down unconstitutional laws, suppress unconstitutionally obtained evidence, issue stays of proceedings, and order *Charter* damages.[208] Lawmakers and police officers get the message and adjust their conduct accordingly.[209] The law then evolves through constitutional dialogue as Parliament enacts new laws that conform, or not, to the Supreme Court of Canada's decisions.[210] The process then repeats. Consider how this type of constitutional dialogue pushes Parliament to improve its laws by ensuring that they meet the Constitution's requirements, respect individuals' rights, or safeguard people's interests.

However, when it comes to street-level police powers, most of this dialogic process never happens.[211] Leaving aside the Supreme Court of Canada's early jurisprudence that required Parliament to create certain warrants in order for police action to be lawful, there is little constitutional dialogue related to street-level law enforcement.[212] This creates two serious problems. First, the absence of constitutional dialogue in street-level policing means that neither Parliament nor courts will refine these powers over time. As a result, the branches of government will not engage in the typical back-and-forth process that can safeguard rights optimally.[213] Since judges create common law powers, these powers will not be struck down as unconstitutional, refined by Parliament, and rescrutinized by courts. Since judges determine whether police powers are constitutional, Parliament has no reason to impose stricter requirements than what the Court mandates, especially if it generates political risks.[214] Second, since Parliament and courts avoid constitutional dialogue related to street-level police powers, individuals cannot rely on these branches of government to control police misconduct effectively. As previous sections have shown, courts impose weak transparency and oversight mechanisms on the police.[215] Furthermore, the judiciary has failed to provide sufficient public and private law remedies to address police impropriety.[216] Parliament, for its part, will not touch common law police powers with a ten-foot pole.

Yet if courts create police powers that give rise to domination and legislators do nothing to constrain these powers, to whom should individuals turn for protection? In some cases, they turn to human rights tribunals.[217] Increasingly, though, individuals turn to themselves and to the media in order to counteract domination.[218] Since formal legal mechanisms fail to control police misconduct adequately, individuals develop their own informal mechanisms to achieve this aim.[219] Two examples illustrate this point. First, consider the rise of counter-surveillance to mitigate domination. The term "counter-surveillance" refers to contexts where individuals film the police in order to ensure greater transparency in police interactions and to promote the accountability of officers.[220] In many senses, counter-surveillance maximizes the visibility of street-level police encounters that are otherwise unseen by the judiciary and by the broader public.[221] When officers are filmed, they are made aware of the risks of behaving arbitrarily, the importance of acting lawfully, and the necessity of drafting reports accurately.[222] Empirical research studies also show that officers behave differently when they are aware that they are being filmed.[223] Additionally, the rise of smartphones and their video-recording capabilities provide highly probative evidence in formal legal proceedings.[224] Counter-surveillance, therefore, may provide strong checks and balances against domination.

Second, there are cop-watching organizations where individuals form groups that "patrol their neighbourhoods, monitor police conduct, and create videos of what they see."[225] Although cop-watching groups are prevalent in US cities, they also exist in Canadian cities.[226] Historically, cop-watching groups have emerged as a means to protect marginalized persons against over-policing and discrimination.[227] Jocelyn Simonson notes that counter-surveillance and cop watching are different.[228] Counter-surveillance tends to be a reactive response to police action in a particular case.[229] Cop watching, on the other hand, aims to deter over-policing practices, de-escalate police interventions, and document police encounters.[230] These three aims – deterrence, de-escalation, and documentation – endeavour to provide informal protection against domination precisely because existing legal mechanisms fail to do so.

Viewed this way, self-help mechanisms are a response to the judiciary's tendency to expand police powers while constraining freedom and political equality. At their root, informal over-sight mechanisms aim to counter the arbitrariness and unchecked power that exemplify domination in street-level policing.

Conclusion

This chapter has argued that together, the ancillary powers doctrine, judicially authorized police powers, and regulatory offences result in a one-way ratchet in criminal procedure. It has explained how this tendency stems from two phenomena. First, the Supreme Court of Canada expanded the scope of police powers in a manner that restricts liberty and equality. But it did not impose adequate transparency and oversight mechanisms on law enforcement. Second, while expanding police powers, the Court failed to develop new public and private law remedies to prevent and rectify police impropriety. This chapter also has shown how the ancillary powers doctrine increases domination and undermines political equality, which in turn decreases trust in the police. It has demonstrated why Parliament and courts fail to protect adequately individuals against domination by the police. Its conclusion provides an account of why individuals develop their own informal self-help mechanisms to protect themselves against domination.

Going forward, how can Parliament and the Supreme Court of Canada better protect individuals' republican freedom and political equality? As a first step, the Court could abandon the ancillary powers doctrine that has altered the judiciary's role within Canadian criminal procedure.[231] The Court could also send the following strong message to Parliament: so long as common law police powers lack adequate transparency and oversight measures, these powers are constitutionally suspect.[232] Additionally, the Supreme Court of Canada could overrule its prior decisions that authorize arbitrary police action, such as random vehicle stops, and that are prone to unchecked interference.[233] This approach is beneficial for three reasons: first, it can re-establish the Supreme Court's counter-majoritarian role in criminal procedure;[234] second, it can incentivize Parliament to codify and legislate street-level police powers;[235] and, third, it can catalyze a new era of constitutional dialogue related to police powers – dialogue that can better safeguard individuals against domination.[236]

This approach would also address some of the fundamental objections to the ancillary power doctrine: its inconsistency with the separation of powers, its conflict with the rule of law, and its tendency to create powers that are enforced disparately and discriminatorily.[237] To be clear, even if this proposal is implemented, it will not – and cannot – eliminate discrimination and racial profiling in the justice system. Yet Parliament and the judiciary can still alleviate some of the most objectionable aspects of the ancillary powers doctrine and its associated police powers, both of which contribute to domination. Furthermore, to counteract the growth of police powers in criminal procedure, the Supreme Court of Canada could broaden the scope of public and private law remedies for police misconduct. Various options are available, many of which have been discussed at length elsewhere.[238] The Court, for instance, could expand section 15 of the *Charter*'s role in criminal law and procedure, increase the quantum of damages for police impropriety, and authorize class action proceedings for systemic wrongdoing by the police, among others.[239] By addressing the features that give rise to a one-way ratchet in criminal procedure, Parliament and the Court could better counteract domination in policing.

Conclusion

As can be seen, the ancillary powers doctrine has had a profound impact on Canadian police and society. It has helped shape policing in Canada and, importantly, has received mixed reviews as to its utility in the common law. Chapter 1 considered police powers in their infancy – how these powers were shaped and understood over the course of centuries. It also proposed the idea that policing is a necessary part of the social fabric. Indeed, Chapter 1 put forth the idea that police powers are a natural consequence of living in close proximity to one another. The role of the constable is derived from centuries of jurisprudence and legal edicts. From a historical perspective, it appears as though the constable represents the relationship that exists between the community and police. Chapter 1 suggested that this relationship is vital and perpetually redefined, depending on the needs of society at a particular moment in time. Thus, legislation can only go so far in articulating the full extent of police powers. The common law has been and will be a key part of developing police powers. Policing, after all, can be characterized as discretionary and fluid. It requires quick decision-making and fast action when circumstances create an impetus for such action.

However, Chapter 1 also highlighted how policing practices have undeniably brushed up against the rights and values of society. As a consequence, the common law has recognized the inalienable rights that are bestowed upon citizens of a democracy. History shows us that these rights are perpetually threatened by policing practices. Judges have continuously grappled with the line that must be drawn between the state's interests and the liberty and property rights of the individual. The historical overview in Chapter 1 presented a view of the police that is multifaceted and prone to change. In prior eras, the police have served as tax collectors, firefighters, and community watchmen, among other things. In today's modern police force, an officer's duties and powers are tied to police work – that is, the prevention and investigation of crime. Yet the officer's role of serving the community has not changed. Common law jurisprudence from England and Ireland shows us that an officer has an obligation to protect the public. Police powers, it is noted in *Humphries v Connor,* are an obligation that binds the officer to see that "the peace is preserved and that he is to do everything that is necessary for that purpose."[1]

But when does an officer's obligations toward preserving the peace, preventing crime, and protecting lives and property infringe unjustifiably on an individual's rights? Since the advent of the ancillary powers doctrine, jurists have grappled with this question. Chapter 2 explained that the *Canadian Charter of Rights and Freedoms* stands between unfettered state power and our civil liberties.[2] Its framers found the need to constitutionalize various rights and freedoms to create checks and balances on state conduct, such as the policing of the community. Thus, Chapter 1's emphasis on the relationship between the police and the community is complicated in post-*Charter* jurisprudence as courts continue their reliance on the ancillary powers doctrine. Chapter 2 showed us how the *Waterfield* test has been utilized to expand police powers, notwithstanding the *Charter*'s protective force over our civil liberties.[3] Whether police conduct that is reviewed is reasonable and necessary became the refrain in the Supreme Court's articulation of common law police powers. The *Dedman* Court laid the groundwork for the consistent use of the ancillary powers doctrine for years to come.[4] Chief Justice Brian Dickson's dissent in *Dedman* implicitly asked future courts to be wary of the courtroom becoming a gateway for the *ex post facto* justification of unauthorized police conduct. Dickson CJ warned that the police should not be able to achieve their goals by any means necessary.

Waterfield remained very narrow in its scope in the British common law. It has yet to be used in the British legal system to expand ancillary police powers. Its usage is dissimilar in the context of the Canadian justice system. Perhaps an example of this uniquely Canadian bent on *Waterfield* is found in the nexus between the cases of *Dedman* and *R v Orbanski.*[5] The ruling in *Dedman,* which established that officers could stop a driver at a check stop under the common law, was used to justify the questioning of the driver's sobriety in *Orbanski*. Simply put, the common law operates to incrementally expand the recognized power in *Dedman*. The common law, as we know, operates on *stare decisis*. Thus, the articulation of *Waterfield* in *Dedman* has led to the proliferation of police powers in the Canadian common law.

In Chapter 3, we were presented with a fruitful discussion of search incident to arrest and the way in which the ancillary powers doctrine has helped to develop this common law police power. The Supreme Court of Canada's reliance on police search powers under the common law reinforces the idea that the ancillary powers doctrine can coexist with adjacent principles and doctrines in the criminal law. This is a testament to *Waterfield*'s flexibility. However, this same characteristic that is its strength is also, arguably, protracting its use by the judiciary as the Supreme Court has been unable, or unwilling, to deviate from the ancillary powers doctrine in any meaningful way over the decades that it has been applied to novel police conduct.

The growth of police powers in the common law, as highlighted in Chapter 4, is observable in the case law. This growth can be seen at all levels of court. Its far-reaching impact on judicial review of *Charter* applications suggests that Dickson CJ and others may have been correct in their warnings that the use of *Waterfield* usurps the judiciary's role as guardians of the Constitution. What the data in Chapter 4 shows us is that each generation of a power leads to exponential deployment of that power in the justice system. This pandora-like phenomenon has had an immeasurable impact on the pervasiveness of low-visibility stops in policing practices, which, in turn, has disproportionately impacted racialized and Indigenous communities in Canada. The issues presented in Chapter 4 are centred on the discretionary and quasi-judicial power of the police in the wake of the ancillary powers doctrine. This role has deviated, in some respects, from the original intentions of the common law. The growth of the discretionary role of police may have delayed meaningful reform in policing.

Interestingly, the Supreme Court has signalled a shift in its approach to high-profile cases concerning police powers. *Fleming*, as discussed in previous chapters, is a bellwether in the case law. It shows a Supreme Court that was willing to rein back its generation and deployment of powers by choosing not to recognize a highly questionable form of policing – that is, to arrest a law-abiding citizen – which should receive the highest scrutiny by courts when common law powers are concerned. In *R v McColman*, the Supreme Court, once again, returned to Dickson CJ's oft-repeated proclamation that police conduct not authorized by the common law or statute is unjustifiable.

As such, the *McColman* Court told us that uncertainty in the law is not an excuse for the police to rely on *ex post facto* rulings to justify their misconduct. Instead, police must err on the side of caution when the law is uncertain.

Chapter 5 looked at some of the proportionality constraints imposed by the *Waterfield* test. As part of their proportionality analysis, courts evaluate the importance of an ancillary police power, its impact on liberty, and whether it is necessary for officers to restrict liberty to fulfill a police duty. It argued that the ancillary powers doctrine's proportionality test is flawed in many respects and employs a weaker proportionality framework compared to section 1 of the *Charter*. The ancillary powers doctrine's proportionality framework has fundamental problems that can undermine the legitimacy of common law police powers. However, as Chapters 6 and 7 suggested, the problems with policing and police powers are systemic and widespread. Chapter 6 presented a historical overview of the relationship between police and racialized communities. This relationship is a far cry from the community presence of British policing from centuries past. Instead, Chapter 6 identified how public perceptions of police bias differ between racialized communities and their white counterparts. Notwithstanding efforts to reform police practices, negative perceptions of police bias in racialized communities have remained a constant.

Studies have shown that racial profiling is a serious issue in Canadian policing. Chapter 6 presented the results of empirical research to support the widely held assertion that racialized minorities are more likely to be stopped by police than their white counterparts. Police investigative techniques that we read about in case law are only one part of the story. What Chapter 6 highlighted is that low-visibility stops have affected racialized communities disproportionately. Thus, investigative techniques, such as investigative detention and roadside stops, are having a detrimental impact on the welfare of racialized communities. Further to this, the relationship between the police and racialized communities does not reflect the adage that police are serving their community. Further, Chapter 6 identified the psychological harm that over-policing has on racialized communities and documented how it contributes to their over-criminalization. Chapter 6 then called for serious reforms on the issue of the stop-and-search practices of police.

Chapter 7 showed how the ancillary powers doctrine resembles a one-way ratchet that expands police powers and restricts constitutional rights. It demonstrated how the ancillary powers doctrine and judicially created police powers expose individuals to a unilateral threat of interference; a form of domination that the republican theory of freedom brings to light. Chapter 7 also considered how ancillary police powers affect the public's perception of law enforcement. It elucidated how proactive police encounters can corrode individuals' trust of the police – a reality that the Supreme Court of Canada overlooks when it employs the ancillary powers doctrine. Chapter 7 then explained how the judicial and legislative branches do not control police misconduct adequately. As a result, members of the public resort increasingly to informal mechanisms, such as counter-surveillance and cop-watching groups, to increase transparency and accountability in law enforcement. Chapter 7's concluding sections contended that the Supreme Court of Canada should stop creating common law police powers and, instead, return to its role as the guardian of constitutional rights. More specifically, the Court should abandon the ancillary powers doctrine and send a strong message that existing common law police powers are unconstitutional unless they incorporate sufficient transparency and accountability safeguards.

This book has also laid the groundwork for future research into the ancillary powers doctrine in Canadian law. The judiciary's authority to create police powers – and common law police powers more generally – raises profound theoretical and practical concerns for Indigenous persons, which is an area of research that requires significant scrutiny. The Cotter report for Statistics Canada notes a number of troubling empirical findings in this context:

> Indigenous people were more likely to have had contact with police in the previous 12 months, when compared with the non-Indigenous, non-visible minority population ... Indigenous people, who were much more likely to have had prior contact with Canadian criminal courts, had similar perceptions to non-Indigenous, non-visible minority people. The exception was the ability of the courts to ensure a fair trial for the accused, which Indigenous people perceived less favourably ... Indigenous people, in turn, were much more likely than non-Indigenous, non-visible minority people to cite serious problems or disputes with the police or justice system ... Indigenous women were more likely than Indigenous men to have experienced one or more serious problems or disputes in the past 3 years.[6]

The nexus between ancillary police powers and Indigenous persons gives rise to an array of novel research questions that should be examined in the future. For instance, what is the relationship between the state's fiduciary relationship with Indigenous persons and the ancillary powers doctrine? How do ancillary police powers contribute to the over-policing and over-incarceration of Indigenous persons? How do these realities impact Indigenous persons' constitutional right to equality and their distinct *Charter*-protected rights and interests? Furthermore, how does the ancillary powers doctrine affect the goal of reconciliation and to what extent do common law police powers undermine this goal? Together, the historical context of colonialism and its ongoing effects, Indigenous persons' discrete constitutional rights, their unique fiduciary relationship with the state, the reality of over-incarceration, and other considerations highlight the need for future research that connects these issues to the ancillary powers doctrine.

We expect that as we delve into the issues of detention and arrest encounters with persons who are Indigenous, like the policing of Black persons, findings will empirically reflect the perceptions of Indigenous persons as recounted by Cotter in his report for Statistics Canada.[7] This in itself would correlate with the risks of prejudice and bias that would necessitate jurisprudential adjustments. In delving into the discourse on bias, the dimensions of race, gender, class, and the conscious or unconscious influence that shape decisions – in this case, the police – may lead to unfair or flawed judgments. As defined by the American Psychological Association (APA), cognitive bias is akin to "partiality," reflecting an inclination or predisposition for or against something.[8] The APA draws a connection between bias and prejudice, characterizing prejudice as a negative attitude formed prior to any direct experience with an individual or group.[9] Prejudices encompass an affective component, ranging from mild nervousness to outright hatred, a cognitive component involving assumptions and beliefs, including stereotypes, and a behavioral component that manifests as negative actions, such as discrimination and violence. These biases often resist change, distorting the prejudiced individual's perception of information related to the targeted group.

The synergy between prejudice and bias is evident, with a notable aspect being their tendency to operate covertly and subconsciously in the modern context rather than manifesting explicitly.[10] It is this subtle nature that renders cognitive bias insidious; individuals frequently refrain from vocalizing their biases, and, in many cases, they remain blissfully unaware of their own biases. Researchers underscore the challenge in recognizing and correcting bias, emphasizing its often subtle and implicit nature.[11] Anderson's findings further underscore the pervasiveness of bias and other cognitive pitfalls at every stage of a criminal investigation, heightening the risk of wrongful convictions. This underscores the imperative to scrutinize and address these intricate dynamics within the realm of police-citizen encounters.[12]

The danger of bias and prejudice in the earliest stages of contact with police has proximate harmful effects, perhaps correlating with findings in the Cotter report.[13] As Tanovich argues, judicial decision-makers, in order to determine relevance, will use "logic, common sense and experience" to guide decision-making.[14] These forms of reasoning bring with them a high degree of reliance on bias and stereotypes.[15] When bias, prejudice, myth, and stereotype inform the police-person encounter, the breeding ground for disproportionate impacts on racialized communities is strengthened and a link to wrongful conviction could manifest.[16] Indeed, current attempts to create an independent commission for remediating wrongful convictions contain language directly addressing prejudices against Indigenous and Black persons in the context of miscarriages of justice: section 5(e) of an *Act to Amend the Criminal Code* mandates that the established commission must take into account "the distinct challenges that applicants who belong to certain populations face in obtaining a remedy for a miscarriage of justice, with particular attention to the circumstances of Indigenous or Black applicants."[17]

The viewpoints that have been presented in the chapters of this book paint a picture of police powers that is complex and nuanced. The various authors have asked us to consider policing from the viewpoint of the police, the individual, and the community that the police serve. We have also presented findings and conclusions that have been reached from scrutinizing the case law data. In the end, we can admit and acknowledge that serious issues in policing are not new, nor are efforts to reform policing practices. What we can appreciate is that the justice system has as much of a responsibility to rebuke unjustifiable police conduct as the legislators. Reform cannot come from one aspect of the legal system. It must arrive by way of a holistic effort of numerous stakeholders, lawmakers, and judges who condemn police practices that fall outside the scope of statutory and common law authorization. Furthermore, police practices, whose legality remains unclear, must be addressed with clarity and precision to avoid harmful impacts on racialized and Indigenous communities across Canada.

Notes

Introduction

1 *Fleming v Ontario*, 2019 SCC 45, [2019] 3 SCR 519 at paras 57–100, 75 [*Fleming*].
2 Quoted in Janice Tibbetts, "Court's Youth Crime Decision a Blow to Tory Crime Agenda," *National Post* (16 May 2008), online: <http://www.nationalpost.com>.
3 The test was introduced in *R v Waterfield; R v Lynn*, [1963] 2 ALL ER 659 (CA) [*Waterfield*], and famously deployed in the Canadian context in *Dedman v The Queen*, [1985] 2 SCR 2, 20 DLR (4th) 321 [*Dedman*].
4 James Stribopoulos, "In Search of Dialogue: The Supreme Court, Police Powers and the Charter" (2002) 31 Queen's LJ 35 at 35.
5 Richard Jochelson, "Crossing the Rubicon: Of Sniffer Dogs, Justifications, and Pre-emptive Deference" (2007–08) 13:2 Rev Const Stud 67 at 89–90; Stribopoulos, *supra* note 4 at 8, 55.
6 Jochelson, *supra* note 5.
7 *Ibid* at 93. See also Margit Cohn & Mordechai Kremnitzer, "Judicial Activism: A Multi-dimensional Model" (2005) 18 Can JL & Jur 333 at 347.
8 Jochelson, *supra* note 5 at 96. See generally Martin Loughlin, *Public Law and Political Theory* (Oxford: Clarendon Press, 1992) at 205–29. For an earlier treatment, see Ronald Dworkin, *Taking Rights Seriously* (London: Duckworth, 1997) at 134.
9 *Police and Criminal Evidence Act 1984* (UK), c 60, which delineates the exercise by police officers of statutory powers to search a person or a vehicle without first making an arrest; the need for a police officer to make a record of a stop or encounter; the details of police powers to search premises and to seize and retain property found on premises and persons; the requirements for the detention, treatment, and questioning by police officers of suspects not related to terrorism in police custody; the main methods used by the police to identify people in connection with the investigation of offences and the keeping of accurate and reliable criminal records; the tape recording of interviews with suspects in the police station; the visual recording with sound of interviews with

suspects; and specialized powers of arrest and the requirements for the detention, treatment, and the questioning of suspects related to terrorism in police custody by police officers.

10 Herbert L Packer, "Two Models of the Criminal Process" (1964) 113:1 U Pa L Rev 1.

11 Patricia Monture, "Standing against Canadian Law: Naming Omissions of Race, Culture, and Gender" in E Comack, ed, *Locating Law: Race/Class/Gender/Sexuality Connections* (Winnipeg: Fernwood, 2014) 68. See also John Borrows, *Recovering Canada: The Resurgence of Indigenous Law* (Toronto: University of Toronto Press, 2002).

12 Aboriginal Justice Inquiry (AJI), *Final Report of the Aboriginal Justice Implementation Commission* (Winnipeg: AJI, 2001), online: <http://www.ajic.mb.ca/reports/final_toc.html>.

13 *Ibid* (this work has been theorized aptly in Glen Coulthard, "Beyond Recognition: Indigenous Self Determination as Prefigurative Practice" in Leanne Simpson, ed, *Lighting the Eighth Fire: The Liberation, Resurgence, and Protection of Indigenous Nations* (Winnipeg: Arbeiter Ring Press, 2008) 187.

14 Terry Skolnik, "Racial Profiling and the Perils of Ancillary Police Powers" (2021) 99:2 Can Bar Rev 429.

15 Ibid at 436. See also generally Kent Roach, "Making Progress on Understanding and Remedying Racial Profiling" (2004) 41:4 Alta L Rev 895.

16 Ontario Human Rights Commission (OHRC), *Under Suspicion: Research and Consultation Report on Racial Profiling in Ontario* (Toronto: OHRC, 2017); Victor Armony, Mariam Hassaoui & Massimiliano Mulone, "Les interpellations policières à la lumière des identités racisées des personnes interpellées: Analyse des données du Service de Police de la Ville de Montréal (SPVM) et élaboration d'indicateurs de suivi en matière de profilage racial" (Montreal, August 2019). See generally Scot Wortley, *Halifax, Nova Scotia: Street Checks Report* (Halifax: Nova Scotia Human Rights Commission, 2019).

17 Adam Cotter, "Perceptions of and Experiences with Police and the Justice System among the Black and Indigenous Populations in Canada," 16 February 2022, online: https://www150.statcan.gc.ca/n1/en/catalogue/85-002-X202200100003.

18 *Ibid*.

19 J. Cobbina-Dungy et al, "'Defund the Police': Perceptions among Protesters in the 2020 March on Washington" (2022) 21 Criminology & Public Policy 1, online: https://onlinelibrary.wiley.com/doi/10.1111/1745-9133.12571.

20 *Canadian Charter of Rights and Freedoms*, Part 1 of the *Constitution Act, 1982*, being Schedule B to the *Canada Act 1982* (UK), 1982, c 11.

21 *Ordinance for the Preservation of the Peace; Statute of Winchester. Statute of Winchester*, 13 Edw. 1, Stat. 2, c 1, 2, 4, 6.

22 *Constitution Act, 1867* (UK), 30 & 31 Vict, c 3.

23 *Waterfield, supra* note 3.

24 *Dedman, supra* note 3.

25 *R v Orbanski; R v Elias*, 2005 SCC 37; *R v Godoy*, [1999] 1 SCR 311 at para 2, 41 OR (3d) 95.

26 *R v MacDonald*, 2014 SCC 3.

27 *R v Mann*, 2004 SCC 52.

28 *R v Kang-Brown*, 2008 SCC 18; *R v AM* [2008] 1 SCR 569, 2008 SCC 19; *R v Clayton*, 2007 SCC 32.

29 *Cloutier v Langlois*, [1990] 1 SCR 158, SCJ No 10.

30 *R v Golden*, 2001 SCC 83.

31 *R v Stillman*, [1997] 1 SCR 607, 144 DLR (4th) 193.

32 *R v Saeed*, 2016 SCC 24.

33 *R v Caslake*, [1998] 1 SCR 51, 155 DLR (4th); *R v Fearon*, 2014 SCC 77.

34 *Fleming, supra* note 1.

Chapter 1: The Common Law Constable

Epigraph: O'Rourke v Schacht, [1976] 1 SCR 53 at 65–66.

1 Winnipeg Police Service, "Statistical Report" (2022) at 5, 9, 38, online: Annual Reports <https://www.winnipeg.ca/media/2436> [perma. cc/UF3U-4AN9].

2 *Ibid* at 28.

3 Livio Di Matteo, "Police and Crime Rates in Canada" (2014) at 6, online: *Fraser Institute* <https://www.fraserinstitute.org/sites/default/files/police-and-crime-rates-in-canada. pdf> [perma.cc/AGV5-4RXT]. Citing Public Safety Canada, 2013: 5; Standing Committee on Public Safety and National Security, Economics of Policing (Committee Report) (Ottawa: House of Commons, 2014) at 15–17. See also David Bayley, "What Do the Police Do?" in William Salusbury, Joy Mott & Tim Newburn, eds, *Themes in Contemporary Policing* (London, UK: Police Foundation, 1996) at 29–41; Richard V Ericson, *Reproducing Order: A Study of Police Patrolwork* (Toronto: University of Toronto Press, 1982) at 5–6.

4 The earliest meaning given to the word "policy" in the *Oxford English Dictionary* includes in 1387 "an organized and established system or form of government or administration."

5 Virginia J Hunter, *Policing Athens: Social Control in the Attic Lawsuits, 420–320 BC* (Princeton, NJ: Princeton University Press, 1993). For the same time frame in India, see Anupam Sharma, "The Police in Ancient India" (2004) 65 Indian J Political Science 1 at 101–10.

6 Christopher J Fuhrmann, *Policing the Roman Empire: Soldiers, Administration, and Public Order (30 BC–476 AD)* (New York: Oxford University Press, 2012). See also Roger S Bagnall, "Army and Police in Roman Upper Egypt" 14 *Journal of the American Research Center in Egypt* (1977), 67–86.

7 The editors of *Encyclopaedia Brittanica* specify "shire" (date not specified). See *Encyclopaedia Britannica*, online: <https://www.britannica.com/topic/shire-British-government -unit> [perma.cc/6GH7-K3Z9].

8 Philip Stenning, *Legal Status of the Police: A Study Paper* (Ottawa: Law Reform Commission of Canada, 1981) at 16 [emphasis added]. See also William Lambard, *Duties of Constables, Borsholder, Tithingmen and Such Other Low Ministers of the Peace* (London: Printed by Miles Flesher, Io Haviland, and Robert Young, the assignees of Iohn Moore Esquire, 1631).

9 The *Grand Connétable de France* was one of the original five great officers of the Crown of France, established by King Philip I in 1060 AD, with Albéric de Montmorency becoming the first constable.

10 Robert Gardiner, *The Complete Constable: Directing All Constables, Headboroughs, Tithingmen, Churchwardens, Overseers of the Poor, Surveyors of the Highways, and Scavengers, in the Duty of Their Several Offices, According to the Power Allowed Them by the Laws and Statutes: Continued to This Present Time* (London: Assigns of Richard and Edward Atkins, 1736) at 13–14. See also Mathew Hale, *Historia Placitorum Coronæ: The History of the Pleas of the Crown, by Sir Matthew Hale ... Now First Published from His Lordship's Original Manuscript, and the Several References to the Records Examined by the Originals, with Large Notes. By Sollom Emlyn ... to Which Is Added a Table of the Principal Matters in Two Volumes* (In the Savoy: E and R Nutt, and R Gosling, assigns of Edward Sayer, Esq; for F Gyles, T Woodward, and C Davis, 1736).

11 *Criminal Code*, RSC 1985, c C-46.
12 Carl Stephenson & Frederick George Marcham, *Sources of English Constitutional History: A Selection of Documents from AD 600 to the Present* (New York: Harper & Brothers, 1937) at 139.
13 *Ibid* at 173. The *Statute of Winchester of 1285* (UK), 13 Edw I, c 2. It was also known as the *Statute of Winton*, enacted by King Edward I of England, who reformed the system of Watch and Ward (watchmen) of the Assize of Arms of 1252 and revived the jurisdiction of the local courts. It received royal assent on 8 October 1285.
14 Stephenson & Marcham, *supra* note 12 at 174.
15 Quoted in DeLloyd Guth, "The Traditional Common-Law Constable" in David Schneiderman & RC Macleod, eds, *Police Powers in Canada: The Evolution and Practice of Authority* (Toronto: University of Toronto Press, 1994) 3 at 6.
16 *Ibid*.
17 See e.g., *R v Kang-Brown*, 2008 SCC 18 at para 51, citing reasons of Abella J in *R v Clayton*, 2007 SCC 32 at para 22.
18 See generally, notes 11–17. Common Law Duties, *Op cit*, note 60.
19 Lambard, *supra* note 8.
20 *Humphries v Connor*, [1864] 17 ICLR 1 (CA) [*Humphries*].
21 At that time, the orange lily was seen as a marker of the Orange Order and a reminder of the Battle of Boyne (1690s), which marked a Protestant victory over the Catholics.
22 *Humphries, supra* note 20 at 6. See also *Minto v McKay*, [1987] NZCA 19, [1987] 1 NZLR 374 (where this passage was cited by Bisson J with approval).
23 *Cooke v Nethercote*, [1835] 6 Car. & P. 744, sub nom *Cook v Nethercote*, 172 ER 1443.
24 *R v Browne*, [1841] 1 C&M 314, sub nom *R v Browne*, 174 ER 522.
25 *Kyle v Bell*, [1836] 1 M&W 519, sub nom *Ingle v Bell*, 150 ER 539. See also *Cohen v Huskisson*, [1837] 2 M&W 477, 150 ER 845 at 847 (Court of Exch).
26 *R v Hogan*, [1837] 8 Car. & P. 171, sub nom *R v Hagan*, [1837] 173 ER 445 [*Hogan*].
27 *Humphries, supra* note 20 at 7.
28 *Ibid* [emphasis added].
29 *O'Kelly v Harvey*, [1883] 14 LR Ir 105 (CA).
30 *Ibid* at 109–10 [emphasis added].
31 *Thomas v Sawkins*, [1935] 2 KB 249. See also AJ Goodhart, "*Thomas v Sawkins*: A Constitutional Innovation" (1936) 6:1 Cambridge LJ 22.
32 *Duncan v Jones*, [1936] 1 KB 218 (DC). For a similar Commonwealth decision, see also *Burton v Power*, [1940] NZLR 305 (SC).
33 *Haynes v Harwood*, [1935] 1 KB 146 at 162 (CA), per Maugham LJ, aff'ing [1934] 2 KB 240 [*Haynes*].
34 Stenning, *supra* note 8 at 146. See also Hale, *supra* note 10 at 94.
35 *Entick v Carrington*, [1765] 19 St Tr 1030 (CP) [*Entick*].
36 Law Reform Commission of Canada, *Police Powers Search and Seizure in Criminal Law Enforcement* (Ottawa: Law Reform Commission of Canada, 1983) at 16.
37 *Ibid; Criminal Code*, SC 1892, c 29. See now RSC 1985, c 46.
38 *Entick, supra* note 35. This principle of legality is elaborated on by AV Dicey: "[E]very official, from the Prime Minister down to a constable or collector of taxes, is under the same responsibility for every act done without legal justification." AV Dicey, *Law of the Constitution (1885)*, 10th ed (London: Macmillan Education, 1959) at 153.
39 *R v Barnett*, [1829] 3 Car. & P. 600, 172 ER 563. See also *R v Jones*, [1834] 6 Car. & P. 343, 172 ER 1296; *R v Kinsey*, [1836] 7 Car. & P. 447, 173 ER 198.
40 *R v O'Donnell*, [1835] 7 Car. & P. 138, 173 ER 61.

41 *Ibid* at 61 (ER), reasons of Patterson J.
42 *Dillon v O'Brien and Davis*, [1887] 20 LR Ir 30, 16 Cox CC 245.
43 *R v Lushington, Ex paret Otto* [1894] 1 QB 420 at 423.
44 *Ibid*.
45 *Bessell v Wilson* (1853), 1 El. & Bl. 489, 118 ER 518, 17 JP 52 (QB).
46 *Ibid* at 52 (17 JP).
47 *Leigh v Cole*, [1853] 6 Cox CC 329.
48 *Ibid* at 332 [emphasis added].
49 Guth, *supra* note 14 at 9 (who states: "Because most of this royal centralization entered the common law by parliamentary statute, the constable's duties were specified in writing, no longer customary and discretionary at a magistrate's order").
50 *Ibid*.
51 Jacob Giles, "Constable" in *A New Law-Dictionary Containing the Interpretation and Definition of Words* (London: E and R Nutt and R Gosling, 1729). An equally long list of duties for French police officers can be found in Augustin Julien Alletz, *Dictionnaire de Police Modern*, 2nd ed (Paris: Antoine Bavoux, 1823). Augustin Alletz was the police commissioner for Paris in 1820, and the duties assigned to the municipal police included:

> Harmful projections on the public highway; brawls and gatherings; nighttime noises that disturb the peace of the citizens; the tumult in the public meetings; verification of weights and measures; the wholesomeness of edibles and medicines; fires, epidemics, epizootics, and others calamitous plagues; the foolish and the furious left at liberty; the verification of registers of landlords and hoteliers; the maintenance of public morals; the display of obscene objects; carriages and horses and the accidents which they may occasion; precautions to be taken by roofers and other workers, etc [translation from original French by the author].

52 *An Act for Improving the Police in and near the Metropolis* (UK), 1829, 10 Geo 4, c 44. It was shortened in 1896 to the *Metropolitan Police Act, 1829*.
53 Patrick Colquhoun, *A Treatise on the Police of the Metropolis, Etc*, 2nd ed (London: H Fry, 1796) at 357, 428–35. See also subsequent editions.
54 Richard Mayne, *Metropolitan Police General Orders and Instruction Books*, 1829, as quoted in Jennifer Hilton, "Instructions to the New Police" (1977) 50:1 Police 23. Often attributed to Sir Robert Peel, who was Home Secretary at the time the *Metropolitan Police Act* was passed; it is believed that the principles were drafted by the first commissioners. See UK Government, "Definition of Policing by Consent" (Home Office FOI Release), online: *UK Government* <https://www.gov.uk/government/publications/policing-by-consent/definition-of-policing-by-consent>.
55 *Constitution Act, 1867* (UK), 30 & 31 Vict, c 3.
56 This includes the unwritten principles: "[B]ehind the written word ... an historical lineage stretching back through the ages, which aids in the consideration of the underlying constitutional principles. These principles inform and sustain the constitutional text: they are the vital unstated assumptions upon which the text is based." *Reference re Secession of Quebec*, [1998] 2 SCR 217 at para 49. It is these unwritten norms, recognized and affirmed by the preamble to the *Constitution Act, 1867*, "which [serve] as the grand entrance hall to the castle of the Constitution, that the true source of our commitment to this foundational principle is located." *Reference re: Remuneration of Judges of the Provincial Court of Prince Edward Island*, [1997] 3 SCR 3, at para 106.
57 *Constitution Act, 1867* (UK), 30 & 31 Vict, c 3.
58 *Town Officers Act*, SNS 1765, c 1.

59 Donald Fyson, *Magistrates, Police and People: Everyday Criminal Justice in Quebec and Lower Canada, 1764–1837* (Toronto: Osgoode Society, 2006). See also Keith Mercer, *Rough Justice, Policing Crime and the Origins of the Newfoundland Constabulary, 1729–1871* (St. John's: Flanker Press, 2021); Jonathan Swainger, *The Notorious Georges: Crime and Community in British Columbia's Northern Interior, 1909–1925* (Vancouver: UBC Press, 2023).

60 *Parish and Town Officers Act 1793* (UK), 33 Geo 3, c 2. See Statutes of Upper Canada 1800, 40 Geo 3, c 1.

61 Article 32 of the *Laws of Assiniboia*, passed by the Governor and Council of Assiniboia on the 11th April, 1862 (Fort Garry, NWT: Office of The Nor'-Wester, Red River Settlement, 1862), stated:

> Efficient householders, not exceeding twelve in number, to remain in office for a term of three years from the 1st of September following the date of their appointment, shall be appointed constables on the last Thursday in each year by the magistrates, specially assembled for the purpose; and every constable so appointed must take the following oath: "I swear by God, as I shall answer to God at the great day of Judgment, that I shall, till lawfully discharged from my office of constable, for the district of Assiniboia, be always ready at all hazards to serve and execute all legal writs, and to maintain public peace and security; and that I shall, to the utmost of my ability, obey all laws and all lawful authorities within and for the said district, and induce all others to obey the same, and that I shall do my best to become acquainted with all local regulations.

62 CT Griffith, B Whitelaw & RB Parent, *Canadian Police Work* (Toronto: ITP Nelson, 1999) at 5.

63 John Burchill, President, Winnipeg Police Museum and Historical Society, and Executive Support Officer, Manitoba Association Chiefs of Police, personal communication, 5 May 2023 [documents on file with author].

64 *Ibid.*

65 James Robert Gowan, with notes by James Patton, *The Canadian Constables' Assistant* (Barrie: JW Young, 1852) at 15 [emphasis added]. See also Adam Wilson, QC, *The Constable's Guide: A Sketch of the Office of Constable* (Toronto: Maclear, 1859); Joseph Ritson, Esquire, *The Office of Constable* (London: Whieldon & Butterworth, 1791); *Re in Trespass of Assault, Battery and Imprisonment*, [1593] 79 ER 1135 (KB) (in which Chief Justice Popham stated that "a Constable was one of the most ancient offices in the realm for conservation of the peace, and by his office he is a conservator of the peace").

66 *Ibid.*

67 *An Act respecting Police of Canada, 1868* (Can.), c 73.

68 *Police Act*, SQ 1870, c 39; *Police Act*, SM 1871, c 33. Both statutes are nearly identical, outlining the duties of police officers as those that

> [S]hall be hereafter assigned to constables in relation to the preservation of the peace, the prevention of crime, and of offences against the laws of the dominion or of the province, or against the by-laws of the municipality in which they may be stationed or lawfully ordered to act, and the apprehension of criminals and offenders and others who may be lawfully taken into custody ... And for these purposes, and in the performance of all the duties assigned to them by or under the authority of this act, they shall have all the powers, authority, protection and privileges, which any constable now has or shall hereafter by law have ...

69 *Police Services Act*, RSO 1990, c P.15 [*Police Services Act* RSO] [emphasis added]; *Community Safety and Policing Act*, SO 2019, c 1.

70 See *Police Services Act*, CCSM, c P94.5 [*Police Services Act* CCSM] (s 24(1) for municipal officers and s 18(2) for Royal Canadian Mounted Police officers); *Police Act*, SNS 2004, c 31, s 42(1)(a) [*Police Act* SNS]; *Police Act*, RSBC 1996, c 367 [*Police Act* RSBC] (s 38(1)(a) for municipal officers and s 10(1) for RCMP officers); *Royal Newfoundland Constabulary Act*, SNL 1992, c R-17, s 8(3) [*Royal Newfoundland Constabulary Act* SNL]; *Police Services Act* RSO, *supra* note 69 (s 42(3) and s 82(3) when the *Community Safety and Policing Act*, *supra* note 69, is proclaimed in force); *Police Act*, RSPEI 1988, c P-11.1, s 15(2) [*Police Act* RSPEI].

71 See *Police Services Act* CCSM, *supra* note 70, s 25; *Police Act* SNS, *supra* note 70, s 42(2); *Police Act*, RSA 2000, c P-17, s 38(1); *Police Act*, CQLR 2000, c P-13.1, s 48; *Police Act* RSBC, *supra* note 70, s 34(2), 7(2); *Royal Newfoundland Constabulary Act* SNL, *supra* note 70, s 8(1); *Police Services Act* RSO, *supra* note 70, s 42(1); *Police Act*, SS 1990, c P-15.01, s 36(2); *Police Act* RSPEI, *supra* note 70, s 13; *Royal Canadian Mounted Police Act*, RSC 1985, c R-10, s 18; *Police Act*, SNB 1977, c P-9.2, s 12(1); *Police Act*, RSQ, c P-13.1, s 48 (generally) and s 93 (Indigenous police forces).

72 *Cady v Dombrowski*, 413 US 433 at 441 (1973).

73 *Nicholson v Avon*, [1991] 1 VR 212, leave to appeal High Court denied (AustLII); *United States v Rohrig*, 98 F (3d) 1506 (6th Cir 1996). See also *City of Fargo v Lee (et al)*, 580 NW (2d) 580 (Supt Ct ND 1998); *Commonwealth v Kiser*, 724 NE (2d) 348 (Mass CA 2000).

74 *R v Martin* (1995), 97 CCC (3d) 241, 1995 CanLII 1003 at para 16 (BCCA) (CanLII), aff'd *R v Martin*, [1996] 1 SCR 463. The Court also stated that police officers "are expected to perform aid and succour functions [support in times of hardship and distress] above and beyond the duties specified in the [*Police Act*]." 1995 CanLII 1003 at para 16 (BCCA) (CanLII).

75 *United States v Lancellotti*, 145 F (3d) 1342 (9th Cir 1998). See also *R v Jamieson*, 2002 BCCA 411 (where entry may be necessary to contain the risk of property damage due to vandalism, fire, water, or power).

76 *R v Johnston*, 2004 BCCA 148 at 183.

77 *R v Hern*, 1994 ABCA 65. See also *R v Dreysko* (1990), 110 AR 317 (CA); *R v Nguyen*, [2000] BCJ No 2728 (SC); *R v Gibson*, 2003 BCSC 1572.

78 *Haynes*, *supra* note 33.

79 *United States v Smith*, 522 F (3d) 305 (3rd Cir 2008), quoting *United States v Rodriguez-Morales*, 929 F (2d) 780 at 784–85 (1st Cir 1991), cert denied 112 S Ct 868 (1992).

80 *Brigham City v Stuart*, 547 US 398 at 406 (2006) (where the Court stated: "[T]he role of a peace officer includes preventing violence and restoring order, not simply rendering first aid to casualties; an officer is not like a boxing [or hockey] referee, poised to stop a bout only if it becomes too one-sided").

81 *R v Howell* (1981), 73 Cr App R 31 (CA).

82 *R v Ringler*, 2004 ONCJ 104. But see *R v Ritch and Mynott*, 2015 ONSC 5433 (where the evidence did not show the need for immediacy or that exigent circumstances existed).

83 *R v Waterfield; R v Lynn*, [1963] 2 ALL ER 659 (CA) [*Waterfield*]. Despite its reception and integration into Canadian jurisprudence for more than fifty years, *Waterfield* has not been without its criticisms. See Richard Jochelson & David Ireland, *Privacy in Peril: Hunter v Southam and the Drift from Reasonable Search Protections* (Vancouver: UBC Press, 2019) at 79 (where my colleague states: "[T]he test [is] being used as a gap filling measure to expand police powers on a case-by-case basis"). However, the government has never intervened during those fifty years to modify or legislate a different test. As noted by Mark Carter, "if our elected representatives are satisfied with certain common law rules, then there is no reason for them to enshrine or alter them in statute. If there is any

currency left in Edward Coke's view that the common law represents 'that which hath been refined and perfected by all the wisest men in former succession of ages,' legislators may be acting prudently by leaving it as unaltered as possible." Mark Carter, "Non-Statutory Criminal Law and the Charter: The Application of the Swain Approach in *R v Daviault*" (1995) 59:2 Sask L Rev 241 at 242.

84 *Ibid* at 171 [emphasis added].

85 *Ibid* at 171.

86 *Ibid* at 171.

87 *R v Stenning*, [1970] SCR 631, [1970] RCS 631.

88 *Criminal Code, 1953–54* (Can.), c 51, s 232(2).

89 *Police Act*, RSO 1960, c 298.

90 *R v Knowlton*, 1973 CanLII 148 (SCC), [1974] SCR 443.

91 *Criminal Code, 1953–54* (Can.), s 118(a), [1970] RSC, c C-34.

92 *Ibid* at 447–48.

93 New Zealand courts have also applied the *Waterfield* test. The Supreme Court of New Zealand has found that while police actions must be tested against the requirements of the *Bill of Rights Act 1990, No 109*, the requirements of the common law as stated in *Waterfield* are consistent with the act (specifically, that both the common law and the *Bill of Rights Act* require that police officers act reasonably). See *Ngan v The Queen*, [2007] NZSC 105 at para 22, [2008] 2 NZLR 48, per Blanchard for a majority of the Court, concurring opinions by Tipping and McGrath JJ. The difference, according to Tipping J, is that under *Waterfield* the police had to act "lawfully," whereas under the *Bill of Rights Act* they had to act "reasonably." See also *Tuato v R*, [2011] NZCA 278 at paras 14–17.

Chapter 2: The Supreme Court's Embrace of the Ancillary Powers Doctrine

1 *Canadian Charter of Rights and Freedoms*, Part 1 of the *Constitution Act, 1982*, being Schedule B to the *Canada Act 1982* (UK), 1982, c 11.

2 *Hunter et al v Southam Inc*, [1984] 2 SCR 145, 11 DLR (4th) 641 [*Southam*].

3 *R v Waterfield; R v Lynn*, [1963] 2 ALL ER 659 (CA) [*Waterfield*].

4 *R v Stenning*, [1970] SCR 631, [1970] RCS 631; *R v Knowlton*, 1973 CanLII 148 (SCC), [1974] SCR 443.

5 *R v Clayton*, 2007 SCC 32 at para 75 [*Clayton*].

6 *Dedman v The Queen*, [1985] 2 SCR 2, 20 DLR (4th) 321 [*Dedman*].

7 *Ibid*.

8 Even though the SCC's hearing of *Dedman* occurred after the enactment of the *Charter*, the Court didn't expressly deal with a *Charter* claim because the events of the case occurred before 1982.

9 *Dedman, supra* note 6 at para 50. We have previously discussed the ways in which the majority deviated from the precedent of the British doctrine of ancillary powers in Richard Jochelson, "Crossing the Rubicon: Of Sniffer Dogs, Justifications, and Preemptive Deference" (2008) 13:2 Rev Const Stud 67 at 209. See also Richard Jochelson, "Ancillary Issues with *Oakes*: The Development of the *Waterfield* Test and the Problem of Fundamental Constitutional Theory" (2013) 43:3 Ottawa L Rev 355 at 365, where he notes:

> Therefore, in the evolution of the Waterfield test we see the Supreme Court's recent willingness to use the test as a means of creating police powers. We also see an increasing tendency by the Court to view Waterfield as a means to constitutionally inoculate a police power; as a quasi-Oakes test of justification. This constitutional function of the Waterfield test has not been without anxiety for some members of the Court. The

next section will briefly explore further the connection between Waterfield and Oakes and describe some of the tensions raised by dissenters in the Court who seem to object to the proliferation of Waterfield as a constitutional standard of sorts.

10 *Dedman, supra* note 6.
11 *Ibid,* headnote.
12 *Ibid* at para 51; *Criminal Code,* RSC 1985, c C-46.
13 *Dedman, supra* note 6 at para 31.
14 *Ibid* at para 12, citing the dissenting opinion in *R v Biron,* [1976] SCR 56 at 64–65.
15 *Dedman, supra* note 6 at para 20, citing *Waterfield, supra* note 3.
16 *Dedman, supra* note 6 at para 13, citing the reasons of Martin JA in *R v Dedman* (1981), 32 OR (2d) 641, 122 DLR (3d) 655 ("[n]o one is entitled to impose any physical restraint upon the citizen except as authorized by law, and this principle applies as much to police officers as to anyone else").
17 *Highway Traffic Act,* RSO 1990, c H.8.
18 *Ibid* at para 68.
19 *Ibid* at para 13.
20 *Ibid* at para 66, citing *Waterfield, supra* note 3 at 661–62.
21 *Johnson v Phillips,* [1975] 3 All ER 682 [*Philips*].
22 *Dedman, supra* note 6 at para 69. Factors considered included the importance of performance of the duty to the public good; the necessity of the interference with the individual's liberty for the performance of the duty; and the extent of the interference with the individual liberty.
23 *Ibid.*
24 *Ibid.*
25 *Ibid* at para 15.
26 *Ibid* at para 24 citing *Wiretap Reference,* [1984] 2 SCR 697 at 718–19, 14 DLR (4th) 546.
27 *Dedman, supra* note 6 at para 35.
28 *Ibid* at para 3.
29 *Ibid* at para 26.
30 *Ibid* at para 25.
31 Richard Jochelson & David Ireland, *Privacy in Peril* (Vancouver: UBC Press, 2019) at 78.
32 *Dedman, supra* note 6 at para 30.
33 *R v Orbanski; R v Elias,* 2005 SCC 37 [*Orbanski*].
34 *Ibid* at para 25.
35 *Ibid* at para 45.
36 *Ibid.*
37 *Ibid* at para 43; *Highway Traffic Act,* CCSM, c H60.
38 *Orbanski, supra* note 33 at para 45.
39 *Ibid* at para 45, citing *Dedman, supra* note 6 at para 69.
40 *Orbanski, supra* note 33.
41 *Ibid* at paras 37, 50.
42 *Ibid* at paras 55–60.
43 *Ibid* at para 70.
44 *Ibid* at para 82, citing Wilson J in *R v Jacoy,* [1988] 2 SCR 548 at 563, 89 NR 61.
45 *Orbanski, supra* note 33 at para 58, citing *R v Bartle,* [1994] 3 SCR 173 at 191, 172 NR 1.
46 *Orbanski, supra* note 33 at para 82.
47 *Ibid* at para 82.
48 *Ibid* at para 79.
49 *Ibid* at paras 79–80.

50 *Ibid* at para 69.
51 *Ibid* at para 81.
52 *Semayne's Case*, [1588–1774] All ER Rep 62. See also *R v Tessling*, 2004 SCC 67, citing Lord H Brougham, *Historical Sketches of Statesment Who Flourished in the Time of George III* (London: Richard Griffin, 1855) at 42:

> The poorest man may in his cottage bid defiance to all the forces of the crown. It may be frail – its roof may shake – the wind may blow through it – the storm may enter – the rain may enter – but the King of England cannot enter – all his force dares not cross the threshold of the ruined tenement. So be it – unless he has justification by law.

53 *R v Godoy*, [1999] 1 SCR 311, 41 OR (3d) 95 [*Godoy*].
54 *Ibid* at para 2.
55 *Ibid* at para 13.
56 *Police Services Act*, RSO 1990, c P.15, s 42(1)(c) (statutory duty of assisting victims of crime).
57 *Ibid*, s 42(2) (general duties ascribed to a common law constable).
58 *R v Simpson*, 1993 CarswellOnt 83 at para 55 (CA) [*Simpson*].
59 *Godoy, supra* note 53 at para 22.
60 *Southam, supra* note 2.
61 *Ibid* at 147.
62 *Ibid* at 159.
63 *Ibid*.
64 *R v Edwards*, [1996] 1 SCR 128 at para 45, 132 DLR (4th) 31.
65 *R v Collins*, [1987] 1 SCR 265 at 278, SCJ No 15.
66 Jochelson & Ireland, *supra* note 31 at 100.
67 *R v MacDonald*, 2014 SCC 3 [*MacDonald*].
68 *Ibid* at paras 26–27.
69 *Ibid* at para 36 [citations omitted].
70 *Ibid* at para 39.
71 *Ibid* at para 32.
72 *Ibid* at para 42.
73 *Ibid* at para 39.
74 *Ibid* at para 29, citing *R v Mann*, 2004 SCC 52 at para 36 [*Mann*].
75 *MacDonald, supra* note 67 at para 48; *R v Collins*, [1987] 1 SCR 265.
76 But see the dissent in *MacDonald, ibid*, who state that

> [e]very day, throughout this country, police officers put their lives and safety at risk in order to preserve and protect the lives and safety of others. In return, they are entitled to know that when potentially dangerous situations arise, the law permits them to conduct minimally intrusive safety searches to alleviate the risks they face. That is the fundamental bargain we, as a society, have struck with the police – and it is a fundamental commitment upon which the police are entitled to rely (at para 64).

77 *Ibid* at para 64.
78 *Fleming v Ontario*, 2019 SCC 45 at para 5 [*Fleming*].
79 *Cloutier v Langlois*, [1990] 1 SCR 158 at 181–82, SCJ No 10.
80 *Dedman, supra* note 4 at 35.
81 *Ibid*.
82 *Mann, supra* note 74 at para 27; *Simpson, supra* note 58.
83 *Simpson, supra* note 58 at para 58 [emphasis added].

84 *Ibid* at para 61.
85 *Mann, supra* note 74 at 30.
86 *Ibid* at para 27.
87 *Ibid* at para 34.
88 *Ibid* at para 47.
89 *Ibid* [emphasis added].
90 *Ibid* at para 40.
91 *Ibid* at paras 44–45.
92 *Ibid* at para 40.
93 *Ibid* at para 46–61.
94 *Police Services Act, supra* note 56.
95 *Clayton, supra* note 5, citing *R v Clayton*, 2005 CarswellOnt 1061 at para 56 (CA).
96 *Clayton, supra* note 5 at para 102.
97 *Ibid* at para 61.
98 *Ibid; R v Oakes*, [1986] 1 SCR 103, SCJ No 7.
99 *Clayton, supra* note 5 at para 89.
100 *R v Kang-Brown*, 2008 SCC 18 at para 1.
101 *Ibid* at para 6.
102 *Ibid* at para 7.
103 *Ibid* at para 14.
104 *Ibid* at para 15.
105 *Ibid* at para 17.
106 *Ibid* at para 22.
107 *Ibid* at para 54.
108 *Ibid*.
109 *Ibid* at para 22.
110 *Ibid* at para 51.
111 *Ibid*.
112 *Ibid* at para 182.
113 *Ibid*.
114 *Ibid* at para 184.
115 *Ibid* at para 192.
116 *Ibid* at para 60.
117 *Fleming, supra* note 78 at para 1.
118 *Ibid* at para 57.
119 Albeit no reference was made to the decision of *Humphries v Connor*, [1864] 17 ICLR 1 (CA), where a police officer was justified in removing an orange lily from the button-hole of a woman's jacket. As no arrest was made in that case, preventive action short of arrest, including temporary detention and seizure of property, may still be a part of the common law. In fact, the power endorsed by *Humphries v Connor* "continues to be part of the common law of Australia," at least for those individuals who are wittingly or unwittingly provocateurs. *Binsaris v Northern Territory*, [2020] HCA 22 at paras 39–40, per Gageler JA.
120 *Ibid* at para 42.
121 *Fleming, supra* note 78 at para 57.
122 *Ibid* at para 60.
123 *Ibid* at para 64.
124 *Ibid* at para 65.
125 *Ibid*, headnote.

126 *Ibid* at para 83.
127 *Ibid* at paras 89.
128 *Ibid* at para 90.
129 *Ibid* at para 95.
130 *Ibid* at para 98.
131 *Ibid* at para 82.

Chapter 3: Search Incident to Arrest

1 *R v Waterfield; R v Lynn*, [1963] 2 ALL ER 659 (CA) [*Waterfield*]; *Gottschalk v Hutton* (1921), 17 Alta LR 347, 66 DLR 499 (Alta SC App Div); *R v McDonald* (1932), 26 Alta LR 460, 59 CCC 56 (Alta SC, App Div); *R v Morrison* (1987), 20 OAC 230, 35 CCC (3d) 437; *R v Miller* (1987), 62 OR (2d) 97, 38 CCC (3d) 252 (Ont CA); *Gordon v Denison* (1895), 22 OAR 315, 1895 WL 8710; *Welch v Gilmour* (1955), 111 CCC 221, 1955 Carswell BC 190 (BCSC); *R v Brezack*, [1949] OR 888, [1950] 2 DLR 265 (Ont CA); *Laporte v Laganière* (1972), 29 DLR (3d) 651, 8 CCC (2d) 343 (Qc SC); *Reynen v Antonenko* (1975), 54 DLR (3d) 124, 20 CCC (2d) 342 (Alta SC); *R v Rao* (1984), 46 OR (2d) 80, 9 DLR (4th) 542 (Ont CA); *Rousseau v The Queen*, [1985] 2 SCR 38; *R v Lerke* (1986), 43 Alta LR (2d), 24 CCC (3d) 129; *R v Beare*, [1988] 2 SCR 387, 55 DLR (4th) 481; *R v Debot*, [1989] 2 SCR 1140, 52 CCC (3d) 193.

2 Interestingly, *Cloutier v Langlois*, [1990] 1 SCR 158, SCJ No 10 [*Cloutier*], does not cite *Waterfield* directly; it instead cites *Dedman v The Queen*, [1985] 2 SCR 2, 20 DLR (4th) 321 [*Dedman*], indirectly linking search incident to arrest to the common law:

> In determining the exact scope of a police power derived from the common law, this Court often had recourse to considerations of principle, and the weighing of the competing interests involved (*Eccles v Bourque*, [1975] 2 SCR 739, *Dedman v The Queen*, [1985] 2 SCR 2, and *R v Landry*, [1986] 1 SCR 145). Competing interests are important factors in determining the limits of a common law power. When the power in question comes into conflict with individual freedoms, it is first necessary to decide whether the power falls within the general scope of the duty of peace officers. This duty, clearly identified, must historically have been recognized by the courts as tending to promote the effective application of the law. Secondly, the Court must determine whether an invasion of individual rights is justified. In this regard, Le Dain J. in *Dedman* defined what he meant by "justifiable use of the power" in question (at para 10).

3 John Burchill notes that in *R v Barnett* (1829), [1928] 172 ER 563, "the historical roots of the power to search incident to arrest date back nearly 200 years where it was implied that police officers may seize property from an arrested person if it is connected with the charge against him." John Burchill, "Stripping Matters to the [Central] Core: Searching Electronic Devices Incident to Arrest" (2009) 33:2 Man LJ 263 at para 7. He also reiterates that the deep roots of the incident-to-arrest power are also apparent in *United States v Robinson*, 414 US 218 at 235 (1973), where the Court notes that "[t]he authority to search the person incident to a lawful custodial arrest, while based upon the need to disarm and to discover evidence, does not depend on what a court may later decide was the probability in a particular arrest situation that weapons or evidence would in fact be found upon the person of the suspect. A custodial arrest of a suspect based on probable cause is a reasonable intrusion under the Fourth Amendment; that intrusion being lawful, a search incident to the arrest requires no additional justification. It is the fact of the lawful arrest which establishes the authority to search, and we hold that in the case of a lawful custodial arrest a full search of the person is not only an exception to

the warrant requirement under the Fourth Amendment, but is also a 'reasonable' search under that Amendment" (at para 13). See also *Bessell v Wilson* (1853), [1911] 118 ER 518 (KB); *Leigh v Cole*, [1853] 6 Cox CC 329; *Yakimishyn v Bileski*, [1946] 3 DLR 390 at para 181, 86 CCC 179 (MBKB); *R v Brezack*, [1949] OR 888 at para 101, [1950] 2 DLR 265 (ONCA). For further clarification of the search power's long history, see Steven Penney, "Unreasonable Search and Seizure and Section 8 of the Charter: Cost-Benefit Analysis in Constitutional Interpretation" (2013) 62 SCLR 101 at para 76 (QL).

4 *Dillon v O'Brien and Davis*, [1887] 20 LR Ir 30, 16 Cox CC 245.

5 *Dedman, supra* note 2.

6 *Cloutier, supra* note 2.

7 Richard Jochelson & David Ireland, *Privacy in Peril* (Vancouver: UBC Press, 2019) at 105–6.

8 *Cloutier, supra* note 2 at para 47.

9 *Hunter et al v Southam Inc*, [1984] 2 SCR 145 at para 29, 11 DLR (4th) 641.

10 *Cloutier, supra* note 2 at para 51.

11 *Ibid.*

12 *Canadian Charter of Rights and Freedoms*, Part 1 of the *Constitution Act, 1982*, being Schedule B to the *Canada Act 1982* (UK), 1982, c 11.

13 *Cloutier, supra* note 2 at para 17.

14 *Ibid* at para 3.

15 *Ibid* at para 50.

16 *Ibid* at para 60.

17 *Ibid.*

18 *Ibid.*

19 *Ibid.*

20 *Ibid.*

21 *Ibid* at para 61.

22 *Ibid* at para 62.

23 *Ibid* at para 68.

24 *Ibid.*

25 *R v Golden*, 2001 SCC 83.

26 *Ibid* at para 30.

27 *Ibid* at para 39.

28 *Ibid* at para 26.

29 *Ibid* at para 99.

30 *Ibid* at para 101.

31 *Ibid* at para 99.

32 *Ibid* at para 102.

33 *Ibid* at para 5.

34 *R v Stillman*, [1997] 1 SCR 607, 144 DLR (4th) 193.

35 *Ibid* at para 33.

36 *Ibid* at para 46.

37 *Ibid* at para 47.

38 *R v Saeed*, 2016 SCC 24.

39 *Ibid* at para 18.

40 *Ibid* at para 47.

41 *Ibid* at para 59.

42 *Ibid* at para 75.

43 *Ibid.*

44 *Ibid* at para 54.
45 *Ibid* at para 78.
46 *Ibid*, headnote.
47 *Ibid*.
48 *R v Caslake*, [1998] 1 SCR 51, 155 DLR (4th).
49 *Ibid* at para 3.
50 *Ibid* at para 25.
51 *Ibid*.
52 *Ibid* at para 17.
53 *Ibid* at para 26.
54 *Ibid* at paras 42–43.
55 *R v Fearon*, 2014 SCC 77 [*Fearon* SCC].
56 *Ibid* at para 4.
57 *Ibid* at para 58.
58 *Ibid* at para 51, citing *R v Vu*, 2013 SCC 60 at paras 41–44.
59 *Fearon* SCC, *supra* note 55 at para 58.
60 *Ibid* at para 83.
61 *Ibid* at paras 28, 33.
62 *R v Fearon*, 2010 ONCJ 645 at para 44.
63 *Fearon* SCC, *supra* note 55 at para 88.
64 *Ibid* at para 171.
65 *Ibid* at para 132.
66 *Ibid*, headnote.
67 *Ibid* at para 176.
68 *R v Stairs*, 2022 SCC 11 [*Stairs*].
69 *Controlled Drugs and Substances Act*, SC 1996, c 19.
70 *Stairs*, *supra* note 68 at para 5.
71 *Ibid* at para 8.
72 *Ibid* at paras 72, 78, 80.
73 *Ibid* at para 85.
74 *Ibid* at para 114.
75 *Ibid* at para 128.
76 As an example of a declination of novel police powers, see *Fleming v Ontario*, 2019 SCC 45.
77 Jochelson & Ireland, *supra* note 7 at 136.

Chapter 4: An Empirical Analysis of Ancillary Power Generation and Deployment

1 *Canadian Charter of Rights and Freedoms*, Part 1 of the *Constitution Act, 1982*, being Schedule B to the *Canada Act 1982* (UK), 1982, c 11 [*Charter*].
2 *Hunter et al v Southam Inc*, [1984] 2 SCR 14, 11 DLR (4th) 641.
3 *Charter*, *supra* note 1, s 1.
4 Beverley McLachlin, "The Role of Judges in Modern Society" (5 May 2001), online: *Supreme Court of Canada*, https://perma.cc/S39Z-4TSQ.
5 Adam Molnar & Ian Warren, "Lawful Illegality: Authorizing Extraterritorial Police Surveillance" (2020) 18:3 Surveillance & Society 357.
6 Richard Jochelson et al, "Generation and Deployment of Common Law Police Powers by Canadian Courts and the Double-Edged Charter" (2020) 20 Critical Criminology 107 at 110.

7 *R v Mann*, 2004 SCC 52 at para 18 [*Mann*].
8 *Dedman v The Queen*, [1985] 2 SCR 2, 20 DLR (4th) 321 [*Dedman*].
9 *Ibid* at para 4.
10 *Controlled Drugs and Substances Act*, SC 1996, c 19.
11 *Mann, supra* note 7.
12 James Stibopoulos, "The Limits of Judicially Created Police Powers: Investigative Detention after *Mann*" (2006) 52 CLQ 299 at 304.
13 *R v Waterfield; R v Lynn*, [1963] 2 ALL ER 659 (CA); Richard Jochelson, "Ancillary Issues with *Oakes:* The Development of the *Waterfield* Test and the Problem of Fundamental Constitutional Theory" (2013) 43 Ottawa L Rev 355 at 362.
14 *R v Brown*, 64 OR (3d) 161, [2003] OJ No 1251.
15 David Tanovich, "The Colourless World of *Mann*" (2004) 21 Criminal Reports (6th) 47 at 47–48.
16 Amar Khoday, "Ending the Erasure? Writing Race into the Story of Psychological Detentions – Examining *R v Le*" (2021) 100 SCLR (2d) 165 at 166. Some have alluded to the *Mann* case as being a prime example where Indigenous identity was used to profile a suspect. See Elsa Kaka, "The Supreme Court of Canada's Justification of *Charter* Breaches and Its Effect on Black and Indigenous Communities" (2020) 4 Man LJ 117 at 128–29:

> On December 23, 2000, shortly before midnight, two police officers were alerted to a break and enter occurring in a neighbourhood near downtown Winnipeg. The person committing the break and enter was suspected by the witness to be "Zachary Parisienne" and was described as being "a 21-year-old Aboriginal male, approximately five feet eight inches tall, weighing about 165 pounds, clad in a black jacket with white sleeves" ... The Court ultimately held that the police were empowered to detain Mann for investigative purposes and search him for protective purposes ... *The issue with the Supreme Court's decision in Mann is that it reads as though there is no awareness of the social science pertaining to the racial dimensions of investigative detentions: that it effectively erases the racial aspects of the legal issue ... When one examines the history of police violence and racial profiling, it becomes understandable that Indigenous peoples would feel pressured to comply with the police's demands.* [emphasis added]).

17 *R v Le*, 2019 SCC 34 at 95 [*Le*]; *Fleming v Ontario*, 2019 SCC 45 at para 5 [*Fleming*].
18 *Le, supra* note 17 [citation omitted].
19 Between 2008 and 2011, police filled out 1.25 million Field Information Reports on 788,000 individuals, according to a *Toronto Star* investigation. See Patty Winsa & Jim Rankin, "Known to Police: Toronto Police Stop and Document Black and Brown People Far More Than Whites," *Toronto Star* (21 August 2013), online: <https://www.thestar.com/news/insight/2012/03/09/known_to_police_toronto_police_stop_and_document_black_and_brown_people_far_more_than_whites.html> [perma.cc/6TZ5-FKDH].
20 *Fleming, supra* note 17 at para 5.
21 Felicity Bell, "Empirical Research in Law" (2016) 25:2 Griffith L Rev 267.
22 *Ibid*.
23 Bell, *supra* note 22 at 275.
24 Craig Allen Nard, "Empirical Legal Scholarship: Reestablishing a Dialogue between the Academy and Profession" (1995) Faculty Publications 341 at 349.
25 Bell, *supra* note 22 at 273, citing Kylie Burns & Terry C Hutchinson, "The Impact of 'Empirical Facts' on Legal Scholarship and Legal Research Training" (2009) 43:2 The Law Teacher 153.

26 Richard Jochelson et al, "Generation and Deployment of Common Law Police Powers by Canadian Courts and the Double-Edged *Charter*" (2020) 28 Critical Criminology 107.

27 The 2018–20 dataset should be approached cautiously when considered in comparison with the preceding time frames, given how small it is relative to the others. See also *ibid*, at Table 2.

28 See Jochelson et al, *supra* note 6 at 117.

29 See *ibid* at 122.

30 *Dedman, supra* note 8, headnote.

31 *R v Kang-Brown*, 2008 SCC 18.

32 *Ibid* at para 4.

33 *R v Orbanski; R v Elias*, 2005 SCC 37 at para 82.

34 *Ibid* at para 81.

35 *Fleming, supra* note 17 at para 55.

36 *Ibid* at para 76.

37 Jochelson, *supra* note 13 at 115.

38 *R v McKenzie*, 2022 MBCA 3, application for leave denied, 2022 CanLII 58765 (SCC) [*McKenzie*].

39 *R v McColman*, 2021 ONCA 382 [*McColman* ONCA]; *R v McColman*, 2023 SCC 8 [*McColman* SCC].

40 *R v Stairs*, 2022 SCC 11 [*Stairs*].

41 *McKenzie, supra* note 40 at para 10.

42 *Ibid* at para 13, citing *R v MacKenzie*, 2013 SCC 50 at para 35; *Mann, supra* note 7 at para 45.

43 *McKenzie, supra* note 40 at para 47.

44 *Ibid* at para 32. See also *Mann, supra* note 7 at para 40; *R v Clayton*, 2007 SCC 32 at paras 29–30.

45 *McKenzie, supra* note 40 at para 49.

46 *Ibid* at para 51; *R v MacDonald*, 2014 SCC 3.

47 *McKenzie, supra* note 40 at para 53.

48 *Ibid*.

49 *Stairs, supra* note 42.

50 *McColman* ONCA, *supra* note 41 at para 27.

51 *Highway Traffic Act*, RSO 1990, c H.8.

52 *McColman* ONCA, *supra* note 41 at para 49, citing *Fleming, supra* note 17 at para 41.

53 *McColman* ONCA, *supra* note 41 at para 50, citing *Fleming, supra* note 17 at para 42.

54 *McColman* ONCA, *supra* note 41 at para 64.

55 *Ibid* at para 68.

56 *Ibid* at para 73.

57 *Ibid* at para 75, citing *Fleming, supra* note 17 at para 84.

58 *McColman* ONCA, *supra* note 41.

59 *Ibid* at para 70.

60 *Ibid*.

61 *McColman* SCC, *supra* note 41 at para 20.

62 *Ibid* at para 63.

63 *Ibid*.

64 *Ibid* at para 75.

65 *R v Grant*, 2009 SCC 32.

66 *Ibid* at para 72.

67 Michael Plaxton, "Police Powers after Dicey" (2012) 38:1 Queen's LJ 99 at 136.

68 *Ibid*.

69 *R v Simpson*, 1993 CarswellOnt 83 (CA).

70 See Coretta Phillips & Benjamin Bowling, "Racism, Ethnicity and Criminology: Developing Minority Perspectives" (2002) 43:2 Brit J Crim 269; RS Engel & JM Canlon, "Examining the Influence of Drivers' Characteristics during Traffic Stops with Police: Results from a National Survey" (2004) 21 Justice Quarterly 49; Scott Wortley & Akwasi Owusu-Bempah, "The Usual Suspects: Police Stop and Search Practices in Canada" (2011) 21:4 Policing & Society 395.

71 Ontario Human Rights Commission, "A Disparate Impact" (August 2020), online (pdf): <https://www.ohrc.on.ca/sites/default/files/A%20Disparate%20Impact%20-%20TPS %20inquiry%20%28updated%20January%202023%29.pdf>.

72 *Ibid* at 2.

73 Wortley & Owusu-Bempah, *supra* note 72 at 403.

74 *Ibid*.

75 Kaka, *supra* note 16 at 120. Kaka also notes that

> There are countless examples of police officers failing to properly investigate crimes committed against Indigenous women, as was noted by The National Inquiry into Missing and Murdered Indigenous Women and Girls. The police have also been responsible for committing heinous acts against Indigenous peoples; often at the direction of the state. For example, the RCMP committed genocide against Indigenous communities when they ripped Indigenous children away from their families and forced them to attend Indian Residential Schools. It was the police that enforced the confinement of Indigenous peoples to reserves, as per the Indian Act (at 120–21 [citations omitted]).

76 Malini Vijaykumar, "A Crisis of Conscience: Miscarriages of Justice and Indigenous Defendants in Canada" (2018) 51 UBC L Rev 159 at 166.

77 See e.g., Leah Combs, "Healing Ourselves: Interrogating the Underutilization of Sections 81 & 84 of the Corrections and Conditional Release Act" (2018) 41:3 Man LJ 163. For media accounts, see Colin Freeze, "More Than One-Third of People Shot to Death over a Decade by RCMP Officers Were Indigenous," *Globe and Mail* (17 November 2019), online: <http://www.theglobeandmail.com/canada/article-more-than-one-third-of -people-shot-to-death-over-a-decade-by-rcmp/> [perma.cc/U8JT-UCS3].

78 Kaka, *supra* note 16 at 122.

79 David Milward, *Reconciliation and Indigenous Justice: A Search for Ways Forward* (Halifax: Fernwood, 2022).

80 Dan Zakreski, "Saskatoon Police Removed 'Starlight Tours' Section from Wikipedia, Student Says," *CBC News* (31 March 2016), online: <https://perma.cc/K5H5-TKW2>.

81 Truth and Reconciliation Commission of Canada, *Calls to Action* (Winnipeg: Truth and Reconciliation Commission of Canada, 2012).

82 See Milward, *supra* note 81.

Chapter 5: The Doctrine's Proportionality Problem

1 *R v Waterfield; R v Lynn*, [1963] 2 ALL ER 659 (CA); *Fleming v Ontario*, 2019 SCC 45 at para 54 [*Fleming*]; Richard Jochelson, "Crossing the Rubicon: Of Sniffer Dogs, Justifications, and Preemptive Deference" (2008) 13:2 Rev Const Stud 209 at 220–21 (noting that both doctrines incorporate proportionality considerations).

2 *Fleming, supra* note 1 at para 45; *Dedman v The Queen,* [1985] 2 SCR 2 at 35, 20 DLR (4th) 321 [*Dedman*]; Vanessa MacDonnell, "Assessing the Impact of the Ancillary Powers Doctrine on Three Decades of *Charter* Jurisprudence" (2012) 57 SCLR (2d) 225 at 236–37.

3 *Fleming, supra* note 1 at para 54; *R v MacDonald,* 2014 SCC 3 at para 37 [*MacDonald*].

4 *MacDonald, supra* note 3 at para 37.

5 *Canadian Charter of Rights and Freedoms,* Part 1 of the *Constitution Act, 1982,* being Schedule B to the *Canada Act 1982* (UK), 1982, c 11 [*Charter*]; *Fleming, supra* note 1 at para 54, citing John Burchill, "A Horse Gallops Down a Street: Policing and the Resilience of the Common Law" (2018) 41:1 Man LJ 161 at 174–75. The *Oakes* test stems from *R v Oakes,* [1986] 1 SCR 103, SCJ No 7 [*Oakes*]. It provides the applicable proportionality test for s 1 of the *Charter.*

6 Terry Skolnik, "Racial Profiling and the Perils of Ancillary Police Powers" (2021) 99:2 Can Bar Rev 429 at 454 [Skolnik, "Racial Profiling"].

7 *Ibid* at 448–53.

8 See discussion later in this chapter.

9 See discussion later in this chapter.

10 James Stribopoulos, "In Search of Dialogue: The Supreme Court, Police Powers and the *Charter*" (2005) 31:1 Queen's LJ 1 at 53–55.

11 See discussion later in this chapter.

12 See e.g., David Harris, "Across the Hudson: Taking the Stop and Frisk Debate beyond New York City" (2013) 16:4 NYUJ Legis & Pub Pol'y 853 at 854–55.

13 Skolnik, "Racial Profiling," *supra* note 6 at 436–38; Terry Skolnik & Fernando Belton, "*Luamba* et la fin des interceptions routières aléatoires" (2023) 101:3 Can B Rev 671 at 695–98.

14 See discussion later in this chapter.

15 Moshe Cohen-Eliya & Iddo Porat, "Proportionality and Justification" (2014) 64:3 UTLJ 458 at 462–63.

16 See e.g., *Fleming, supra* note 1 at para 54, citing Richard Jochelson, "Ancillary Issues with *Oakes:* The Development of the *Waterfield* Test and the Problem of Fundamental Constitutional Theory" (2012) 43:3 Ottawa L Rev 355 at 366–67.

17 *Fleming, supra* note 1 at para 42; *MacDonald, supra* note 3 at para 81; Terry Skolnik & Vanessa MacDonnell, "Policing Arbitrariness: *Fleming v Ontario* and the Ancillary Powers Doctrine" (2021) 100 SCLR (2d) 187 at 201.

18 *Dedman, supra* note 2 at 35; *MacDonald, supra* note 3 at paras 35–36; *Fleming, supra* note 1 at para 55.

19 *Fleming, supra* note 1 at para 45.

20 *Dedman, supra* note 2 at 35. Quotation is taken from *Fleming, supra* note 1 at para 54.

21 Moshe Cohen-Eliya & Iddo Porat, "Proportionality and the Culture of Justification" (2011) 59:2 Am J Comp L 463 at 466–67.

22 *Ibid.*

23 Alice Ristroph, "Proportionality as a Principle of Limited Government" (2005) 55:2 Duke LJ 263 at 265.

24 *Ibid.*

25 Cohen-Eliya & Porat, *supra* note 21 at 469.

26 Aharon Barak, "A Judge on Judging: The Role of a Supreme Court in a Democracy" (2002) 116:1 Harv L Rev 19 at 147–48.

27 *Ibid;* Mark Tushnet, *Weak Courts, Strong Rights: Judicial Review and Social Welfare Rights in Comparative Constitutional Law* (Princeton, NJ: Princeton University Press, 2007) at ix (describing strong-form judicial review).

28 Alexander Bickel, *The Least Dangerous Branch: The Supreme Court at the Bar of Politics* (New Haven, CT: Yale University Press, 1962) at 16–17.

29 See e.g., Vicki Jackson, "Constitutional Law in an Age of Proportionality" (2015) 124:8 Yale LJ 3094 at 3142–44.

30 *Ibid.*

31 *Ibid.*

32 Aharon Barak, "Proportionality and Principled Balancing" (2010) 4:1 L & Ethics of Human Rights 1 at 5–6; Matthias Klatt & Moritz Meister, *The Constitutional Structure of Proportionality* (Oxford: Oxford University Press, 2012) at 8–10.

33 Jackson, *supra* note 29 at 3111–12.

34 Robert Alexy, "Constitutional Rights and Proportionality" (2014) 22 Revus: J Constitution Theory & Philosophy of Law 51 at 52–53.

35 Charles-Maxime Panaccio, "In Defence of Two-Step Balancing and Proportionality in Rights Adjudication" (2011) 24:1 Can JL & Jur 109 at 113.

36 Barak, *supra* note 32 at 6.

37 Jochelson, *supra* note 1 at 220–21; Ryan Liss, "Whose Right Is It Anyway? Adjudicating *Charter* Rights in the Context of Multiple Rights Holders" (2020) 94 SCLR (2d) 271 at 293–94.

38 *Fleming, supra* note 1 at para 47.

39 *Ibid;* Skolnik & MacDonnell, *supra* note 17 at 193.

40 See e.g., *MacDonald, supra* note 3 at para 47.

41 Terry Skolnik, "Rééquilibrer le rôle de la Cour Suprême de Canada en procédure criminelle" (2022) 67:3 McGill LJ 259 at 262, 268 [Skolnik, "Rééquilibrer"].

42 Skolnik, "Racial Profiling," *supra* note 6 at 439–44; Monica Bell, "Anti-Segregation Policing" (2020) 95:3 NYUL Rev 650 at 687 (discussing collective harms); Jocelyn Simonson, "Police Reform through a Power Lens" (2021) 130 Yale LJ 778 at 812; Kami Chavis Simmons, "The Legacy of Stop and Frisk: Addressing the Vestiges of a Violent Police Culture" (2014) 49:3 Wake Forest L Rev 849 at 855–56.

43 Skolnik, "Racial Profiling," *supra* note 6 at 454.

44 Tom Tyler, "From Harm Reduction to Community Engagement: Redefining the Goals of American Policing in the Twenty-First Century" (2017) 111 Nw UL Rev 1537 at 1547; Skolnik & Belton, *supra* note 13 at 686.

45 Rod Brunson, "'Police Don't Like Black People': African-American Young Men's Accumulated Police Experiences" (2007) 6:1 Criminology & Public Policy 71 at 73–75, 94–95.

46 *Ibid;* Patricia Warren, "Perceptions of Police Disrespect during Vehicle Stops: A Race-Based Analysis" (2011) 57:3 Crime & Delinquency 356 at 359–60.

47 Madeleine Novich & Alyssa Zduniak, "Violence Trending: How Socially Transmitted Content of Police Misconduct Impacts Reactions toward Police among American Youth" in Bailey, Flynn & Henry (eds), *The Emerald International Handbook of Technology-Facilitated Violence and Abuse* (Bingley: Emerald, 2021) at 279–83.

48 Wesley Skogan, "Asymmetry in the Impact of Encounters with Police" (2006) 16:2 Policing & Society 99 at 105.

49 Terry Skolnik, "Criminal Justice Reform: A Transformative Agenda" (2022) 59:3 Alta L Rev 631 at 642.

50 Skolnik, "Racial Profiling," *supra* note 6 at 438.
51 Ontario Human Rights Commission (OHRC), *Under Suspicion: Research and Consultation Report on Racial Profiling in Ontario* (Toronto: OHRC, 2017) at 40; Valerio Baćak & Kathryn Nowotny, "Race and the Association between Police Stops and Depression among Young Adults: A Research Note" (2020) 10:3 Race & Justice 363 at 355–56; Dylan Jackson et al, "Unpacking Racial/Ethnic Disparities in Emotional Distress among Adolescents during Witnessed Police Stop" (2021) 69 J Adolescent Health 248 at 248.
52 See e.g., Lisa Walter, "Eradicating Racial Stereotyping from Terry Stops: The Case for an Equal Protection Exclusionary Rule" (2000) 71:1 U Colo L Rev 255 at 285–86.
53 Skolnik, "Racial Profiling," *supra* note 6 at 436–37.
54 Lorne Foster, Les Jacobs & Bobby Siu, *Race Data and Traffic Stops in Ottawa, 2013–2015: A Report on Ottawa and the Police Districts* (Ottawa: Ottawa Police Service, 2016) at 3–5; Timothy Appleby, "Kingston Police More Likely to Stop Blacks, Study Finds," *Globe and Mail* (27 May 2005).
55 Steven Hayle, Scot Wortley & Julian Tanner, "Race, Street Life, and Policing Implications for Racial Profiling" (2016) 58 Can J Corr 322 at 341–42.
56 *Ibid* at 328–29, 332.
57 Scot Wortley, *Halifax, Nova Scotia: Street Checks Report* (Halifax: Nova Scotia Human Rights Commission, 2019) at 39–40.
58 *Luamba c Procureur général du Québec*, 2022 QCCS 3866 at paras 3, 275–78, 605 [*Luamba*]. See also Holly Cabrera, "Terrebonne Police, City Slammed with $205K Lawsuit for Systemic Discrimination," *CBC News* (4 January 2023), online: <https://www.cbc.ca/news/canada/montreal/black-while-driving-monsanto-terrebonne-police-1.6703471>.
59 David Harris, "Driving While Black and All Other Traffic Offenses: The Supreme Court and Pretextual Traffic Stops" (1997) 87 J Crim L & Criminology 544 at 570.
60 See e.g., Tom Tyler, Jeffrey Fagan & Amanda Geller, "Street Stops and Police Legitimacy: Teachable Moments in Young Urban Men's Legal Socialization" (2014) 11:4 J Empirical Leg Stud 751 at 776; Tom Tyler, Jonathan Jackson & Avital Mentovich, "The Consequences of Being an Object of Suspicion: Potential Pitfalls of Proactive Police Contact" (2015) 12:4 J Empirical Leg Stud 602 at 615–16.
61 Jordan Blair Woods, "Decriminalization, Police Authority, and Routine Traffic Stops" (2015) 62:3 UCLA L Rev 672 at 745.
62 *Ibid*; David Harris, "The Stories, the Statistics, and the Law: Why Driving While Black Matters" (1999) 84:2 Minn L Rev 265 at 273; Adero Jernigan, "Driving While Black: Racial Profiling in America" (2000) 24 Law & Psychol Rev 127 at 135–36.
63 *Luamba*, *supra* note 58 at para 180.
64 Skolnik, "Racial Profiling," *supra* note 6 at 446–53.
65 James Stribopoulos, "Packer's Blind Spot: Low Visibility Encounters and the Limits of Due Process versus Crime Control" in François Tanguay-Renaud & James Stribopoulos, eds, *Rethinking Criminal Law Theory: New Canadian Perspectives in the Philosophy of Domestic, Transnational, and International Criminal Law* (Oxford: Hart, 2012) 193 at 201; Joseph Goldstein, "Police Discretion Not to Invoke the Criminal Process: Low-Visibility Decisions in the Administration of Justice" (1960) 69:4 Yale LJ 543 at 543.
66 Skolnik, "Rééquilibrer," *supra* note 41 at 278; Terry Skolnik, "Policing in the Shadow of Legality: Pretext, Leveraging, and Investigation Cascades" (2022) 60 Osgoode Hall LJ 505 at 517–18.
67 Skolnik, "Rééquilibrer," *supra* note 41 at 278.
68 Terry Skolnik, "Three Stages of Criminal Justice Remedies" (2024) UBC L Rev (forthcoming).

69 Cass Sunstein, "The Most Knowledgeable Branch" (2016) 164 U Pa L Rev 1607 at 1608.
70 *Ibid* at 1613–14; Terry Skolnik, "Hot Bench: A Theory of Appellate Adjudication" (2020) 61:4 Boston College L Rev 1271 at 1308.
71 Sunstein, *supra* note 69 at 1613–14.
72 *Ibid.*
73 Cass Sunstein, "Foreword: Leaving Things Undecided" (1996) 110 Harv L Rev 4 at 18–19; Cass Sunstein, *One Case at a Time: Judicial Minimalism on the Supreme Court* (Cambridge, MA: Harvard University Press, 2001) at 49–50.
74 Skolnik & Belton, *supra* note 13 at 679, 689.
75 Skolnik, "Rééquilibrer," *supra* note 41 at 278–85.
76 For an overview, see Gerald Frug, "Judicial Power of the Purse" (1978) 126:4 U Pa L Rev 715 at 715–16, citing Alexander Hamilton, "Federal No. 78," in *The Federalist Papers* (New York: Palgrave Macmillan, 2009) at 236 ("[t]he judiciary, on the contrary, has no influence over either the sword or the purse; no direction either of the strength or of the wealth of the society; and can take no active resolution whatever").
77 For an overview of these concerns, see Emmett Macfarlane, "Positive Rights and Section 15 of the *Charter*: Addressing a Dilemma" (2018) 38 NJCL 147 at 150; Alana Klein, "Judging as Nudging: New Governance Approaches for the Enforcement of Constitutional Social and Economic Rights" (2008) 39:2 Colum HRLR 351 at 360.
78 Steve Coughlan, "Common Law Police Powers and the Rule of Law" (2007) 47 Criminal Reports (6th) 266 at 266–67.
79 See e.g., Wortley, *supra* note 57; Foster, Jacobs & Siu, *supra* note 54.
80 *R v Ladouceur*, [1990] 1 SCR 1257, SCJ No 53 [*Ladouceur*]; *Luamba, supra* note 58.
81 *Ladouceur, supra* note 80 at 1288–89.
82 *Ibid* at 1278–83.
83 *Ibid* at 1276–78.
84 *Ibid* at 1278–89.
85 *Ibid* at 1279–83.
86 *Ibid* at 1283–84.
87 *Ibid* at 1286.
88 *Ibid* at 1287.
89 *Ibid.*
90 *Ibid.*
91 *Ibid.*
92 Skolnik & Belton, *supra* note 13 at 679, 689.
93 *Ladouceur, supra* note 80 at 1286; OHRC, *supra* note 51 at 40.
94 Skolnik & Belton, *supra* note 13 at 696–98.
95 *Luamba, supra* note 58 at para 869.
96 *Ibid* at paras 601–832.
97 *Ibid* at paras 702–4, 762–74, 830–32.
98 *Ibid* at paras 152–468.
99 *Ibid* at paras 391–462, citing, e.g., Wortley, *supra* note 57; Foster, Jacobs & Siu, *supra* note 54.
100 *Luamba, supra* note 58 at paras 681–94.
101 *Ibid* at paras 693–97.
102 Skolnik, "Racial Profiling," *supra* note 6 at 454 (discussing the ancillary powers doctrine and proportionality).
103 Cohen-Eliya & Porat, *supra* note 21 at 466–67.
104 *Ibid;* Barak, *supra* note 26 at 147–48.

105   See e.g., *R v Perka*, [1984] 2 SCR 232 at 246, SCJ No 40; Terry Skolnik, "Three Problems with Duress and Moral Involuntariness" (2016) 63:1–2 Crim LQ 124 at 127.

106   Terry Skolnik, "Use of Force and Criminalization" (2021) 85:3 Alb L Rev 663 at 665–69 [Skolnik, "Use of Force"].

107   See e.g., *ibid* at 677 (discussing how criminalization is presumptively wrong because it limits freedom without consent). Similar arguments apply to the presumptive wrongfulness of police coercion.

108   *Ibid* at 664–65.

109   *Ibid.*

110   *Ibid.*

111   *Ibid* at 679–84 (discussing the necessity and reasonableness constraints in the context of criminalization).

112   See David Beatty, *The Ultimate Rule of Law* (Oxford: Oxford University Press, 2004) at 176.

113   George Letsas, "Proportionality as Fittingness: The Moral Dimension of Proportionality" (2018) 71:1 Current Leg Probs 53 at 70 (describing the moral dimension of proportionality as the fit between an actor's normative role and their reasons for acting given that role).

114   See e.g., Sujit Choudhry, "So What Is the Real Legacy of *Oakes?* Two Decades of Proportionality Analysis under the *Canadian Charter*'s Section 1" (2006) 34 SCLR (2d) 501 at 501–2, 506 (describing rights as presumptively important and limitations as exceptional); Alec Stone Sweet & Jud Mathews, "Proportionality Balancing and Global Constitutionalism" (2008) 47:1 Colum J Transnat'l L 72 at 75–76. See also *Charter, supra* note 5, s 1; *Oakes, supra* note 5 at para 62.

115   Skolnik, "Use of Force," *supra* note 106 at 664–65, 679.

116   *Ibid.*

117   Steven Penney, "Driving While Innocent: Curbing the Excesses of the 'Traffic Stop' Power" (2019) 24:3 Can Crim L Rev 339 at 360–61.

118   See e.g., Skolnik & MacDonnell, *supra* note 17 at 198–99.

119   Skolnik, "Rééquilibrer," *supra* note 41 at 291–92.

120   David A Sklansky, "Traffic Stops, Minority Motorists, and the Future of the Fourth Amendment" (1997) 1997 Sup Ct Rev 271 at 272; Seth Stoughton, "Principled Policing: Warrior Cops and Guardian Officers" (2016) 51:3 Wake Forest L Rev 611 at 668.

121   Barak, *supra* note 26 at 147–48.

122   See discussion earlier in this chapter.

123   Aliza Cover, "Cruel and Invisible Punishment: Redeeming the Counter-Majoritarian Eighth Amendment" (2014) 79:3 Brook L Rev 1141 at 1147–48.

124   Skolnik, "Racial Profiling," *supra* note 6 at 452.

125   See discussion earlier in this chapter.

Chapter 6: Ancillary Police Powers and the Black Experience in Canada

1   Leanne Weber & Ben Bowling, eds, *Stop and Search: Police Power in Global Context* (New York: Routledge, 2014).

2   CR Epp, S Maynard-Moody & DP Haider-Markel, *Pulled Over: How Police Stops Define Race and Citizenship* (Chicago: University of Chicago Press, 2014).

3   SD Mastrofski, MD Reisig & JD McCluskey, "Police Disrespect toward the Public: An Encounter-Based Analysis" (2002) 40:3 Criminology 519.

4   Brad W Smith & Malcolm D Holmes, "Police Use of Excessive Force in Minority Communities" (2014) 61:1 Social Problems 83.

5 Clayton James Mosher, *Discrimination and Denial: Systemic Racism in Ontario's Legal and Criminal Justice Systems, 1892–1961* (Toronto: University of Toronto Press, 1998) at 170.

6 A Milan & K Tran, "Blacks in Canada: A Long History" (2008) 72 Can Social Trends 2. See also T Chui, K Tran & H Maheux, *Canada's Ethnocultural Mosaic: The 2006 Census (2008)*, Catalogue no 97-562-X (Ottawa: Statistics Canada, 2008).

7 Akwasi Owusu-Bempah, *Black Males' Perceptions of and Experiences with the Police in Toronto* (PhD Dissertation, University of Toronto, 2014) at 2, online: <https://tspace. library.utoronto.ca/handle/1807/68227> [hdl.handle.net/1807/68227].

8 Daiva K Stasiulis, "Minority Resistance in the Local State: Toronto in the 1970s and 1980s" (1989) 12:1 Ethnic & Racial Studies 63 at 67, online: <https://doi.org/10.1080/0 1419870.1989.9993623>.

9 *Ibid*.

10 Owusu-Bempah, *supra* note 7 at 3.

11 *Metropolitan Police Force Complaints Project Act*, SO 1981, c 43.

12 Owusu-Bempah, *supra* note 7 at 3.

13 *Police Services Act*, RSO 1990, c P.15; Wasun, "A Short History of Community Organizing against Police Brutality in Toronto: The History of BADC and Beyond," *BASICS* (20 March 2008), online: <basicsnewsletter.blogspot.com/2008/03/short-history-of-police -brutality-in.html> [perma.cc/HE8M-XSPC].

14 Ontario, Race Relations and Policing Task Force, *The Report of the Race Relations and Policing Task Force* (Ottawa: Queen's Printer, 1989) (Clare Lewis) at 1, online: <https:// www.siu.on.ca/pdfs/clare_lewis_report_1989.pdf> [perma.cc/9R5B-CYWM].

15 *Ibid* at 23.

16 *Ibid* at 212; Ontario, Special Investigations Unit, *Review Report on the Special Investigations Unit Reforms Prepared for the Attorney General of Ontario* (Toronto: Attorney General of Ontario, 2003) (George W Adams) at 9, online: <https://www.siu.on.ca/pdfs/adams_ report_ii.pdf> [perma.cc/JRJ7–4BPB].

17 Ontario, Ipperwash Inquiry, *Police Use of Force in Ontario: An Examination of Data from the Special Investigations Unit – Final Report* (Toronto: Attorney General of Ontario, 2006) (Scot Wortley) at 28–31, online: <https://www.attorneygeneral.jus.gov.on.ca/inquiries/ ipperwash/policy_part/projects/pdf/AfricanCanadianClinicIpperwashProject_ SIUStudybyScotWortley.pdf> [perma.cc/VA6S-9PJY].

18 Jim Rankin et al, "Singled Out," *Toronto Star* (19 October 2002), online: <https://www. thestar.com/news/gta/knowntopolice/2002/10/19/singled-out.html> [perma.cc/555Z -T4LC]; Jim Rankin et al, "Police Target Black Drivers," *Toronto Star* (20 October 2002), online: <https://www.thestar.com/news/gta/raceandcrime/2002/10/20/police-target -black-drivers-star-analysis-of-traffic-data-suggests.html> [perma.cc/8YR8-AWWR] [Rankin et al, "Police Target Black Drivers"].

19 Rankin et al, "Police Target Black Drivers," *supra* note 18.

20 *Ibid*.

21 *Ibid*.

22 *Ibid*.

23 Carol Tator & Frances Henry, *Racial Profiling in Canada: Challenging the Myth of 'a Few Bad Apples'* (Toronto: University of Toronto Press, 2006) at 5, online: <https://doi.org/ 10.3138/9781442678972>.

24 *Ibid* at 133.

25 Philip Mascoll & Jim Rankin, "Racial Profiling Exists: Promises of Internal Probe Fell Flat," *Toronto Star* (31 March 2005).

26 Jim Rankin, "When Good People Are Swept Up with the Bad," *Toronto Star* (6 February 2010), online: <https://www.thestar.com/news/gta/2010/02/06/when_good_people_are_ swept_up_with_the_bad.html> [perma.cc/65PU-JKVD]; Jim Rankin, "Carded: Probing a Racial Disparity," *Toronto Star* (6 February 2010).

27 *Ibid.*

28 Scot Wortley, "Justice for All? Race and Perceptions of Bias in the Ontario Criminal Justice System: A Toronto Survey" (1996) 38:4 Can J Crim 439 at 449.

29 Scot Wortley & Akwasi Owusu-Bempah, "Unequal before the Law: Immigrant and Racial Minority Perceptions of the Canadian Criminal Justice System" (2009) 10:4 J Intl Migration & Integration 447 at 465.

30 *Ibid.*

31 Scot Wortley, Akwasi Owusu-Bempah & Huibin Lin, *Race and Criminal Injustice: An Examination of Public Perceptions of and Experiences with the Ontario Criminal Justice System,* report prepared on behalf of the Canadian Association of Black Lawyers and funded by Legal Aid Ontario (Toronto: Ryerson University Faculty of Law, 2021) at 46, online: <perma.cc/649G-76FE>.

32 Gervan Fearon & Carlyle Farrell, "Perceptions of the Toronto Police and Impact of Rule Changes under Regulation 58/16: A Community Survey" (2019) at 16, 25, online (pdf): *Toronto Police Service Board* <https://tpsb.ca/consultations-and-publications/items-of -interest?task=download.send&id=612&catid=2&m=0> [perma.cc/PV6B-QRUX].

33 *Ibid* at 25.

34 *Ibid* at 16, 20.

35 *Ibid* at 29.

36 Wortley & Owusu-Bempah, *supra* note 30 at 462–64.

37 Akwasi Owusu-Bempah & Paul Millar, "Research Note: Revisiting the Collection of 'Justice Statistics by Race' in Canada" (2010) 25:1 CJLS 97 at 99, online: <https://doi. org/10.1017/S0829320100010231>.

38 Lysandra R Marshall, *Racial Disparities in Police Stops in Kingston, Ontario: Democratic Racism and Canadian Racial Profiling in Theoretical Perspective* (PhD Dissertation, University of Toronto, 2017) at 75, online: <https://tspace.library.utoronto.ca/handle/ 1807/77464> [hdl.handle.net/1807/77464].

39 Ontario, Kingston Police Services Board, *Police Stop Search Activities in Kingston, Ontario: Results from the Data Collection Pilot Project* (Kingston: Kingston Police Services Board, 2005) (Scot Wortley & Lysandra Marshall).

40 *Ibid.*

41 *Ibid.*

42 Catherine Porter, "Kingston Race Study Attacked: Report Tracked Police Arrests, Critics Dispute Claim of Racial Bias," *Toronto Star* (8 June 2005) A04, online: *Ottawa Men's Centre* <http://www.ottawamenscentre.com/news/20050609_kingston.htm> [perma.cc/35FR-CTPZ].

43 Owusu-Bempah, *supra* note 7 at 11.

44 Tator & Henry, *supra* note 23 at 16.

45 *Aiken v Ottawa Police Services Board,* 2013 HRTO 901 at paras 1, 29.

46 Lorne Foster, Les Jacobs & Bobby Siu, "Race Data and Traffic Stops in Ottawa, 2013–2015: A Report on Ottawa and the Police Districts" in Lorne Foster et al, eds, *Racial Profiling and Human Rights in Canada: The New Legal Landscape* (Toronto: Irwin Law, 2018) 353 at 354.

47 *Ibid* at 355.

48 Ontario Human Rights Commission (OHRC), *OHRC Response to the Race Data and Traffic Stops in Ottawa Report* (Toronto: OHRC, 2016) s 3, online: <www.ohrc.on.ca/en/book/export/html/19676> [perma.cc/4PVS-AH3P].

49 Patty Winsa & Jim Rankin, "Known to Police: Toronto Police Stop and Document Black and Brown People Far More Than Whites," *Toronto Star* (9 March 2012), online: <https://www.thestar.com/news/insight/2012/03/09/known_to_police_toronto_police_stop_and_document_black_and_brown_people_far_more_than_whites.html> [perma.cc/V962-P25S].

50 *Ibid*.

51 Patty Winsa & Jim Rankin, "Police Service Board Decision on 'Carding' Stuns Activists," *Toronto Star* (14 April 2012), online: <https://www.thestar.com/news/gta/2012/04/14/police_service_board_decision_on_carding_stuns_activists.html> [perma.cc/U8QC-2MMW].

52 Nova Scotia Human Rights Commission, *Nova Scotia Street Checks Report: Appendix A and B* (Halifax: Nova Scotia Human Rights Commission, 2019) (Scot Wortley & Akwasi Owusu-Bempah) at 76–77, online: <humanrights.novascotia.ca/sites/default/files/editor-uploads/appendixab.docx> [perma.cc/YX35-WA7G].

53 Simon Little, "Audit Finds 94% Drop in Street Checks by Vancouver Police: Critics Renew Call for Ban," *Global News* (18 February 2021), online: <https://globalnews.ca/news/7649562/vancouver-street-check-audit/> [perma.cc/MD7U-9ZJW].

54 Robynne Neugebauer-Visano, "Kids, Cops, and Colour: The Social Organization of Police-Minority Youth Relations" in Gary M O'Bireck, ed, *Not a Kid Anymore: Canadian Youth, Crime, and Subcultures* (Scarborough, ON: Nelson Canada, 1996) 283 at 293.

55 Carl E James, "'Up to No Good': Black on the Streets and Encountering Police" in Vic Satzewich, ed, *Racism and Social Inequality in Canada: Concepts, Controversies, and Strategies of Resistance* (Toronto: University of Toronto Press, 1998) 157 at 166.

56 *Ibid*.

57 Owusu-Bempah, *supra* note 7 at 133.

58 *Ibid*.

59 Delores Jones-Brown, "Forever the Symbolic Assailant: The More Things Change, The More They Remain the Same" (2007) 6:1 Criminology & Public Policy 103 at 109, online: <https://perma.cc/EGL2-HG8X>.

60 Owusu-Bempah, *supra* note 7 at 134.

61 CE James, "'Singled Out': Being a Black Youth in the Suburbs," in L Foster, L Jacobs & B Siu, eds, *Racial Profiling and Human Rights in Canada: The New Legal Landscape* (Toronto: Irwin Law, 2018) at 133.

62 *Ibid* at 149.

63 *Ibid*.

64 OHRC, *Paying the Price: The Human Cost of Racial Profiling* (Toronto: OHRC, 2003), online: <https://www3.ohrc.on.ca/sites/default/files/attachments/Paying_the_price%3A_The_human_cost_of_racial_profiling.pdf> [perma.cc/RNX6-663W] [OHRC, *Paying the Price*]; Christopher J Williams, "Obscurantism in Action: How the Ontario Human Rights Commission Frames Racial Profiling" (2006) 38:2 Can Ethnic Studies 1.

65 Roots of Youth Violence Inquiry, *The Review of the Roots of Youth Violence: Findings, Analysis and Conclusions,* vol 1 (Ottawa: Queen's Printer, 2008) (Roy McMurtry & Alvin Curling); Roots of Youth Violence Inquiry, *The Review of the Roots of Youth Violence: Community Perspectives Report,* vol 3 (Ottawa: Queen's Printer, 2008) (Roy McMurtry & Alvin Curling).

66 Ontario Regulation 58/16: Collection of Identifying Information in Certain Circumstances – Prohibition and Duties, January 1, 2017.

67 Fearon & Farrell, *supra* note 34 at 55.

68 Nova Scotia Human Rights Commission, *Nova Scotia Street Checks Report* (Halifax: Nova Scotia Human Rights Commission, 2019) (Scot Wortley) at 6–8, online: <https://humanrights.novascotia.ca/sites/default/files/editor-uploads/halifax_street_checks_report_march_2019_0.pdf> [perma.cc/X7PV-9WWK].

69 *Ibid* at 6.

70 David M Tanovich, *The Colour of Justice: Policing Race in Canada* (Toronto: Irwin Law, 2006) at 35–36.

71 Owusu-Bempah, *supra* note 7 at 164.

72 *Ibid* at 189–92.

73 *Ibid* at 186–88

74 Personal interview with the author, quoted in *ibid*.

75 *Ibid* at 59–60.

76 Elijah Anderson, *Streetwise: Race, Class, and Change in an Urban Community* (Chicago: University of Chicago Press, 1990); Alice Goffman, "On the Run: Wanted Men in a Philadelphia Ghetto" (2009) 74:3 American Sociological Rev 339; Alyasah Ali Sewell, Kevin A Jefferson & Hedwig Lee, "Living under Surveillance: Gender, Psychological Distress, and Stop-Question-and-Frisk Policing in New York City" (2016) 159 Social Science & Medicine 1 at 2, online: <https://doi.org/10.1016/j.socscimed.2016.04.024>.

77 Sewell, Jefferson & Lee, *supra* note 78 at 6–9.

78 *Ibid* at 9–10.

79 *Ibid*.

80 *Ibid*.

81 *Ibid* at 9.

82 Amanda Geller et al, "Aggressive Policing and the Mental Health of Young Urban Men" (2014) 104:12 American J Public Health 2321 at 2322, online: <https://www.ncbi.nlm.nih.gov/pmc/articles/PMC4232139/pdf/AJPH.2014.302046.pdf> [perma.cc/7W3A-Y649].

83 *Ibid*.

84 *Ibid* at 2324.

85 *Ibid* at 2324–25.

86 *Ibid* at 2324.

87 OHRC, *Paying the Price, supra* note 66 at 56.

88 Defined as youth who reported selling drugs on ten or more occasions in the previous twelve months.

89 S Wortley & J Tanner, "Inflammatory Rhetoric? Baseless Accusations? Responding to Gabor's Critique of Racial Profiling Research in Canada" (2005) 47:3 Can J Criminology & Crim Justice 581 at 586.

90 J Rankin, S Contenta & A Bailey, "Toronto Marijuana Arrests Reveal 'Startling' Racial Divide," *Toronto Star* (6 July 2017), online: <https://www.thestar.com/news/insight/2017/07/06/toronto-marijuana-arrests-reveal-startling-racial-divide.html>.

91 *Ibid*.

92 HA Hamilton et al, "Ethnoracial Differences in Cannabis Use among Native-Born and Foreign-Born High School Students in Ontario" (2018) 17:2 J Ethnicity in Substance Abuse 123.

93 Lisa D Moore & Amy Elkavich, "Who's Using and Who's Doing Time: Incarceration, the War on Drugs, and Public Health" (2008) 98:5 Am J Public Health 782, online:

<https://doi.org/10.2105/ajph.2007.126284>; Michelle Alexander, "The War on Drugs and the New Jim Crow" (2010) 17:1 Race, Poverty & the Environment 75, online: <https://perma.cc/ADV8-JVAY>; Elizabeth Hinton, *From the War on Poverty to the War on Crime* (Cambridge, MA: Harvard University Press, 2017); Elizabeth Hinton & DeAnza Cook, "The Mass Criminalization of Black Americans: A Historical Overview" (2021) 4 Annual Rev Criminology 261.

94 Scot Wortley & Akwasi Owusu-Bempah, "The Usual Suspects: Police Stop and Search Practices in Canada" (2011) 21:4 Policing & Society 395 at 403, online: <https://doi.org/10.1080/10439463.2011.610198>.

95 TR Tyler & J Fagan, "Legitimacy, Compliance and Cooperation: Procedural Justice and Citizen Ties to the Law" (2008) 6:1 Ohio State J Crim L 231.

96 SH Decker & RL Smith, "Police Minority Recruitment: A Note on Its Effectiveness in Improving Black Evaluations of the Police" (1980) 8:6 J Criminal Justice 387. See also C Kaukinen & S Colavecchia, *Public Perceptions of the Courts: An Examination of Attitudes toward the Treatment of Victims and Accused* (Ottawa: Canadian Criminal Justice Association, 1999).

97 Tom R Tyler, "Justice, Self-Interest, and the Legitimacy of Legal and Political Authority" in JJ Mansbridge, ed, *Beyond Self-Interest* (Chicago: University of Chicago Press, 1990) 171. See also GD LaFree, *Losing legitimacy: Street Crime and the Decline of Social Institutions in America* (Boulder, CO: Westview Press, 1998).

98 K Russell, *The Racial Hoax as Crime: The Law as Affirmation* (Indianapolis: Indiana State Bar Association, 1996).

99 J Del Toro et al, "The Criminogenic and Psychological Effects of Police Stops on Adolescent Black and Latino Boys" (2019) 116:17 Proceedings of the National Academy of Sciences 8261.

100 Anthony N Doob & Rosemary Gartner, "Understanding the Impact of Police Stops" (2017) at A22, online (pdf): *Centre for Criminology and Sociolegal Studies* <https://www.crimsl.utoronto.ca/sites/crimsl.utoronto.ca/files/DoobGartnerPoliceStopsReport-17Jan2017r.pdf> [perma.cc/73YK-MQTS].

Chapter 7: The Doctrine as a One-Way Ratchet

1 *R v Kang-Brown*, 2008 SCC 18 at para 6 [*Kang-Brown*].

2 *Dedman v The Queen*, [1985] 2 SCR 2, 20 DLR (4th) 321 [*Dedman*] (creating the police power to conduct roadblocks); *R v Mann*, 2004 SCC 52 [*Mann*] (creating the police power to conduct investigative detentions and to conduct preventive pat-down searches). For an overview of police powers, see Terry Skolnik, "Policing in the Shadow of Legality: Pretext, Leveraging, and Investigation Cascades" (2022) 60 Osgoode Hall LJ 505.

3 *R v Ladouceur*, [1990] 1 SCR 1257, SCJ No 53 [*Ladouceur*]. Note, however, that the Superior Court of Quebec recently struck down the constitutionality of random traffic stops. See *Luamba c Procureur général du Québec*, 2022 QCCS 3866 [*Luamba*].

4 *Criminal Code*, RSC 1985, c C-46, s 495; *Trespass to Property Act*, RSO 1990, c T.21, s 9, 10.

5 *Highway Traffic Act*, RSO 1990, c H.8, s 142 (signalling turns and stops), s 62 (lights required on all motor vehicles), s 144(22–27) (jaywalking).

6 See e.g., City of Ottawa, Bylaw No 2007-266, *Idling Control* (June 13, 2007) s 2; City of Saskatoon, Bylaw No 8354, *Public Spitting, Urination and Defecation Prohibition, 2004* (July 29, 2019), s 3.

7 *R v Beaudry*, 2007 SCC 5 at para 37 [*Beaudry*].

8 *Fleming v Ontario*, 2019 SCC 45 at para 82 [*Fleming*].

9 *Beaudry, supra* note 7 at paras 37–38.
10 Samuel Walker, *Taming the System: The Control of Discretion in Criminal Justice, 1950–1990* (Oxford: Oxford University Press, 1993) at 23–25.
11 On the criminal law's tendency to function as a one-way ratchet, see Aziz Huq, "Fourth Amendment Gloss" (2018) 113:4 Nw UL Rev 701 at 739–40; William Stuntz, "The Pathological Politics of Criminal Law" (2001) 100:3 Mich L Rev 505 at 509.
12 Terry Skolnik, "Racial Profiling and the Perils of Ancillary Police Powers" (2021) 99:2 Can Bar Rev 429 at 456–63 [Skolnik, "Racial Profiling"].
13 Terry Skolnik, "Rééquilibrer le rôle de la Cour Suprême de Canada en procédure criminelle" (2022) 67:3 McGill L J 259 at 278–84 [Skolnik, "Rééquilibrer"].
14 *Ladouceur, supra* note 3.
15 Rick Libman, "Is Presuming Guilt for Regulatory Offences Still Constitutional but Wrong? *R v Wholesale Travel Group Inc.* and Section 1 of the *Charter of Rights and Freedoms* 20 Years After" (2012) 43:3 Ottawa L Rev 455 at 459.
16 On domination, see Philip Pettit, *Republicanism: A Theory of Freedom and Government* (Oxford: Oxford University Press, 1999) [Pettit, *Republicanism*].
17 John Burchill, "A Horse Gallops Down a Street: Policing and the Resilience of the Common Law" (2018) 41:1 Man LJ 161 at 183.
18 Colton Fehr, "Criminal Law and Digital Technologies: An Institutional Approach to Rule Creation in a Rapidly Advancing and Complex Setting" (2019) 65:1 McGill LJ 67 at 89–91.
19 These three concerns are discussed more in depth in Skolnik, "Racial Profiling," *supra* note 12 at 433–35.
20 James Stribopoulos, "In Search of Dialogue: The Supreme Court, Police Powers and the *Charter*" (2005) 31 Queen's LJ 1 at 53–55 [Stribopoulos, "Search of Dialogue"]; Alexandre Boucher, François Lacasse & Thierry Nadon, "La création de la détention pour enquête en common law: Dérive jurisprudentielle ou évolution nécessaire? Un point de vue pragmatique" (2009) 50:3–4 C de D 770 at 773.
21 Skolnik, "Rééquilibrer," *supra* note 13 at 261–62.
22 *Ibid.*
23 James Stribopoulos, "A Failed Experiment: Investigative Detention: Ten Years Later" (2003) 41:2 Alta L Rev 335 at 382–83; Skolnik, "Racial Profiling," *supra* note 12.
24 Richard Jochelson et al, "Generation and Deployment of Common Law Police Powers by Canadian Courts and the Double-Edged *Charter*" (2020) 28 Critical Criminology 107 at 122.
25 Frank Cross, "The Error of Positive Rights" (2001) 48 UCLA L Rev 857 at 914.
26 Stribopoulos, "Search of Dialogue," *supra* note 20 at 48.
27 Skolnik, "Racial Profiling," *supra* note 12 at 461.
28 *Ibid.*
29 Stribopoulos, "Search of Dialogue," *supra* note 20 at 48.
30 Steve Coughlan, "Common Law Police Powers and the Rule of Law" (2007) 47 Criminal Reports (6th) 266 at 267.
31 Martin Friedland, "Reforming Police Powers: Who's in Charge?" in David Schneiderman & RC MacLeod, eds, *Police Powers in Canada: The Evolution and Practice of Authority* (Toronto: University of Toronto Press, 1994) 100 at 103–4.
32 Steve Coughlan, "*Charter* Protection against Unlawful Police Action: Less Black and White Than It Seems" (2012) 57 SCLR (2d) 205 at 207–8.

33 *Ibid.*
34 David Tanovich, "The Colourless World of *Mann*" (2004) 21 Criminal Reports (6th) 47 at 47–48.
35 Skolnik, "Racial Profiling," *supra* note 12 at 456–63.
36 *Ibid.*
37 Akwasi Owusu-Bempah & Scot Wortley, "Race, Crime, and Criminal Justice in Canada" in Sandra Bucerius & Michael Tonry, eds, *The Oxford Handbook of Ethnicity, Crime, and Immigration* (Oxford: Oxford University Press, 2014) 281 at 281–82, 286–87.
38 See e.g., Scot Wortley, *Halifax, Nova Scotia: Street Checks Report* (Halifax: Nova Scotia Human Rights Commission, 2019); Victor Armony, Mariam Hassaoui & Massimiliano Mulone, "Les interpellations policières à la lumière des identités racisées des personnes interpellées: Analyse des données du Service de Police de la Ville de Montréal (SPVM) et élaboration d'indicateurs de suivi en matière de profilage racial," Montreal, August 2019, at 7–11.
39 Akwasi Owusu-Bempah & Paul Millar, "Research Note: Revisiting the Collection of Justice Statistics by Race in Canada" (2010) 25:1 CJLS 97 at 98.
40 Terry Skolnik & Vanessa MacDonnell, "Policing Arbitrariness: *Fleming v Ontario* and the Ancillary Powers Doctrine" (2021) 100 SCLR (2d) 187 at 192–94.
41 *Fleming, supra* note 8 at para 42.
42 Skolnik, "Racial Profiling," *supra* note 12 at 455–56. However, there are some exceptions. For instance, the government of Quebec codified the random traffic stop power following *Ladouceur, supra* note 3. See *Luamba, supra* note 3 at paras 54–55.
43 Jochelson et al, *supra* note 24 at 116.
44 *Ibid.*
45 *Ibid.*
46 Stribopoulos, "Search of Dialogue," *supra* note 20 at 70–71.
47 Skolnik, "Racial Profiling," *supra* note 12 at 455–56; Oona Hathaway, "Path Dependence in the Law: The Course and Pattern of Legal Change in a Common Law System" (2001) 86:2 Iowa L Rev 601 at 604–5.
48 Skolnik, "Racial Profiling," *supra* note 12 at 455–56.
49 *Ibid* at 432.
50 *Ibid* at 456.
51 *Ibid* at 452.
52 See e.g., Richard Jochelson, "Crossing the Rubicon: Of Sniffer Dogs, Justifications, and Preemptive Deference" (2008) 13:2 Rev Const Stud 209 at 236. Jochelson notes that the ancillary powers doctrine avoids the policy debate inherent to the legislative process. However, new police powers also avoid the political blowback associated with enacting them.
53 Huq, *supra* note 11 at 739–40. Other scholars explain how the criminal law functions as a one-way ratchet more generally. See William Stuntz, "The Pathological Politics of Criminal Law" (2001) 100:3 Mich L Rev 505 at 509; Terry Skolnik, "The Tragedy of the Criminal Justice Commons" (2025) 58 UC Davis L Rev (forthcoming).
54 Coughlan, *supra* note 32 at 206–10.
55 *Ibid.*
56 *R v Grant,* 2009 SCC 32 at paras 54–56 [*Grant*]; *R v Collins,* [1987] 1 SCR 265 at para 23, SCJ No 15.
57 Coughlan, *supra* note 30 at 206–10.

58 *Ibid.*
59 The arguments and examples provided in this section were originally advanced in Skolnik, "Rééqulibrer," *supra* note 13 at 278–84.
60 *Ibid;* Kent Roach, "Making Progress on Understanding and Remedying Racial Profiling" (2004) 41:4 Alta L Rev 895 at 897–98; Tim Quigley, "Brief Investigatory Detentions: A Critique of *R v Simpson*" (2004) 41:4 Alta L Rev 935 at 948–49, cited in Roach, *ibid.*
61 *Canadian Charter of Rights and Freedoms,* Part 1 of the *Constitution Act, 1982,* being Schedule B to the *Canada Act 1982* (UK), 1982, c 11.
62 For an overview of *Charter* damages, see Kent Roach, "A Promising Late Spring for *Charter* Damages: *Ward v Vancouver*" (2011) 29 NJCL 145 at 152–53.
63 *Vancouver (City) v Ward,* 2010 SCC 27 [*Ward*].
64 *Ibid* at paras 7–8.
65 *Ibid* at para 64.
66 *Ibid* at para 73.
67 *R v Golden,* 2001 SCC 83 at para 83 [*Golden*].
68 *Ward, supra* note 63 at para 73.
69 *Ibid* at para 71.
70 Skolnik, "Rééqulibrer," *supra* note 13 at 282–83. On the anchoring effect, see Amos Tversky & Daniel Kahneman, "Judgment under Uncertainty: Heuristics and Biases" (1974) 185 Science 1124 at 1128–29.
71 Thomas Mussweiler, Birte Englich & Fritz Strack, "Anchoring Effect" in Rüdiger F Pohl, ed, *Cognitive Illusions: A Handbook on Fallacies and Biases in Thinking, Judgment, and Memory* (New York: Psychology Press, 2012) 183 at 185.
72 Chris Guthrie, Jeffrey Rachlinski & Andrew J Wistrich, "Blinking on the Bench: How Judges Decide Cases" (2007) 93 Cornell L Rev 1 at 19.
73 *Ibid.*
74 Tversky & Kahneman, *supra* note 70 at 1128–29.
75 Jennifer Robbennolt & Christina Studebaker, "Anchoring in the Courtroom: The Effects of Caps on Punitive Damages" (1999) 23:3 L & Human Behavior 353 at 368–69.
76 *Ibid.*
77 See e.g., *Joseph v Meier,* 2020 BCSC 778 at paras 87–91; *Stewart v Toronto (Police Services Board),* 2020 ONCA 255 at para 147; *Fleming, supra* note 8 at para 28; *Fong v British Columbia (Minister of Justice),* 2019 BCSC 263 at paras 440–43; *Mason v Turner,* 2016 BCCA 58 at para 9.
78 *Ibid.*
79 *Elmardy v Toronto Police Services Board,* 2017 ONSC 2074 at para 40 (awarding fifty thousand dollars in *Charter* damages). Note that few decisions have accorded a similar amount.
80 Ranjan Agarwal & Joseph Marcus, "Where There Is No Remedy, There Is No Right: Using *Charter* Damages to Compensate Victims of Racial Profiling" (2015) 34:1 NJCL 75 at 94.
81 *Seneca College of Applied Arts and Technology v Bhadauria,* [1981] 2 SCR 181 at 194–95, 124 DLR (3d) 193.
82 *Ibid.*
83 Mariève Lacroix, "Civil Liability of Police Forces: The Impact of the Quebec Charter and Punitive Damages" (2017) 51 RJTUM 547 at 576–77; Skolnik, "Rééqulibrer," *supra* note 13 at 281–82.
84 Don Stuart, "The Charter Balance against Unscrupulous Law and Order Politics" (2012) 57 SCLR (2d) 13 at 28.

85 Kent Roach, "Remedies for Discriminatory Profiling" in Kent Roach & Robert J Sharpe, eds, *Taking Remedies Seriously* (Montreal: Canadian Institute for the Administration of Justice, 2009) 391 at 403–5 [Roach, "Remedies for Discriminatory Profiling"].

86 Terry Skolnik, "Criminal Justice Reform: A Transformative Agenda" (2022) 59:3 Alta L Rev 631 at 657.

87 *Grant, supra* note 56, *Canadian Charter*, s 24(2).

88 I Bennett Capers, "Policing, Place, and Race" (2009) 44 Harv CR-CLL Rev 43 at 73.

89 Skolnik, "Rééqulibrer," *supra* note 13 at 290–93. See the overview in Rosemary Cairns Way, "Incorporating Equality into the Substantive Criminal Law: Inevitable or Impossible?" (2005) 4:2 JL & Equality 203 at 215–18.

90 *Ontario (Attorney General) v G*, 2020 SCC 38.

91 *Ibid* at para 8.

92 *Ibid* at paras 8–10.

93 *Ibid.*

94 *Ibid.*

95 See e.g., David Tanovich, "Applying the Racial Profiling Correspondence Test" (2017) 64 Crim LQ 359 at 362–8; Steven Hayle, Scot Wortley & Julian Tanner, "Race, Street Life, and Policing: Implications for Racial Profiling" (2016) 58:3 Can J Corr 322 at 325–26.

96 *R v Le*, 2019 SCC 3 [*Le*]; *R v Ahmad*, 2020 SCC 11.

97 Skolnik, "Rééquilibrer," *supra* note 13 at 278–84.

98 Isaiah Berlin, "Two Concepts of Liberty" in Henry Hardy, ed, *Liberty* (Oxford: Oxford University Press, 2002) 166 at 169.

99 *Ibid;* Charles Larmore, "Liberal and Republican Conceptions of Freedom" in Daniel Weinstock & Christian Nadeau, eds, *Republicanism: History, Theory, and Practice* (London: Frank Cass, 2004) 96 at 98.

100 Oren Ben-Dor, *Constitutional Limits and the Public Sphere: A Critical Study of Bentham's Constitutionalism* (London: Hart, 2000) at 258.

101 *Gosselin v Quebec (Attorney General)*, 2002 SCC 84 at paras 80–84.

102 On the republican theory of freedom, see Pettit, *Republicanism, supra* note 16.

103 Philip Pettit, *Just Freedom: A Moral Compass for a Complex World* (London: Norton, 2014) at 5.

104 *Ibid* at 4.

105 Pettit, *Republicanism, supra* note 16 at 22–23.

106 Philip Pettit, *On the People's Terms: A Republican Theory and Model of Democracy* (Cambridge: Cambridge University Press, 2012) at 7 [Pettit, *On the People's Terms*].

107 *Ibid.*

108 Tarunabh Khaitan, *A Theory of Discrimination Law* (Oxford: Oxford University Press, 2015) at 98–99.

109 Larmore, *supra* note 99 at 85.

110 Pettit, *Republicanism, supra* note 16 at 22–23.

111 *Ibid.*

112 Pettit, *On the People's Terms, supra* note 106 at 64.

113 *Ibid.*

114 *Ibid.*

115 *Ibid.*

116 Pettit, *Republicanism, supra* note 16 at 32.

117 Terry Skolnik, "Freedom and Access to Housing: Three Conceptions" (2018) 35 Windsor YB Access Just 226 at 237.

118 *Ibid.*
119 Pettit, *Republicanism, supra* note 16 at 58.
120 *Ibid* at 32.
121 Eoin Daly, "Freedom as Non-Domination in the Jurisprudence of Constitutional Rights" (2015) 28 Can JL & Jur 289 at 293.
122 Pettit, *Republicanism, supra* note 16 at 57.
123 *Ibid.*
124 Eric Miller, "Challenging Police Discretion" (2015) 58 How LJ 521 at 536–37.
125 Philip Pettit, "Criminalization in Republican Theory" in RA Duff et al, eds, *Criminalization: The Political Morality of the Criminal Law* (Oxford: Oxford University Press, 2014) 132 at 138–39 [Pettit, "Criminalization"].
126 *Ibid.*
127 *Ibid.*
128 *Ibid.*
129 *Ibid.*
130 *Ibid.*
131 Fabian Schuppert, "Non-Domination, Non-Alienation and Social Equality: Towards a Republican Understanding of Equality" (2015) 18:4 Critical Rev Intl Social & Political Philosophy 440 at 445.
132 Terry Skolnik, "Homelessness and Unconstitutional Discrimination" (2019) 15 JL & Equality 69 at 94 [Skolnik, "Homelessness"].
133 *Ibid;* Fabian Wendt, "Slaves, Prisoners, and Republican Freedom" (2011) 17 Res Publica 175 at 177–78.
134 Frank Lovett & Philip Pettit, "Neorepublicanism: A Normative and Institutional Research Program" (2009) 12 Annual Rev Political Science 11 at 14.
135 Skolnik, "Homelessness," *supra* note 132 at 75; Horacio Spector, "Four Conceptions of Freedom" (2010) 38:6 Political Theory 780 at 797–98.
136 Philip Pettit, "Law and Liberty" in Samantha Besson & José Luis Martí, eds, *Law and Republicanism* (Oxford: Oxford University Press, 2009) 39 at 44.
137 Quentin Skinner, "Freedom as the Absence of Arbitrary Power" in Cecile Laborde & John Maynor, eds, *Republicanism and Political Theory* (Oxford: Blackwell, 2008) 83 at 99, cited in Spector, *supra* note 135.
138 Skolnik, "Rééquilibrer," *supra* note 13 at 278–85; José Luis Martí, "The Republican Democratization of Criminal Law and Justice" in Besson & Martí, *supra* note 136, 124 at 133.
139 James Stribopoulos, "Packer's Blind Spot: Low Visibility Encounters and the Limits of Due Process versus Crime Control" in François Tanguay-Renaud & James Stribopoulos, eds, *Rethinking Criminal Law Theory: New Canadian Perspectives in the Philosophy of Domestic, Transnational, and International Criminal Law* (Oxford: Hart, 2012) 193 at 196 [Stribopoulos, "Packer's Blind Spot"].
140 Debra Livingston, "Police Discretion and the Quality of Life in Public Places: Courts, Communities, and the New Policing" (1997) 97 Colum L Rev 551 at 592.
141 David Tanovich, "E-Racing Racial Profiling" (2004) 41:4 Alta L Rev 905 at 929–30.
142 Gabriella Jamieson, "Using Section 24(1) *Charter* Damages to Remedy Racial Discrimination in the Criminal Justice System" (2017) 22 Appeal: Rev Current L & L Reform 71 at 90–91.
143 I Bennett Capers, "Criminal Procedure and the Good Citizen" (2018) 118 Colum L Rev 653 at 696–98; Eric J Miller, "Police Encounters with Race and Gender" (2015) 5:4 UC Irvine L Rev 735 at 750.

144 Seth Stoughton, "Principled·Policing: Warrior Cops and Guardian Officers" (2016) 51:3 Wake Forest L Rev 611 at 655.

145 Alice Ristroph, "The Constitution of Police Violence" (2017) 64 UCLA L Rev 1182 at 1185, 1189, 1192.

146 Rachel Abanonu, "De-escalating Police-Citizen Encounters" (2018) 27:3 Southern California Rev L & Social Justice 239 at 255.

147 Josh Bowers, "Annoy No Cop" (2017) 166 U Pa L Rev 129 at 172; Stoughton, *supra* note 144 at 655.

148 Janice Nadler, "No Need to Shout: Bus Sweeps and the Psychology of Coercion" (2002) 2002:1 Sup Ct Rev 153 at 195–97; David Kessler, "Free to Leave: An Empirical Look at the Fourth Amendment's Seizure Standard" (2008) 99:1 J Crim L & Criminology 51 at 60–64.

149 See also Eric Miller, "Encountering Resistance: Contesting Policing and Procedural Justice" (2016) U Chicago Legal F 295 at 341–42 (describing domination in policing contexts).

150 *Le, supra* note 96; *Mann, supra* note 2.

151 *Le, supra* note 96 at para 95, citing Ontario Human Rights Commission (OHRC), *A Collective Impact: Interim Report on the Inquiry into Racial Profiling and Racial Discrimination of Black Persons by the Toronto Police Service* (Toronto: Government of Ontario, 2018) at 21–27.

152 *Le, supra* note 96 at paras 85–97.

153 *Grant, supra* note 56 at para 169.

154 David Tanovich, "Using the *Charter* to Stop Racial Profiling: The Development of an Equality-Based Conception of Arbitrary Detention" (2002) 40:2 Osgoode Hall LJ 145 at 166; Ekow Yankah, "Pretext and Justification: Republicanism, Policing, and Race" (2019) 40 Cardozo L Rev 1543 at 1547–49.

155 *Dedman, supra* note 2; *Ladouceur, supra* note 3.

156 *Ladouceur, supra* note 3 at 1280.

157 *Ibid* at 1288–89.

158 Sujit Choudhry & Kent Roach, "Racial and Ethnic Profiling: Statutory Discretion, Constitutional Remedies, and Democratic Accountability" (2003) 41:1 Osgoode Hall LJ 1 at 17–18.

159 David Harris, "Driving While Black and All Other Traffic Offenses: The Supreme Court and Pretextual Traffic Stops" (1997) 87 J Crim L & Criminology 544 at 545; David Sklansky, "Traffic Stops, Minority Motorists, and the Future of the Fourth Amendment" (1997) 1997 Sup Ct Rev 271 at 273.

160 Pettit, "Criminalization," *supra* note 125 at 142.

161 John Braithwaite & Philip Pettit, *Not Just Deserts: A Republican Theory of Criminal Justice* (Oxford: Oxford University Press, 1992) at 93–94.

162 Steven Penney, "Driving While Innocent: Curbing the Excesses the 'Traffic Stop' Power" (2019) 24 Can Crim L Rev 339 at 360–61.

163 See the overview in Angelina Britt-Spells, "Effects of Perceived Discrimination on Depressive Symptoms among Black Men Residing in the United States: A Meta-Analysis" (2016) 12:1 American J Men's Health 52 at 55; Monica Bell, "Police Reform and the Dismantling of Legal Estrangement" (2017) 126 Yale LJ 2054 at 2066–67 (describing legal estrangement).

164 For a similar argument, see Daniel Susser, "Predictive Policing and the Ethics of Pre-emption" in Ben Jones & Eduardo Mendieta, eds, *The Ethics of Policing: New Perspectives on Law Enforcement* (New York: New York University Press, 2021) 268 at 284.

165 Lu-in Wang, "Race as Proxy: Situational Racism and Self-Fulfilling Stereotypes" (2004) 53 DePaul L Rev 1013 at 1046–47.

166 Tom Tyler, "Procedural Justice, Legitimacy, and the Effective Rule of Law" (2003) 30 Crime & Justice 283 at 325.

167 Charles Epp, Steven Maynard-Moody & Donald Haider-Markel, *Pulled Over: How Police Stops Define Race and Citizenship* (Chicago: University of Chicago Press, 2014) at 118–28; Wortley, *supra* note 38 at 41.

168 Wortley, *supra* note 38 at 41.

169 OHRC, *Under Suspicion: Research and Consultation Report on Racial Profiling in Ontario* (Toronto: Government of Ontario, 2017) at 11–12.

170 *Ibid* at 33–35.

171 David Sklansky, "Traffic Stops, Minority Motorists, and the Future of the Fourth Amendment" (1997) 1997 Sup Ct Rev 271 at 312–15, cited in Yankah, *supra* note 154.

172 This argument was advanced in Skolnik, "Racial Profiling," *supra* note 12 at 444–45.

173 Rick Trinkner, Jonathan Jackson & Tom Tyler, "Bounded Authority: Expanding 'Appropriate' Police Behavior beyond Procedural Justice" (2018) 42 L & Human Behavior 280 at 282–83; Rick Trinkner & Tom Tyler, "Legal Socialization: Coercion versus Consent in an Era of Mistrust" (2016) 12 Annual Rev L & Social Science 417 at 428.

174 Aziz Huq, Jonathan Jackson & Tom Tyler, "Legitimating Practices: Revisiting the Predicates of Police Legitimacy" (2017) Brit J Crim 1101 at 1118.

175 *Ibid* at 1102.

176 *Ibid* at 1102, 1104.

177 *Ibid* at 1118 (this example is provided by Aziz Huq, Jonathan Jackson, and Tom Tyler).

178 *Ibid.*

179 Tracey Meares, Tom Tyler & Jacob Gardener, "Lawful or Fair? How Cops and Laypeople Perceive Good Policing" (2015) 105 J Crim L & Criminology 297 at 333–34.

180 Stribopoulos, "Packer's Blind Spot," *supra* note 139 at 196.

181 Huq, Jackson & Tyler, *supra* note 174 at 1102.

182 Wesley Skogan, "Asymmetry in the Impact of Encounters with Police" (2006) 16 Policing & Society 99 at 100.

183 *Ibid.*

184 *Ibid.*

185 Wesley Skogan, "Assessing Asymmetry: The Life Course of a Research Project" (2012) 22 Policing & Society 270 at 272.

186 Rod Brunson, "'Police Don't Like Black People': African American Young Men's Accumulated Police Experiences" (2007) 6:1 Criminal & Public Policy 71 at 72–73; Jacinta Gau & Rod Brunson, "Procedural Justice and Order Maintenance Policing: A Study of Inner-City Young Men's Perceptions of Police Legitimacy" (2010) 27:2 Justice Q 255 at 265.

187 Scot Wortley & Akwasi Owusu-Bempah, "Unequal before the Law: Immigrant and Racial Minority Perceptions of the Canadian Criminal Justice System" (2009) 10 Intl Migration & Integration 447 at 463–64, 468; Scot Wortley & Akwasi Owusu-Bempah, "The Usual Suspects: Police Stop and Search Practices in Canada" (2011) 21 Policing & Society 395 at 401.

188 Ronald Weitzer, "Incidents of Police Misconduct and Public Opinion" (2002) 30 J Criminal Justice 397 at 405; Ronald Wetizer, "American Policing under Fire: Misconduct and Reform" (2015) 52 Society 475 at 475.

189 Felicia Campbell & Pamela Velera, "'The Only Thing New Is the Cameras': A Study of U.S. College Students' Perceptions of Police Violence on Social Media" (2020) 51:7 J Black Studies 654 at 662–64.

190 Ian Weinstein, "The Adjudication of Minor Offenses in New York City" (2004) 31:4 Fordham Urb LJ 1157 at 1163–64.

191 Skolnik, "Racial Profiling," *supra* note 12 at 439–44.

192 *Ibid;* Beverley McLachlin, "Preserving Public Confidence in the Courts and the Legal Profession" (2002) 29:3 Man LJ 277 at 279–87.

193 *Grant, supra* note 56 at para 68.

194 *R v Antic,* 2017 SCC 27 at para 34; *Criminal Code, supra* note 4, s 515(10)(c).

195 *R v Jordan,* 2016 SCC 27 at para 22.

196 *British Columbia (Attorney General) v Provincial Court Judges' Association of British Columbia,* 2020 SCC 20 at para 29.

197 Skolnik, "Racial Profiling," *supra* note 12. See e.g., *Ladouceur, supra* note 3 (random traffic stops); *Mann, supra* note 2 (investigative detentions and frisk searches); *Golden, supra* note 67 (strip-searches).

198 *Terry v Ohio,* 392 US 1 at 25 (1968).

199 Skolnik, "Racial Profiling," *supra* note 12 at 439.

200 *Fleming, supra* note 8 at para 2.

201 Tom Tyler & Jeffrey Fagan, "Legitimacy and Cooperation: Why Do People Help the Police Fight Crime in Their Communities" (2008) 6 Ohio State J Criminal L 231 at 233; Tom Tyler & Jonathan Jackson, "Popular Legitimacy and the Exercise of Legal Authority: Motivating Compliance, Cooperation, and Engagement" (2014) 21 Psychol Pub Pol'y & Law 78 at 79–80.

202 Tom Tyler, Jonathan Jackson & Avital Mentovich, "The Consequences of Being an Object of Suspicion: Potential Pitfalls of Proactive Police Contact" (2015) 12 J Empirical Leg Stud 602 at 625.

203 Skolnik, "Racial Profiling," *supra* note 12 at 431, 442.

204 For a summary of how criminal procedure is portrayed, see e.g., William Stuntz, "The Uneasy Relationship between Criminal Law and Criminal Procedure" (1997) 107:1 Yale LJ 1 at 3.

205 Erik Luna, "Transparent Policing" (2000) 85:4 Iowa L Rev 1107 at 1122.

206 John Hart Ely, *Democracy and Distrust: A Theory of Judicial Review* (Cambridge, MA: Harvard University Press, 1980) at 7–8.

207 Kent Roach, *The Supreme Court on Trial: Judicial Activism or Democratic Dialogue* (Toronto: Irwin Law, 2001) at 188.

208 See e.g., Kent Roach, "Remedies" in Peter Oliver, Patrick Macklem & Nathalie Des Rosiers, eds, *The Oxford Handbook of the Canadian Constitution* (Oxford: Oxford University Press, 2017) 673.

209 Stuntz, *supra* note 204 at 3.

210 Kent Roach, "Constitutional and Common Law Dialogues between the Supreme Court and Canadian Legislatures" (2001) 80 Can Bar Rev 481 at 483.

211 Stribopoulos, "Search of Dialogue," *supra* note 20 at 69–70.

212 *Ibid* at 34; Tim Quigley, "The Impact of the *Charter* on the Law of Search and Seizure" (2008) 40 SCLR (2d) 117 at 126–28. See e.g., *R v Feeney,* [1997] 2 SCR 13 (which gave rise to entry warrants); *R v Wong,* [1990] 3 SCR 36 (which gave rise to general warrants).

213 See e.g., Barry Friedman, "Dialogue and Judicial Review" (1993) 91 Mich L Rev 577 at 655–58.
214 Skolnik, "Racial Profiling," *supra* note 12 at 455–56.
215 *Ibid.*
216 Skolnik, "Rééquilibrer," *supra* note 13 at 278–84.
217 Roach, "Remedies for Discriminatory Profiling," *supra* note 85 at 408–10.
218 Lyndsey Beutin, "Racialization as a Way of Seeing: The Limits of Counter-Surveillance and Police Reform" (2017) 15:1 Surveillance & Society 5 at 8; Jocelyn Simonson, "Filming the Police as an Act of Resistance: Remarks Given at the Smartphoned Symposium" (2016) 10:2 U St Thomas JL & Public Policy 83 at 85–86; Jocelyn Simonson, "Democratizing Criminal Justice through Contestation and Resistance" (2017) 111:6 Nw UL Rev 1609 at 1618–19. Though Simonson speaks of organized cop watching, counter-surveillance fulfills similar ends and constitutes an individual form of cop watching (see notes 203 and on above).
219 Jocelyn Simonson, "Copwatching" (2016) 104:2 Cal L Rev 391 at 413–27.
220 Ben Brucato, "Policing Made Visible: Mobile Technologies and the Importance of Point of View" (2015) 13:3–4 Surveillance & Society 455 at 457–59.
221 Andrew John Goldstein, "Policing's New Visibility" (2010) 50:5 Brit J Crim 914 at 918–19.
222 See e.g., Howard Wasserman, "Recording of and by Police: The Good, the Bad, and the Ugly" (2017) 20:3 J Gender Race & Justice 543 at 543–44.
223 Gregory Brown, "The Blue Line on Thin Ice: Police Use of Force Modifications in the Era of Cameraphones and YouTube" (2016) 56:2 Brit J Crim 293 at 302–3.
224 Holly Campeau, "'Police Culture' at Work: Making Sense of Police Oversight" (2015) 55:4 Brit J Crim 669 at 674–75.
225 Simonson, *supra* note 219 at 408.
226 Laura Huey, Kevin Walby & Aaron Doyle, "Cop Watching in the Downtown Eastside: Exploring the Use of (Counter) Surveillance as a Tool of Resistance" in Laura Huey, Kevin Walby & Aaron Doyle, eds, *Surveillance and Security* (New York: Routledge, 2006) 149 at 150, 152–53.
227 Simonson, *supra* note 219 at 409.
228 *Ibid* at 408–9.
229 *Ibid.*
230 *Ibid* at 409–10.
231 Skolnik, "Racial Profiling," *supra* note 12 at 459–62.
232 *Ibid.*
233 Tanovich, *supra* note 154 at 928–29.
234 Skolnik, "Rééqulibrer," *supra* note 13 at 285–92.
235 Skolnik, "Racial Profiling," *supra* note 12 at 459–62.
236 *Ibid.*
237 *Ibid* at 434–35, 459–62.
238 Skolnik, "Rééqulibrer," *supra* note 13 at 290–92.
239 *Ibid.*

Conclusion

1 *Humphries v Connor*, [1864] 17 CLR 1 (CA).
2 *Canadian Charter of Rights and Freedoms*, Part 1 of the *Constitution Act, 1982*, being Schedule B to the *Canada Act 1982* (UK), 1982, c 11.
3 *R v Waterfield; R v Lynn*, [1963] 2 ALL ER 659 (CA).

4 *Dedman v The Queen,* [1985] 2 SCR 2, 20 DLR (4th) 321.

5 *R v Orbanski; R v Elias,* 2005 SCC 37.

6 Adam Cotter, "Perceptions of and Experiences with Police and the Justice System among the Black and Indigenous Populations in Canada" (16 February 2022), <https://www150. statcan.gc.ca/n1/pub/85-002-x/2022001/article/00003-eng.htm>.

7 *Ibid.*

8 "APA Dictionary of Psychology" (last modified 20 June 2019), online: *American Psychiatric Association* <dictionary.apa.org/bias> [perma.cc/2GY9–67FZ].

9 *Ibid.*

10 Margo Monteith & Anna Woodcock, "Modern Forms of Prejudice" in John M Levine & Michael A Hogg, eds, *Encyclopedia of Group Processes and Intergroup Relations* (Thousand Oaks, CA: Sage, 2010) 571 at 572.

11 Jennifer S Hunt, "Race, Ethnicity, and Culture in Jury Decision Making" (2015) 11 Annual Rev L & Social Science 269 at 269.

12 Kristin J Anderson, *Benign Bigotry: The Psychology of Subtle Prejudice* (Cambridge: Cambridge University Press, 2009) at 116.

13 Cotter, *supra* note 6.

14 David M Tanovich, "Relevance, Social Context and Poverty" (2003) 9 Criminal Reports (6th) 348 at 348.

15 *Ibid.*

16 For the psychological manifestations, see Stephen Porter et al, "Is the Face a Window to the Soul? Investigation of the Accuracy of Intuitive Judgments of the Trustworthiness of Human Faces" (2008) 40:3 Can J Behavioural Science 171.

17 Bill C-40, *An Act to Amend the Criminal Code, to Make Consequential Amendments to Other Acts and to Repeal a Regulation (Miscarriage of Justice Reviews),* 1st Sess, 44th Parl, 2023 (second reading on 21 June 2023).

Bibliography

Legislation and Case Law

Aiken v Ottawa Police Services Board, 2013 HRTO 901.

Bessell v Wilson (1853), [1911] 118 ER 518 (KB).

Bill C-40, *An Act to Amend the Criminal Code, to Make Consequential Amendments to Other Acts and to Repeal a Regulation (Miscarriage of Justice Reviews)*, 1st Sess, 44th Parl, 2023 (second reading on 21 June 2023).

Brigham City v Stuart, 547 US 398 (2006).

British Columbia (Attorney General) v Provincial Court Judges' Association of British Columbia, 2020 SCC 20.

Cady v Dombrowski, 413 US 433 (1973).

Canadian Bill of Rights, SC 1960, c 44.

Canadian Charter of Rights and Freedoms, Part I of the *Constitution Act, 1982*, being Schedule B to the *Canada Act 1982* (UK), 1982, c 11.

City of Fargo v Lee (et al), 580 NW (2d) 580 (Supt Ct ND 1998).

Cloutier v Langlois, [1990] 1 SCR 158, SCJ No 10.

Cohen v Huskisson, [1837] 2 M&W 477, 150 ER 845 (Court of Exch).

Commonwealth v Kiser, 724 NE (2d) 348 (Mass CA 2000).

Community Safety and Policing Act, SO 2019, c 1.

Constitution Act, 1867 (UK), 30 & 31 Vict, c 3.

Cooke v Nethercote, [1835] 6 C&P 744, sub nom *Cook v Nethercote*, 172 ER 1443.

Criminal Code, RSC 1985, c C-46.

Dedman v The Queen, [1985] 2 SCR 2, 20 DLR (4th) 321.

Dillon v O'Brien and Davis, [1887] 20 LR Ir 30, 16 Cox CC 245.

Duncan v Jones, [1936] 1 KB 218 (DC).

Elmardy v Toronto Police Services Board, 2017 ONSC 2074.

Entick v Carrington, [1765] 19 St Tr 1030 (CP).

Fleming v Ontario, 2019 SCC 45 at para 5.

Fong v British Columbia (Minister of Justice), 2019 BCSC 263.

Gordon v Denison (1895), 22 OAR 315, 1895 WL 8710.

Gosselin v Quebec (Attorney General), 2002 SCC 84.

Gottschalk v Hutton (1921), 17 Alta LR 347, 66 DLR 499.

Haynes v Harwood, [1935] 1 KB 146 (CA), [1934] 2 KB 240.

Humphries v Connor, [1864] 17 ICLR 1 (CA).

Hunter et al v Southam Inc, [1984] 2 SCR 145, 11 DLR (4th) 641.

Johnson v Phillips, [1975] 3 All ER 682.

Joseph v Meier, 2020 BCSC 778.

Kyle v Bell, [1836] 1 M&W 519, sub nom *Ingle v Bell*, 150 ER 539.

Laporte v Laganière (1972), 29 DLR (3d) 651, 8 CCC (2d) 343 (Qc SC).

Laws of Assiniboia (1862).

Leigh v Cole, [1853] 6 Cox CC 329.

Luamba c Procureur général du Québec, 2022 QCCS 3866.

Mason v Turner, 2016 BCCA 58.

Ngan v The Queen, [2007] NZSC 105, [2008] 2 NZLR 48.

Nicholson v Avon, [1991] 1 VR 212.

O'Kelly v Harvey, [1883] 14 LR Ir 105.

Ontario (Attorney General) v G, 2020 SCC 38.

Police Act, SQ 1870, c 39.

Police Act, SM 1871, c 33.

Police Act, SNB 1977, c P-9.2.

Police Act, RSPEI 1988, c P-11.1.

Police Act, SS 1990, c P-15.01.

Police Act, RSBC 1996, c 367.

Police Act, RSA 2000, c P-17.

Police Act, CQLR 2000, c P-13.1.

Police Act, SNS 2004, c 31.

Police and Criminal Evidence Act 1984 (UK), c 60.

Police Services Act, CCSM, c P94.5.

Police Services Act, RSO 1990, c P.15.

Re in Trespass of Assault, Battery and Imprisonment, [1593] 79 ER 1135 (KB).

Reference re: Remuneration of Judges of the Provincial Court of Prince Edward Island, [1997] 3 SCR 3.

Reference re Secession of Quebec, [1998] 2 SCR 217.

Reynen v Antonenko (1975), 54 DLR (3d) 124, 20 CCC (2d) 342 (Alta SC).

Royal Canadian Mounted Police Act, RSC 1985, c R-10.

Royal Newfoundland Constabulary Act, 1992, SNL 1992, c R-17.

R v Ahmad, 2020 SCC 11.

R v Antic, 2017 SCC 27 at para 34.

R v Barnett (1829), [1928] 172 ER 563.

R v Bartle, [1994] 3 SCR 173, 172 NR 1.

R v Beare, [1988] 2 SCR 387, 55 DLR (4th) 481.

R v Beaudry, 2007 SCC 5.

R v Brezack, [1949] OR 888, [1950] 2 DLR 265 (Ont CA).

R v Brown, 64 OR (3d) 161, [2003] OJ No 1251.

R v Browne, [1841] 1 C&M 314, sub nom *R v Browne*, 174 ER 522.

R v Caslake, [1998] 1 SCR 51, 155 DLR (4th).

R v Collins, [1987] 1 SCR 265 at 278, SCJ No 15.

R v Clayton, 2007 SCC 32.

R v Debot, [1989] 2 SCR 1140, 52 CCC (3d) 193.

R v Dreysko, (1990) 110 AR 317 (CA).

R v Edwards, [1996] 1 SCR 128 at para 45, 132 DLR (4th) 31.

R v Fearon, 2010 ONCJ 645 at para 44.

R v Fearon, 2014 SCC 77.

R v Feeney, [1997] 2 SCR 13.

R v Gibson, 2003 BCSC 1572.

R v Godoy, [1999] 1 SCR 311, 41 OR (3d) 95.

R v Golden, 2001 SCC 83.

R v Grant, 2009 SCC 32.

R v Hern, (1994) 149 AR 75 (CA), 1994 ABCA 65.

R v Hogan, (1837) 8 C&P 171, sub nom *R v Hagan,* 173 ER 445.

R v Howell, (1981) 73 Cr App R 31 (CA).

R v Jacoy, [1988] 2 SCR 548, 89 NR 61.

R v Jamieson, 2002 BCCA 411.

R v Johnston, 2004 BCCA 148.

R v Jones, [1834], 6 Car & P 343, 172 ER 1296.

R v Jordan, 2016 SCC 27.

R v Kang-Brown, 2008 SCC 18.

R v Kinsey, [1836], 7 Car & P 447, 173 ER 198.

R v Ladouceur, [1990] 1 SCR 1257, SCJ No 53.

R v Le, 2019 SCC 34.

R v Lerke (1986), 43 Alta LR (2d), 24 CCC (3d) 129.

R v Lushington, [1894] 1 QB 420.

R v MacDonald, 2014 SCC 3.

R v MacKenzie, 2013 SCC 50.

R v Mann, 2004 SCC 52.

R v Martin, (1995), 97 CCC (3d) 241, 1995 CanLII 1003 (BCCA).

R v McColman, 2021 ONCA 382.

R v McColman, 2023 SCC 8.

R v McDonald (1932), 26 Alta LR 460, 59 CCC 56 (Alta SC, App Div).

R v McKenzie, 2022 MBCA 3.

R v Miller (1987), 62 OR (2d) 97, 38 CCC (3d) 252 (Ont CA).

R v Morrison (1987), 20 OAC 230, 35 CCC (3d) 437.

R v Nguyen, [2000] BCJ No 2728 (SC).

R v O'Donnell, [1835] 173 ER 61.

R v Oakes, [1986] 1 SCR 103, SCJ No 7.

R v Orbanski; R v Elias, 2005 SCC 37.

R v Perka, [1984] 2 SCR 232 at 246, SCJ No 40.

R v Rao (1984), 46 OR (2d) 80, 9 DLR (4th) 542 (Ont CA).

R v Ringler, 2004 ONCJ 104.

R v Ritch and Mynott, 2015 ONSC 5433.

R v Saeed, 2016 SCC 24.

R v Simpson, 1993 CarswellOnt 83 (CA).

R v Stairs, 2022 SCC 11.

R v Stenning, [1970] SCR 631, [1970] RCS 631.

R v Stillman, [1997] 1 SCR 607, 144 DLR (4th) 193.

R v Tessling, 2004 SCC 67.

R v Vu, 2013 SCC 60.

R v Waterfield; R v Lynn, [1963] 2 ALL ER 659 (CA).

R v Wong, [1990] 3 SCR 36.

Rousseau v The Queen, [1985] 2 SCR 38.

Seneca College of Applied Arts and Technology v Bhadauria, [1981] 2 SCR 181, 124 DLR (3d) 193.

Seymayne's Case, [1588–1774] All ER Rep 62.

Statute of Winchester of 1285 (UK), 13 Edw I, St 2 (Latin: *Statutum Wynton*).

Stewart v Toronto (Police Services Board), 2020 ONCA 255.

Terry v Ohio, 392 US 1 (1968).

Thomas v Sawkins, [1935] 2 KB 249.

Tuato v R, [2011] NZCA 278.

United States v Lancellotti, 145 F (3d) 1342 (9th Cir 1998).

United States v Robinson, 414 US 218 (1973).

United States v Rodriguez-Morales, 929 F (2d) 780 (1st Cir 1991), 112 S Ct 868 (1992).

United States v Rohrig, 98 F (3d) 1506 (6th Cir 1996).

United States v Smith, 522 F (3d) 305 (3rd Cir 2008).

Vancouver (City) v Ward, 2010 SCC 27.

Welch v Gilmour (1955), 111 CCC 221, 1955 CarswellBC 190 (BCSC).

Wiretap Reference, [1984] 2 SCR 697, 14 DLR (4th) 546.

Yakimishyn v Bileski, [1946] 3 DLR 390, 86 CCC 179 (MBKB).

Books and Articles

Abanonu, Rachel. "De-escalating Police-Citizen Encounters" (2018) 27:3 Southern California Rev L & Social Justice 239.

Aboriginal Justice Inquiry (AJI). *Final Report of the Aboriginal Justice Implementation Commission*. Winnipeg: AJI, 2001. <http://www.ajic.mb.ca/reports/final_toc.html>.

Agarwal, Ranjan, and Joseph Marcus. "Where There Is No Remedy, There Is No Right: Using *Charter* Damages to Compensate Victims of Racial Profiling" (2015) 34:1 NJCL 75.

Alexander, Michelle. "The War on Drugs and the New Jim Crow" (2010) 17:1 Race, Poverty & the Environment 75. <https://perma.cc/ADV8-JVAY>.

Alexy, Robert. "Constitutional Rights and Proportionality" (2014) 22 Revus: J Constitutional Theory & Philosophy of Law 51.

Anderson, Elijah. *Streetwise: Race, Class, and Change in an Urban Community*. Chicago: University of Chicago Press, 1990.

Anderson, Kristin J. *Benign Bigotry: The Psychology of Subtle Prejudice*. Cambridge: Cambridge University Press, 2009.

"APA Dictionary of Psychology." *American Psychiatric Association*, last modified 20 June 2019. <http://dictionary.apa.org/bias> [perma.cc/2GY9–67FZ].

Appleby, Timothy. "Kingston Police More Likely to Stop Blacks, Study Finds." *Globe and Mail*, 27 May 2005.

Armony, Victor, Mariam Hassaoui, and Massimiliano Mulone. "Les interpellations policières à la lumière des identités racisées des personnes interpellées: Analyse des données du Service de Police de la Ville de Montréal (SPVM) et élaboration d'indicateurs de suivi en matière de profilage racial." Montreal, August 2019.

Baćak, Valerio, and Kathryn Nowotny. "Race and the Association between Police Stops and Depression among Young Adults: A Research Note" (2020) 10:3 Race & Justice 363.

Bagnall, Roger S. "Army and Police in Roman Upper Egypt" (1977) 14 Journal of the American Research Center in Egypt 67–86.

Barak, Aharon. "A Judge on Judging: The Role of a Supreme Court in a Democracy" (2002) 116:1 Harv L Rev 19.

–. "Proportionality and Principled Balancing" (2010) 4:1 L & Ethics of Human Rights 1.

Bayley, David H. "What Do the Police Do?" In *Themes in Contemporary Policing*, ed. William Salusbury, Joy Mott, and Tim Newburn, 29–41. London: Police Foundation, 1996.

Beatty, David. *The Ultimate Rule of Law.* Oxford: Oxford University Press, 2004.

Bell, Felicity. "Empirical Research in Law" (2016) 25:2 Griffith L Rev 267.

Bell, Monica. "Anti-Segregation Policing" (2020) 95:3 NYU L Rev 650.

–. "Police Reform and the Dismantling of Legal Estrangement" (2017) 126 Yale LJ 2054.

Ben-Dor, Oren. *Constitutional Limits and the Public Sphere: A Critical Study of Bentham's Constitutionalism,* London: Hart, 2000.

Berlin, Isaiah. "Two Concepts of Liberty." In *Liberty,* ed. Henry Hardy, 166–217. Oxford: Oxford University Press, 2002.

Beutin, Lyndsey. "Racialization as a Way of Seeing: The Limits of Counter-Surveillance and Police Reform" (2017) 15:1 Surveillance & Society 5.

Bickel, Alexander. *The Least Dangerous Branch: The Supreme Court at the Bar of Politics.* New Haven, CT: Yale University Press, 1962.

Borrows, John. *Recovering Canada: The Resurgence of Indigenous Law.* Toronto: University of Toronto Press, 2002.

Boucher, Alexandre, François Lacasse, and Thierry Nadon. "La création de la détention pour enquête en common law: Dérive jurisprudentielle ou évolution nécessaire? Un point de vue pragmatique" (2009) 50:3–4 C de D 770.

Bowers, Josh. "Annoy No Cop" (2017) 166 U Pa L Rev 129.

Braithwaite, John, and Philip Pettit. *Not Just Deserts: A Republican Theory of Criminal Justice.* Oxford: Oxford University Press, 1992.

Britt-Spells, Angelina. "Effects of Perceived Discrimination on Depressive Symptoms among Black Men Residing in the United States: A Meta-Analysis" (2016) 12:1 American J Men's Health 52.

Brougham, Lord H. *Historical Sketches of Statesmen Who Flourished in the Time of George III.* Vol. 1. Oxford: Devils in the Detail, 1985.

Brown, Gregory. "The Blue Line on Thin Ice: Police Use of Force Modifications in the Era of Cameraphones and YouTube" (2016) 56:2 Brit J Crim 293.

Brucato, Ben. "Policing Made Visible: Mobile Technologies and the Importance of Point of View" (2015) 13:3–4 Surveillance & Society 455.

Brunson, Rod. "'Police Don't Like Black People': African-American Young Men's Accumulated Police Experiences" (2007) 6:1 Criminology & Public Policy 71.

Burchill, John. "A Horse Gallops Down a Street: Policing and the Resilience of the Common Law" (2018) 41:1 Man LJ 161.

–. President, Winnipeg Police Museum and Historical Society, and Executive Support Officer, Manitoba Association Chiefs of Police. Personal communication, 5 May 2023 [documents on file with author].

–. "Stripping Matters to the [Central] Core: Searching Electronic Devices Incident to Arrest" (2009) 33:2 Man LJ 263.

Burns, Kylie, and Terry C. Hutchinson. "The Impact of 'Empirical Facts' on Legal Scholarship and Legal Research Training" (2009) 43:2 The Law Teacher 153.

Cabrera, Holly. "Terrebonne Police, City Slammed with $205K Lawsuit for Systemic Discrimination." *CBC News*, 4 January 2023. <http://www.cbc.ca/news/canada/montreal/black-while-driving-monsanto-terrebonne-police-1.6703471>.

Cairns Way, Rosemary. "Incorporating Equality into the Substantive Criminal Law: Inevitable or Impossible?" (2005) 4:2 JL & Equality 203.

Callanan, Valerie, and Jared Rosenberger. "Media and Public Perceptions of the Police: Examining the Impact of Race and Personal Experience" (2011) 21:2 Policing & Society 167.

Campbell, Felicia, and Pamela Velera. "'The Only Thing New Is the Cameras': A Study of U.S. College Students' Perceptions of Police Violence on Social Media" (2020) 51:7 J Black Studies 654.

Campeau, Holly. "'Police Culture' at Work: Making Sense of Police Oversight" (2015) 55:4 Brit J Crim 669.

Capers, I. Bennett. "Criminal Procedure and the Good Citizen" (2018) 118 Colum L Rev 653.

Carter, Mark. "Non-Statutory Criminal Law and the Charter: The Application of the Swain Approach in *R v Daviault*" (1995) 59:2 Sask L Rev 241.

Choudhry, Sujit. "So What Is the Real Legacy of *Oakes*? Two Decades of Proportionality Analysis under the *Canadian Charter*'s Section 1" (2006) 34 SCLR (2d) 501.

Choudhry, Sujit, and Kent Roach. "Racial and Ethnic Profiling: Statutory Discretion, Constitutional Remedies, and Democratic Accountability" (2003) 41:1 Osgoode Hall LJ 1.

Chui, T., K. Tran, and H. Maheux. *Canada's Ethnocultural Mosaic: The 2006 Census*. Catalogue no. 97-562-X. Ottawa: Statistics Canada, 2008.

Cobbina-Dungy, J., S. Chaudhuri, A. LaCourse, and C. DeJong. "'Defund the Police': Perceptions among Protesters in the 2020 March on Washington" (2022) 21 Criminology & Public Policy 1. <https://onlinelibrary.wiley.com/doi/10.1111/1745-9133.12571>.

Cohen-Eliya, Moshe, and Iddo Porat. "Proportionality and Justification" (2014) 64:3 UTLJ 458.

–. "Proportionality and the Culture of Justification" (2011) 59:2 Am J Comp L 463.

Cohn, Margit, and Mordechai Kremnitzer. "Judicial Activism: A Multidimensional Model" (2005) 18 Can JL & Jur 333.

Colquhoun, Patrick. *A Treatise on the Police of the Metropolis, Etc.* 2nd ed. London: H. Fry, 1796.

Cotter, Adam. "Perceptions of and Experiences with Police and the Justice System among the Black and Indigenous Populations in Canada." (16 February 2022) 42:1 Juristat 1.

Coughlan, Steve. "*Charter* Protection against Unlawful Police Action: Less Black and White Than It Seems" (2012) 57 SCLR (2d) 205.

–. "Common Law Police Powers and the Rule of Law" (2007) 47 Criminal Reports (6th) 266.

Cover, Aliza. "Cruel and Invisible Punishment: Redeeming the Counter-Majoritarian Eighth Amendment" (2014) 79:3 Brook L Rev 1141.

Cross, Frank. "The Error of Positive Rights" (2001) 48 UCLA L Rev 857.

Daly, Eoin. "Freedom as Non-Domination in the Jurisprudence of Constitutional Rights" (2015) 28 Can JL & Jur 289.

Decker, Scott H., and Russell L. Smith. "Police Minority Recruitment: A Note on Its Effectiveness in Improving Black Evaluations of the Police" (1980) 8:6 J Crim Justice 387.

Del Toro, Juan, Tracey Lloyd, Kim S. Buchanan, Summer Joi Robins, Lucy Zhang Bencharit, Meredith Gamson Smiedt, Kavita S. Reddy, Enrique Rodriguez Pouget, Erin M. Kerrison, and Phillip Atiba Goff. "The Criminogenic and Psychological Effects of Police Stops on Adolescent Black and Latino Boys" (2019) 116:17 Proceedings of the National Academy of Sciences 8261.

DeLloyd, Guth. "The Traditional Common-Law Constable." In *Police Powers in Canada: The Evolution and Practice of Authority*, ed. David Schneiderman and R.C. Macleod, 3–23. Toronto: University of Toronto Press, 1994.

Di Matteo, Livio. "Police and Crime Rates in Canada." *Fraser Institute*, 2014. <https://www.fraserinstitute.org/sites/default/files/police-and-crime-rates-in-canada.pdf> [perma.cc/AGV5–4RXT].

Doob, Anthony N., and Rosemary Gartner. "Understanding the Impact of Police Stops." *Centre for Criminology and Sociolegal Studies*, 2017. <http://www.crimsl.utoronto.ca/sites/crimsl.utoronto.ca/files/DoobGartnerPoliceStopsReport-17Jan2017r.pdf> [perma.cc/73YK-MQTS].

Dripps, Donald. "The Fourth Amendment, the Exclusionary Rule, and the Roberts Court: Normative and Empirical Dimensions of the Over-Deterrence Hypothesis" (2010) 85:1 Chicago-Kent L Rev 209.

Dworkin, Ronald. *Taking Rights Seriously*. London: Duckworth, 1997.

Engel, R., and J. Canlon. "Examining the Influence of Drivers' Characteristics during Traffic Stops with Police: Results from a National Survey" (2004) 21 Justice Quarterly 49.

Epp, Charles, S. Maynard-Moody, and D.P. Haider-Markel. *Pulled Over: How Police Stops Define Race and Citizenship*. Chicago: University of Chicago Press, 2014.

Ericson, Richard V. *Reproducing Order: A Study of Police Patrol Work*. Toronto: University of Toronto Press, 1982.

Fearon, Gervan, and Carlyle Farrell, "Perceptions of the Toronto Police and Impact of Rule Changes under Regulation 58/16: A Community Survey." *Toronto Police Service Board*, 2019. <https://tpsb.ca/consultations-and-publications/items-of-interest?task=download.send&id=612&catid=2&m=0> [perma.cc/PV6B-QRUX].

Fehr, Colton. "Criminal Law and Digital Technologies: An Institutional Approach to Rule Creation in a Rapidly Advancing and Complex Setting" (2019) 65:1 McGill LJ 67.

Foster, Lorne, L.A. Jacobs, B. Siu, and S. Azmi, eds. *Racial Profiling and Human Rights in Canada: The New Legal Landscape*. Toronto: Irwin Law, 2018.

Foster, Lorne, Les Jacobs, and Bobby Siu. *Race Data and Traffic Stops in Ottawa, 2013–2015: A Report on Ottawa and the Police Districts*. Ottawa: Ottawa Police Service, 2016.

Freeze, Colin. "More Than One-Third of People Shot to Death over a Decade by RCMP Officers Were Indigenous." *Globe and Mail*, 17 November 2019. <https://www.theglobeandmail.com/canada/article-more-than-one-third-of-people-shot-to-death-over-a-decade-by-rcmp/>.

Friedland, Martin. "Reforming Police Powers: Who's in Charge?" In *Police Powers in Canada: The Evolution and Practice of Authority*, ed. David Schneiderman and R.C. MacLeod, 100–18. Toronto: University of Toronto Press, 1994.

Friedman, Barry. "Dialogue and Judicial Review" (1993) 91 Mich L Rev 577.

Frug, Gerald. "Judicial Power of the Purse" (1978) 126:4 U Pa L Rev 715.

Fuhrmann, Christopher J. *Policing the Roman Empire: Soldiers, Administration, and Public Order (30 BC–476 AD)*. New York: Oxford University Press, 2012.

Fyson, Donald. *Magistrates, Police and People: Everyday Criminal Justice in Quebec and Lower Canada, 1764–1837*. Toronto: Osgoode Society, 2006.

Gardiner, Robert. *The Complete Constable: Directing All Constables, Headboroughs, Tithingmen, Churchwardens, Overseers of the Poor, Surveyors of the Highways, and Scavengers, in the Duty of Their Several Offices, According to the Power Allowed Them by the Laws and Statutes: Continued to This Present Time*. London: Printed by the Assigns of Richard and Edward Atkins, 1736.

Gau, Jacinta, and Rod Brunson. "Procedural Justice and Order Maintenance Policing: A Study of Inner-City Young Men's Perceptions of Police Legitimacy" (2010) 27:2 Justice Q 255.

Geller, Amanda, Jeffrey Fagan, Tom Tyler, and Bruce G. Link. "Aggressive Policing and the Mental Health of Young Urban Men" (2014) 104:12 American J Public Health 2321. <https://www.ncbi.nlm.nih.gov/pmc/articles/PMC4232139/pdf/AJPH.2014.302046.pdf> [perma.cc/7W3A-Y649].

Giles, Jacob. "Constable." In *A New Law-Dictionary Containing the Interpretation and Definition of Words*. London: E. and R. Nutt and R. Gosling, 1729.

Goffman, Alice. "On the Run: Wanted Men in a Philadelphia Ghetto" (2009) 74:3 American Sociological Rev 339.

Goldstein, Andrew J. "Policing's New Visibility" (2010) 50:5 Brit J Crim 914.

Goldstein, Joseph. "Police Discretion Not to Invoke the Criminal Process: Low-Visibility Decisions in the Administration of Justice" (1960) 69:4 Yale LJ 543.

Gowan, James. *The Canadian Constables' Assistant*. Barrie: J.W. Young, 1852.

Griffith, C.T., B. Whitelaw, and R.B. Parent. *Canadian Police Work*. Toronto: ITP Nelson, 1999.

Guthrie, Chris, Jeffrey Rachlinski, and Andrew J. Wistrich. "Blinking on the Bench: How Judges Decide Cases" (2007) 93 Cornell L Rev 1.

Hale, Mathew. *Historia Placitorum Coronæ. The History of the Pleas of the Crown, by Sir Matthew Hale ... Now First Published from His Lordship's Original Manuscript, and the Several References to the Records Examined by the Originals, with Large Notes. By Sollom Emlyn ... To Which Is Added a Table of the Principal Matters*. In the Savoy: Printed by E. and R. Nutt and R. Gosling, assigns of Edward Sayer, Esq; for F. Gyles, T. Woodward, and C. Davis, 1736.

Hamilton, Alexander. "Federal No. 78." In *The Federalist Papers*. New York: Palgrave Macmillan, 2009.

Hamilton, H.A., A. Owusu-Bempah, A. Boak, and R.E. Mann. "Ethnoracial Differences in Cannabis Use among Native-Born and Foreign-Born High School Students in Ontario" (2018) 17:2 J Ethnicity in Substance Abuse 123.

Harrington, Christine B., and Sally Engle Merry. *The Oxford Handbook of Empirical Legal Research*. Oxford: Oxford University Press, 2010.

Harris, David. "Across the Hudson: Taking the Stop and Frisk Debate beyond New York City" (2013) 16:4 NYU J Legis & Pub Pol'y 853.

–. "Driving While Black and All Other Traffic Offenses: The Supreme Court and Pretextual Traffic Stops" (1997) 87 J Crim L & Criminology 544.

–. "The Stories, the Statistics, and the Law: Why Driving While Black Matters" (1999) 84:2 Minn L Rev 265.

Hart Ely, John. *Democracy and Distrust: A Theory of Judicial Review*. Cambridge, MA: Harvard University Press, 1980.

Hayle, Steven, Scot Wortley, and Julian Tanner. "Race, Street Life, and Policing Implications for Racial Profiling" (2016) 58:3 Can J Corr 322.

Hilton, Jennifer. "Instructions to the New Police" (1977) 50:1 Police 23.

Hinton, Elizabeth. *From the War on Poverty to the War on Crime*. Cambridge, MA: Harvard University Press, 2017.

Hinton, Elizabeth, and DeAnza Cook. "The Mass Criminalization of Black Americans: A Historical Overview" (2021) 4 Annual Rev Criminology 261. <https://www.annual reviews.org/content/journals/10.1146/annurev-criminol-060520-033306>.

Huey, Laura, Kevin Walby, and Aaron Doyle. "Cop Watching in the Downtown Eastside: Exploring the Use of (Counter) Surveillance as a Tool of Resistance." In *Surveillance and Security*, ed. Laura Huey, Kevin Walby, and Aaron Doyle, 149–65. New York: Routledge, 2006.

Hunt, Jennifer. "Race, Ethnicity, and Culture in Jury Decision Making" (2015) 11 Annual Rev L & Social Science 269.

Hunter, Virginia J. *Policing Athens: Social Control in the Attic Lawsuits, 420–320 BC*. Princeton, NJ: Princeton University Press, 1993.

Huq, Aziz. "Fourth Amendment Gloss" (2018) 113:4 Nw UL Rev 701.

Huq, Aziz, Jonathan Jackson, and Tom Tyler. "Legitimating Practices: Revisiting the Predicates of Police Legitimacy" (2017) Brit J Crim 1101.

Jackson, Dylan B., Juan Del Toro, Daniel C. Semenza, Alexander Testa, and Michael G. Vaughn. "Unpacking Racial/Ethnic Disparities in Emotional Distress among Adolescents during Witnessed Police Stops" (2021) 69 J Adolescent Health 248.

Jackson, Vicki. "Constitutional Law in an Age of Proportionality" (2015) 124:8 Yale LJ 3094.

James, Carl E. "'Singled Out': Being a Black Youth in the Suburbs." In *Racial Profiling and Human Rights in Canada: The New Legal Landscape*, ed. L. Foster, L. Jacobs, and B. Siu, 133 -51. Toronto: Irwin Law, 2018.

–. "'Up to No Good': Black on the Streets and Encountering Police." In *Racism and Social Inequality in Canada: Concepts, Controversies, and Strategies of Resistance*, ed. Vic Satzewich, 157–76. Toronto: University of Toronto Press, 1998.

Jamieson, Gabriella. "Using Section 24(1) *Charter* Damages to Remedy Racial Discrimination in the Criminal Justice System" (2017) 22 Appeal: Rev Current L & L Reform 71.

Jernigan, Adero. "Driving While Black: Racial Profiling in America" (2000) 24 Law & Psychol Rev 127.

Jochelson, Richard. "Ancillary Issues with *Oakes:* The Development of the *Waterfield* Test and the Problem of Fundamental Constitutional Theory" (2013) 43:3 Ottawa L Rev 355.

–. "Crossing the Rubicon: Of Sniffer Dogs, Justifications, and Preemptive Deference" (2008) 13:2 Rev Const Stud 209.

Jochelson, Richard, and David Ireland. *Privacy in Peril: Hunter v Southam and the Drift from Reasonable Search Protections*. Vancouver: UBC Press, 2019.

Jochelson, Richard, David Ireland, Ryan Ziegler, Erika Brenner, and Kirsten Kramar. "Generation and Deployment of Common Law Police Powers by Canadian Courts and the Double-Edged *Charter*" (2020) 20 Critical Criminology 107.

Jones-Brown, Delores. "Forever the Symbolic Assailant: The More Things Change, the More They Remain the Same" (2007) 6:1 Criminology & Public Policy 103. <https://onlinelibrary.wiley.com/doi/10.1111/j.1745-9133.2007.00424.x>.

Kaka, Elsa. "The Supreme Court of Canada's Justification of *Charter* Breaches and Its Effect on Black and Indigenous Communities" (2020) 4 Man LJ 117.

Kaukinen, C., and S. Colavecchia. *Public Perceptions of the Courts: An Examination of Attitudes toward the Treatment of Victims and Accused*. Ottawa: Canadian Criminal Justice Association, 1999.

Kessler, David. "Free to Leave: An Empirical Look at the Fourth Amendment's Seizure Standard" (2008) 99:1 J Crim L & Criminology 51.

Khaitan, Tarunabh. *A Theory of Discrimination Law*. Oxford: Oxford University Press, 2015.

Khoday, Amar. "Ending the Erasure? Writing Race into the Story of Psychological Detentions – Examining *R v Le*" (2021) 100 SCLR (2d) 165.

Klatt, Matthias, and Moritz Meister. *The Constitutional Structure of Proportionality*. Oxford: Oxford University Press, 2012.

Klein, Alana. "Judging as Nudging: New Governance Approaches for the Enforcement of Constitutional Social and Economic Rights" (2008) 39:2 Colum HRLR 351.

Lacroix, Mariève. "Civil Liability of Police Forces: The Impact of the Quebec Charter and Punitive Damages" (2017) 51 RJTUM 547.

LaFree, G.D. *Losing Legitimacy: Street Crime and the Decline of Social Institutions in America*. Boulder, CO: Westview Press, 1998.

Lambard, William. *Duties of Constables, Borsholders, Tithingmen and Such Other Low Ministers of the Peace*. London: Printed by Miles Flesher, Io Haviland, and Robert Young, the assignees of Iohn Moore Esquire, 1631.

Larmore, Charles. "Liberal and Republican Conceptions of Freedom." In *Republicanism: History, Theory, and Practice*, ed. Daniel Weinstock and Christian Nadeau, 96–119. London: Frank Cass, 2004.

Law Reform Commission of Canada. *Police Powers Search and Seizure in Criminal Law Enforcement*. Ottawa: Law Reform Commission of Canada, 1983.

Letsas, George. "Proportionality as Fittingness: The Moral Dimension of Proportionality" (2018) 71:1 Current Leg Probs 53.

Libman, Rick. "Is Presuming Guilt for Regulatory Offences Still Constitutional but Wrong? *R v Wholesale Travel Group Inc.* and Section 1 of the *Charter of Rights and Freedoms* 20 Years After" (2012) 43:3 Ottawa L Rev 455.

Liss, Ryan. "Whose Right Is It Anyway? Adjudicating *Charter* Rights in the Context of Multiple Rights Holders" (2020) 94 SCLR (2d) 271.

Little, Simon. "Audit Finds 94% Drop in Street Checks by Vancouver Police: Critics Renew Call for Ban." *Global News*, 18 February 2021. <http://globalnews.ca/news/7649562/vancouver-street-check-audit/> [perma.cc/MD7U-9ZJW].

Livingston, Debra. "Police Discretion and the Quality of Life in Public Places: Courts, Communities, and the New Policing" (1997) 97 Colum L Rev 551.

Loughlin, Martin. *Public Law and Political Theory*. Oxford: Clarendon Press, 1992.

Lovett, Frank, and Philip Pettit. "Neorepublicanism: A Normative and Institutional Research Program" (2009) 12 Annual Rev Political Science 11.

Luna, Erik. "Transparent Policing" (2000) 85:4 Iowa L Rev 1107.

MacDonnell, Vanessa. "Assessing the Impact of the Ancillary Powers Doctrine on Three Decades of *Charter* Jurisprudence" (2012) 57 SCLR (2d) 225.

Macfarlane, Emmett. "Positive Rights and Section 15 of the *Charter*: Addressing a Dilemma" (2018) 38 NJCL 147.

Marshall, Lysandra. *Racial Disparities in Police Stops in Kingston, Ontario: Democratic Racism and Canadian Racial Profiling in Theoretical Perspective*. PhD Dissertation,

University of Toronto, 2017. <http://tspace.library.utoronto.ca/handle/1807/77464> [hdl.handle.net/1807/77464].

Martí, José Luis. "The Republican Democratization of Criminal Law and Justice." In *Legal Republicanism: National and International Perspectives*, ed. Samantha Besson and José Luis Martí, 124–46. Oxford: Oxford University Press, 2009.

Mascoll, Philip, and Jim Rankin. "Racial Profiling Exists: Promises of Internal Probe Fell Flat." *Toronto Star*, 31 March 2005.

Mastrofski, S.D., M.D. Reisig, and J.D. McCluskey. "Police Disrespect toward the Public: An Encounter-Based Analysis" (2002) 40:3 Criminology 519.

McLachlin, Beverley. "Preserving Public Confidence in the Courts and the Legal Profession" (2002) 29:3 Man LJ 277.

–. "The Role of Judges in Modern Society." *Supreme Court of Canada*, 5 May 2001. <https://perma.cc/S39Z-4TSQ>.

Meares, Tracey, Tom Tyler, and Jacob Gardener. "Lawful or Fair? How Cops and Laypeople Perceive Good Policing" (2015) 105 J Crim L & Criminology 297.

Mercer, Keith. *Rough Justice, Policing Crime and the Origins of the Newfoundland Constabulary, 1729–1871*. St. John's, NL: Flanker Press, 2021.

Milan, A., and K. Tran. "Blacks in Canada: A Long History" (2008) 72 Can Social Trends 2.

Miller, Eric. "Challenging Police Discretion" (2015) 58 Howard LJ 521.

–. "Encountering Resistance: Contesting Policing and Procedural Justice" (2016) U Chicago Legal F 295.

Milward, David. *Reconciliation and Indigenous Justice: A Search for Ways Forward*. Halifax: Fernwood, 2022.

Molnar, Adam, and Ian Warren. "Lawful Illegality: Authorizing Extraterritorial Police Surveillance" (2020) 18:3 Surveillance & Society 357.

Monteith, Margo, and Anna Woodcock. "Modern Forms of Prejudice." In *Encyclopedia of Group Processes and Intergroup Relations*, ed. John M. Levine and Michael A. Hogg, 570–75. Thousand Oaks, CA: Sage, 2010.

Monture, Patricia. "Standing against Canadian Law: Naming Omissions of Race, Culture, and Gender." In *Locating Law: Race/Class/Gender/Sexuality Connections*, ed. E. Comack, 68–87. Halifax: Fernwood, 2014.

Moore, Lisa D., and Amy Elkavich. "Who's Using and Who's Doing Time: Incarceration, The War on Drugs, and Public Health" (2008) 98:5 American J Public Health 782. <https://doi.org/10.2105/ajph.2007.126284>.

Mosher, Clayton J. *Discrimination and Denial: Systemic Racism in Ontario's Legal and Criminal Justice Systems, 1892–1961*. Toronto: University of Toronto Press, 1998.

Mussweiler, Thomas, Birte Englich, and Fritz Strack. "Anchoring Effect." In *Cognitive Illusions: A Handbook on Fallacies and Biases in Thinking, Judgment, and Memory*, ed. Rüdiger F. Pohl, 183–200. New York: Psychology Press, 2012.

Nadler, Janice. "No Need to Shout: Bus Sweeps and the Psychology of Coercion" (2002) 1 Sup Ct Rev 153.

Neugebauer-Visano, Robynne. "Kids, Cops, and Colour: The Social Organization of Police-Minority Youth Relations." In *Not a Kid Anymore: Canadian Youth, Crime, and Subcultures*, ed. Gary M. O'Bireck, 283–308. Scarborough, ON: Nelson Canada, 1996.

Nova Scotia Human Rights Commission. *Nova Scotia Street Checks Report*. Authored by Scot Wortley. Halifax: Nova Scotia Human Rights Commission, 2019. <human rights.novascotia.ca/sites/default/files/editor-uploads/halifax_street_checks_report_march_2019_0.pdf> [perma.cc/X7PV-9WWK].

OHRC. *OHRC Response to the Race Data and Traffic Stops in Ottawa Report*. Toronto: OHRC, 2016. <https://www.ohrc.on.ca/en/book/export/html/19676> [perma.cc/4PVS-AH3P].

–. *Paying the Price: The Human Cost of Racial Profiling*. Toronto: OHRC, 2003. <https://www3.ohrc.on.ca/sites/default/files/attachments/Paying_the_price%3A_The_human_cost_of_racial_profiling.pdf> [perma.cc/RNX6–663W].

–. *Under Suspicion: Research and Consultation Report on Racial Profiling in Ontario*. Toronto: OHRC, 2017.

Ontario. *Review Report on the Special Investigations Unit Reforms Prepared for the Attorney General of Ontario*. Authored by George W. Adams. Toronto: Attorney General of Ontario, 2003. <https://www.siu.on.ca/pdfs/adams_report_ii.pdf> [perma.cc/JRJ7–4BPB].

Ontario, Ipperwash Inquiry. *Police Use of Force in Ontario: An Examination of Data from the Special Investigations Unit – Final Report*. Authored by Scot Wortley. Toronto: Attorney General of Ontario, 2006. <http://www.attorneygeneral.jus.gov.on.ca/inquiries/ipperwash/policy_part/projects/pdf/AfricanCanadianClinicIpperwashProject_SIUStudybyScotWortley.pdf> [perma.cc/VA6S-9PJY].

Ontario, Kingston Police Services Board. *Police Stop Search Activities in Kingston, Ontario: Results from the Data Collection Pilot Project*. Authored by Scot Wortley and Lysandra Marshall. Kingston: Kingston Police Services Board, 2005.

Ontario, Race Relations and Policing Task Force. *The Report of the Race Relations and Policing Task Force*. Authored by Clare Lewis. Ottawa: Queen's Printer, 1989. <https://www.siu.on.ca/pdfs/clare_lewis_report_1989.pdf> [perma.cc/9R5B-CYWM].

Ontario Human Rights Commission (OHRC). *A Collective Impact: Interim Report on the Inquiry into Racial Profiling and Racial Discrimination of Black Persons by the Toronto Police Service*. Toronto: Government of Ontario, 2018.

–. *A Disparate Impact*. August 2020. <https://www.ohrc.on.ca/sites/default/files/A%20Disparate%20Impact%20-%20TPS%20inquiry%20%28updated%20January%202023%29.pdf>.

Oona Hathaway. "Path Dependence in the Law: The Course and Pattern of Legal Change in a Common Law System" (2001) 86:2 Iowa L Rev 601.

Owusu-Bempah, Akwasi. *Black Males' Perceptions of and Experiences with the Police in Toronto*. PhD Dissertation, University of Toronto, 2014. <https://tspace.library.utoronto.ca/handle/1807/68227> [hdl.handle.net/1807/68227].

Owusu-Bempah, Akwasi, and Paul Millar. "Research Note: Revisiting the Collection of 'Justice Statistics by Race' in Canada" (2010) 25:1 CJLS 97 at 99. <http://doi.org/10.1017/S0829320100010231>.

Owusu-Bempah, Akwasi, and Scot Wortley. "Race, Crime, and Criminal Justice in Canada." In *The Oxford Handbook of Ethnicity, Crime, and Immigration*, ed. Sandra Bucerius and Michael Tonry, 281–320. Oxford: Oxford University Press, 2014.

Packer, Herbert L. "Two Models of the Criminal Process" (1964) 113:1 U Pa L Rev 1.

Panaccio, Charles-Maxime. "In Defence of Two-Step Balancing and Proportionality in Rights Adjudication" (2011) 24:1 Can JL & Jur 109.

Penney, Steven. "Driving While Innocent: Curbing the Excesses of the 'Traffic Stop' Power" (2019) 24:3 CCLR 339.

–. "Unreasonable Search and Seizure and Section 8 of the Charter: Cost-Benefit Analysis in Constitutional Interpretation" (2013) 62 SCLR 101.

Pettit, Philip. "Criminalization in Republican Theory." In *Criminalization*, ed. R.A. Duff, Lindsay Famer, S.E. Marshall, Massimo Renzo, and Victor Tadros, 132–50. Oxford: Oxford University Press, 2014.

–. *Just Freedom: A Moral Compass for a Complex World*. London: Norton, 2014.
–. "Law and Liberty." In *Law and Republicanism,* ed. Samantha Besson and José Luis Martí, 39–59. Oxford: Oxford University Press, 2009.
–. *On the People's Terms: A Republican Theory and Model of Democracy*. Cambridge: Cambridge University Press, 2012.
–. *Republicanism: A Theory of Freedom and Government*. Oxford: Oxford University Press, 1999.
Phillips, Coretta, and Benjamin Bowling. "Racism, Ethnicity and Criminology: Developing Minority Perspectives" (2002) 43:2 Brit J Crim 269.
Plaxton, Michael. "Police Powers after Dicey" (2012) 38:1 Queen's LJ 99.
Porter, Catherine. "Kingston Race Study Attacked: Report Tracked Police Arrests, Critics Dispute Claim of Racial Bias." *Toronto Star,* 8 June 2005. <http://www.ottawa menscentre.com/news/20050609_kingston.htm> [perma.cc/35FR-CTPZ].
Porter, Stephen, Laura England, Marcus Juodis, Leanne ten Brinke, and Kevin Wilson. "Is the Face a Window to the Soul? Investigation of the Accuracy of Intuitive Judgments of the Trustworthiness of Human Faces" (2008) 40:3 Can J Behavioural Science 171.
Quigley, Tim. "Brief Investigatory Detentions: A Critique of R. v Simpson" (2004) 41:4 Alta L Rev 935.
–. "The Impact of the *Charter* on the Law of Search and Seizure" (2008) 40 SCLR (2d) 117.
Rankin, Jim. "Carded: Probing a Racial Disparity." *Toronto Star,* 6 February 2010.
–. "When Good People Are Swept Up with the Bad." *Toronto Star,* 6 February 2010. <http://www.thestar.com/news/gta/2010/02/06/when_good_people_are_swept_up_ with_the_bad.html> [perma.cc/65PU-JKVD].
Rankin, J., S. Contenta, and A. Bailey. "Toronto Marijuana Arrests Reveal 'Startling' Racial Divide." *Toronto Star,* 6 July 2017. <https://www.thestar.com/news/insight/ 2017/07/06/toronto-marijuana-arrests-reveal-startling-racial-divide.html>.
Rankin, Jim, Jennifer Quinn, Michelle Shephard, Scott Simmie, and John Duncanson. "Police Target Black Drivers." *Toronto Star,* 20 October 2002. <http://www.thestar. com/news/gta/raceandcrime/2002/10/20/police-target-black-drivers-star-analysis-of -traffic-data-suggests.html> [perma.cc/8YR8-AWWR].
–. "Singled Out." *Toronto Star,* 19 October 2002. <http://www.thestar.com/news/gta/ knowntopolice/2002/10/19/singled-out.html> [perma.cc/555Z-T4LC].
Ristroph, Alice. "The Constitution of Police Violence" (2017) 64 UCLA L Rev 1182.
–. "Proportionality as a Principle of Limited Government" (2005) 55:2 Duke LJ 263.
Ritson, Joseph. *The Office of Constable*. London: Whieldon & Butterworth, 1791.
Roach, Kent. "Constitutional and Common Law Dialogues between the Supreme Court and Canadian Legislatures" (2001) 80 Can Bar Rev 481.
–. "Making Progress on Understanding and Remedying Racial Profiling" (2004) 41:4 Alta L Rev 895.
–. "A Promising Late Spring for *Charter* Damages: *Ward v Vancouver*" (2011) 29 NJCL 145.
–. "Remedies." In *The Oxford Handbook of the Canadian Constitution,* ed. Peter Oliver, Patrick Macklem, and Nathalie Des Rosiers, 673–94. Oxford: Oxford University Press, 2017.
–. "Remedies for Discriminatory Profiling." In *Taking Remedies Seriously,* ed. Kent Roach and Robert J. Sharpe, 391–417. Montreal: Canadian Institute for the Administration of Justice, 2009.

–. *The Supreme Court on Trial: Judicial Activism or Democratic Dialogue*. Toronto: Irwin Law, 2001.

Robbennolt, Jennifer, and Christina Studebaker. "Anchoring in the Courtroom: The Effects of Caps on Punitive Damages" (1999) 23:3 L & Human Behavior 353.

Roots of Youth Violence Inquiry. *The Review of the Roots of Youth Violence: Community Perspectives Report*. Authored by Roy McMurtry and Alvin Curling. Vol. 3. Ottawa: Queen's Printer, 2008.

–. *The Review of the Roots of Youth Violence: Findings, Analysis and Conclusions*. Authored by Roy McMurtry and Alvin Curling. Vol. 1. Ottawa: Queen's Printer, 2008.

Russell, K. *The Racial Hoax as Crime: The Law as Affirmation*. Indianapolis: Indiana State Bar Association, 1996.

Schuppert, Fabian. "Non-Domination, Non-Alienation and Social Equality: Towards a Republican Understanding of Equality" (2015) 18:4 Critical Rev Intl Social & Political Philosophy 440.

Sekhon, Nirej. "Police and the Limits of the Law" (2019) 119 Colum L Rev 1711.

Sewell, Alyasah, Kevin A. Jefferson, and Hedwig Lee. "Living under Surveillance: Gender, Psychological Distress, and Stop-Question-and-Frisk Policing in New York City" (2016) 159 Social Science & Medicine 1.

Sharma, Anupam. "The Police in Ancient India" (2004) 1 Indian J Political Science 65.

Simmons, Kami. "The Legacy of Stop and Frisk: Addressing the Vestiges of a Violent Police Culture" (2014) 49:3 Wake Forest L Rev 849.

Simonson, Jocelyn. "Copwatching" (2016) 104:2 Cal L Rev 391.

–. "Democratizing Criminal Justice through Contestation and Resistance" (2017) 111:6 Nw UL Rev 1609.

–. "Filming the Police as an Act of Resistance: Remarks Given at the Smartphoned Symposium" (2016) 10:2 U St Thomas JL & Public Policy 83.

–. "Police Reform through a Power Lens" (2021) 130 Yale LJ 778.

Skinner, Quentin. "Freedom as the Absence of Arbitrary Power." In *Republicanism and Political Theory*, ed. Cecile Laborde and John Maynor, 83–101. Oxford: Blackwell, 2008.

Sklansky, David. "Traffic Stops, Minority Motorists, and the Future of the Fourth Amendment" (1997) 1997 Sup Ct Rev 271.

Skogan, Wesley. "Asymmetry in the Impact of Encounters with Police" (2006) 16:2 Policing & Society 99.

Skolnik, Terry. "Criminal Justice Reform: A Transformative Agenda" (2022) 59:3 Alta L Rev 631.

–. "Freedom and Access to Housing: Three Conceptions" (2018) 35 Windsor YB Access Just 226.

–. "Homelessness and Unconstitutional Discrimination" (2019) 15 JL & Equality 69.

–. "Hot Bench: A Theory of Appellate Adjudication" (2020) 61:4 Boston College L Rev 1271.

–. "Policing in the Shadow of Legality: Pretext, Leveraging, and Investigation Cascades" (2022) 60 Osgoode Hall LJ 505.

–. "Racial Profiling and the Perils of Ancillary Police Powers" (2021) 99:2 Can Bar Rev 429.

–. "Rééquilibrer le rôle de la Cour Suprême de Canada en procédure criminelle" (2022) 67:3 McGill LJ 259.

–. "Three Problems with Duress and Moral Involuntariness" (2016) 63:1–2 Crim LQ 124.

–. "Three Stages of Criminal Justice Remedies" [forthcoming].

–. "Use of Force and Criminalization" (2021) 85:3 Alta L Rev 663.

Skolnik, Terry, and Fernando Belton. "La fin des interceptions au hasard" [forthcoming].

Skolnik, Terry, and Vanessa MacDonnell. "Policing Arbitrariness: *Fleming v Ontario* and the Ancillary Powers Doctrine" (2021) 100 SCLR (2d) 187.

Smith, Brad W., and Malcolm D. Holmes. "Police Use of Excessive Force in Minority Communities" (2014) 61:1 Social Problems 83.

Spector, Horacio. "Four Conceptions of Freedom" (2010) 38:6 Political Theory 780.

Stasiulis, Daiva K. "Minority Resistance in the Local State: Toronto in the 1970s and 1980s" (1989) 12:1 Ethnic & Racial Studies 63. <https://doi.org/10.1080/01419870.1989.9993623>.

Stenning, Philip. *Legal Status of the Police: A Study Paper.* Ottawa: Law Reform Commission of Canada, 1981.

Stephenson, Carl, and Frederick George Marcham. *Sources of English Constitutional History: A Selection of Documents from AD 600 to the Present.* New York: Harper & Brothers, 1937.

Stone Sweet, Alec, and Jud Mathews. "Proportionality Balancing and Global Constitutionalism" (2008) 47:1 Colum J Transnat'l L 72.

Stoughton, Seth. "Principled Policing: Warrior Cops and Guardian Officers" (2016) 51:3 Wake Forest L Rev 611.

Stribopoulos, James. "A Failed Experiment: Investigative Detention: Ten Years Later" (2003) 41:2 Alta L Rev 335.

–. "The Limits of Judicially Created Police Powers: Investigative Detention after Mann" (2006) 52:3–4 Crim LQ 299.

–. "Packer's Blind Spot: Low Visibility Encounters and the Limits of Due Process versus Crime Control." In *Rethinking Criminal Law Theory: New Canadian Perspectives in the Philosophy of Domestic, Transnational, and International Criminal Law,* ed. François Tanguay-Renaud and James Stribopoulos, 193–216. Oxford: Hart, 2012.

–. "In Search of Dialogue: The Supreme Court, Police Powers and the *Charter*" (2005) 31:1 Queen's LJ 1.

Stuart, Don. "The Charter Balance against Unscrupulous Law and Order Politics" (2012) 57 SCLR (2d) 13.

Stuntz, William. "The Pathological Politics of Criminal Law" (2001) 100:3 Mich L Rev 505.

–. "The Uneasy Relationship between Criminal Law and Criminal Procedure" (1997) 107:1 Yale LJ 1.

Sunstein, Cass. "Foreword: Leaving Things Undecided" (1996) 110 Harv L Rev 4.

–. "The Most Knowledgeable Branch" (2016) 164 U Pa L Rev 1607.

–. *One Case at a Time: Judicial Minimalism on the Supreme Court.* Cambridge, MA: Harvard University Press, 2001.

Susser, Daniel. "Predictive Policing and the Ethics of Preemption." In *The Ethics of Policing: New Perspectives on Law Enforcement,* ed. Ben Jones and Eduardo Mendieta, 268–92. New York: New York University Press, 2021.

Swainger, Jonathon. *The Notorious Georges: Crime and Community in British Columbia's Northern Interior, 1909–1925.* Vancouver: UBC Press, 2023.

Tanovich, David. "Applying the Racial Profiling Correspondence Test" (2017) 64 Crim LQ 359.

–. *The Colour of Justice: Policing Race in Canada.* Toronto: Irwin Law, 2006.

–. "The Colourless World of *Mann*" (2004) 21 Criminal Reports (6th) 47.

–. "E-Racing Racial Profiling" (2004) 41:4 Alta L Rev 905.

–. "Relevance, Social Context and Poverty" (2003) 9 Criminal Reports (6th) 348.

–. "Using the *Charter* to Stop Racial Profiling: The Development of an Equality-Based Conception of Arbitrary Detention" (2002) 40:2 Osgoode Hall LJ 145.

Tator, Carol, and Frances Henry. *Racial Profiling in Canada: Challenging the Myth of 'a Few Bad Apples.'* Toronto: University of Toronto Press, 2006. <https://doi.org/10.3138/9781442678972>.

Tibbetts, Janice. "Court's Youth Crime Decision a Blow to Tory Crime Agenda." *National Post,* 16 May 2008. <http://www.nationalpost.com/news/ story.html?id= 0 00>.

Trinkner, Rick, Jonathan Jackson, and Tom Tyler. "Bounded Authority: Expanding 'Appropriate' Police Behavior beyond Procedural Justice" (2018) 42 L & Human Behavior 280.

Trinkner, Rick, and Tom Tyler. "Legal Socialization: Coercion versus Consent in an Era of Mistrust" (2016) 12 Annual Rev L Social Science 417.

Truth and Reconciliation Commission of Canada. *Calls to Action.* Winnipeg: Truth and Reconciliation Commission of Canada, 2012.

Tushnet, Mark. *Weak Courts, Strong Rights: Judicial Review and Social Welfare Rights in Comparative Constitutional Law.* Princeton, NJ: Princeton University Press, 2007.

Tversky, Amos, and Daniel Kahneman. "Judgment under Uncertainty: Heuristics and Biases" (1974) 185 Science 1124.

Tyler, T.R., and J. Fagan. "Legitimacy, Compliance and Cooperation: Procedural Justice and Citizen Ties to the Law" (2008) 6:1 Ohio State J Criminal L 231.

Tyler, Tom. "From Harm Reduction to Community Engagement: Redefining the Goals of American Policing in the Twenty-First Century" (2017) 111 Nw UL Rev 1537.

–. "Justice, Self-Interest, and the Legitimacy of Legal and Political Authority." In *Beyond Self-Interest,* ed. J.J. Mansbridge, 171–79. Chicago: University of Chicago Press, 1990.

–. "Procedural Justice, Legitimacy, and the Effective Rule of Law" (2003) 30 Crime & Justice 283.

Tyler, Tom, and Jeffrey Fagan. "Legitimacy and Cooperation: Why Do People Help the Police Fight Crime in Their Communities" (2008) 6 Ohio State J Criminal L 231.

Tyler, Tom, Jeffrey Fagan, and Amanda Geller. "Street Stops and Police Legitimacy: Teachable Moments in Young Urban Men's Legal Socialization" (2014) 11:4 J Empirical Leg Stud 751.

Tyler, Tom, and Jonathan Jackson. "Popular Legitimacy and the Exercise of Legal Authority: Motivating Compliance, Cooperation, and Engagement" (2014) 21 Psychol Pub Pol'y & L 78.

Tyler, Tom, Jonathan Jackson, and Avital Mentovich. "The Consequences of Being an Object of Suspicion: Potential Pitfalls of Proactive Police Contact" (2015) 12:4 J Empirical Leg Stud 602.

UK Government. "Definition of Policing by Consent" (Home Office FOI Release), *UK Government.* <https://www.gov.uk/government/publications/policing-by-consent/ definition-of-policing-by-consent>.

Vijaykumar, Malini. "A Crisis of Conscience: Miscarriages of Justice and Indigenous Defendants in Canada" (2018) 51 UBC L Rev 159.

Walker, Samuel. *Taming the System: The Control of Discretion in Criminal Justice, 1950– 1990.* Oxford: Oxford University Press, 1993.

Walter, Lisa. "Eradicating Racial Stereotyping from Terry Stops: The Case for an Equal Protection Exclusionary Rule" (2000) 71:1 U Colo L Rev 255.

Wang, Lu-in. "Race as Proxy: Situational Racism and Self-Fulfilling Stereotypes" (2004) 53 DePaul L Rev 1013.

Warren, Patricia. "Perceptions of Police Disrespect during Vehicle Stops: A Race-Based Analysis" (2011) 57:3 Crime & Delinquency 356.

Wasserman, Howard. "Recording of and by Police: The Good, the Bad, and the Ugly" (2017) 20:3 J Gender Race & Justice 543.

Wasun. "A Short History of Community Organizing against Police Brutality in Toronto: The History of BADC and Beyond." *BASICS*, 20 March 2008. <basicsnewsletter. blogspot.com/2008/03/short-history-of-police-brutality-in.html> [perma.cc/ HE8M-XSPC].

Weber, Leanne, and Ben Bowling, ed. *Stop and Search: Police Power in Global Context.* New York: Routledge, 2014.

Weinstein, Ian. "The Adjudication of Minor Offenses in New York City" (2004) 31:4 Fordham Urb LJ 1157.

Weitzer, Ronald. "American Policing under Fire: Misconduct and Reform" (2015) 52 Society 475.

–. "Incidents of Police Misconduct and Public Opinion" (2002) 30 J Criminal Justice 397.

Wendt, Fabian. "Slaves, Prisoners, and Republican Freedom" (2011) 17 Res Publica 175.

Williams, Christopher J. "Obscurantism in Action: How the Ontario Human Rights Commission Frames Racial Profiling" (2006) 38:2 Can Ethnic Studies 1.

Wilson, Adam, QC. *The Constable's Guide: A Sketch of the Office of Constable.* Toronto: Maclear, 1859.

Winsa, Patty, and Jim Rankin. "Known to Police: Toronto Police Stop and Document Black and Brown People Far More Than Whites." *Toronto Star,* 9 March 2012. <https:// www.thestar.com/news/insight/2012/03/09/known_to_police_toronto_police_stop_ and_document_black_and_brown_people_far_more_than_whites.html> [perma. cc/V962-P25S].

–. "Police Service Board Decision on 'Carding' Stuns Activists." *Toronto Star,* 14 April 2012. <http://www.thestar.com/news/gta/2012/04/14/police_service_board_ decision_on_carding_stuns_activists.html> [perma.cc/U8QC-2MMW].

Woods, Jordan. "Decriminalization, Police Authority, and Routine Traffic Stops" (2015) 62:3 UCLA L Rev 672.

Wortley, Scot. *Halifax, Nova Scotia: Street Checks Report.* Halifax: Nova Scotia Human Rights Commission, 2019.

–. "Justice for All? Race and Perceptions of Bias in the Ontario Criminal Justice System: A Toronto Survey" (1996) 38:4 Can J Crim 439.

Wortley, Scot, and Akwasi Owusu-Bempah. "Unequal before the Law: Immigrant and Racial Minority Perceptions of the Canadian Criminal Justice System" (2009) 10:4 J Intl Migration & Integration 447. <https://doi.org/10.1007/s12134-009-0108-x>.

–. "The Usual Suspects: Police Stop and Search Practices in Canada" (2011) 21:4 Policing & Society 395.

Wortley, Scot, Akwasi Owusu-Bempah, and Huibin Lin. *Race and Criminal Injustice: An Examination of Public Perceptions of and Experiences with the Ontario Criminal Justice System.* Report prepared on behalf of the Canadian Association of Black Lawyers and funded by Legal Aid Ontario. Toronto: Ryerson University Faculty of Law, 2021. <https://perma.cc/649G-76FE>.

Wortley, Scot, and J. Tanner. "Inflammatory Rhetoric? Baseless Accusations? Responding to Gabor's Critique of Racial Profiling Research in Canada" (2005) 47:3 Can J Crim & Crim Justice 581.

Yankah, Ekow. "Pretext and Justification: Republicanism, Policing, and Race" (2019) 40 Cardozo L Rev 1543.

Zakreski, Dan. "Saskatoon Police Removed 'Starlight Tours' Section from Wikipedia, Student Says." *CBC News*, 31 March 2016. <https://perma.cc/K5H5-TKW2>.

Index

A.M., R v, 11, 74

Abella, Rosalie: in *Clayton*, 71–72; in *Fearon*, 102; in *Kang-Brown*, 125

Aboriginal Justice Inquiry (AJI), 7, 8

accountability: *Charter* and, 48; counter-surveillance and, 189; for diverse society, 156; information failures and, 147; in low-visibility stops, 109; public control over, 196; Supreme Court and, 196

Act to Amend the Criminal Code, section 5(e), 198

An Act for Improving the Police in and near the Metropolis (1829), 36

Action Committee against Racism, 155

Ahmad, R v, 180

Albert Johnson Defense Committee against Police Brutality, 155

American Psychological Association (APA), 197

ancillary powers: defined, 27; and domination, 183; increase in deployment of, 127; and Indigenous people, 139; in low-visibility contexts, 183

ancillary powers doctrine: about, 6, 192; activism of, 5–6; and arbitrary police discretion, 7; and Black experience, 15–16; in Canada vs. UK, 5; and collective harms, 146; and Constitution, 6, 176–77; court reliance on, 193; and criminal procedure, 176; critiques of, 16, 174–76; in *Dedman*, 5, 10; defences of use of, 174–75; and democracy, 175, 176–77; and discretionary power, 174, 194; and distrust toward police, 190; and domination, 16–17, 182–83, 184–85, 190; and equality, 190; exclusionary rule and, 179; and expansion of powers, 13–14; fair notice regarding, 175; gap-filling rationale, 110; and interference, 14, 16, 195–96; and judicial counter-majoritarian role, 152; and liberty vs. police duty, 126; and necessity, 145–46; and negative freedom/liberty, 180–81; and new powers creation, 5, 125; as one-way ratchet, 16–17, 176–77, 180, 189–90, 195–96; and police reform, 177; proportionality problem, 14–17, 143–53; public cooperation and, 187; and racial profiling, 7–8, 146; and remedial mechanisms, 177–80; and republican freedom, 190; and rule of law, 5, 16, 175, 190; and separation of powers, 175, 190; and state impact on individual interests, 146; and street-level

Printed and bound in Canada

Set in Myriad and Sabon by Artegraphica Design Co. Ltd.

Copy editor: Stacy Belden

Proofreader: Judith Earnshaw

Indexer: Noeline Bridge

Cover designer: Setareh Ashrafologhalai